D0277699

Village and Farmstead

Christopher Taylor

Village and Farmstead

A History of Rural Settlement in England

Book Club Associates, London

This edition published 1983 by Book Club Associates by arrangement with George Philip & Son Ltd, 12–14 Long Acre, London WC2E 9LP

TITLE PAGE ILLUSTRATION **Grange Farm, Stretham, Cambridgeshire. A typical lowland enclosure farmstead built here on newly reclaimed and enclosed fenland soon after 1835.**

Acknowledgements

The author wishes to thank the following for permission to use either photographs, or material on which the drawings are based.

Photographs
Collection of Air Photographs University of Cambridge (Copyright Reserved): 2, 3, 4, 9, 10, 15, 17, 18, 22, 23, 26, 27, 28, 31, 32, 34, 35, 38, 40, 43, 46, 47, 49, 59, 64, 66, 67, 69, 70, 73, 74, 75, 79, 91, 96, 97, 99, 100; Dr R.Muir (Copyright Reserved): title-page, 1, 6, 11, 20, 33, 37, 42, 51, 52, 53, 54, 55, 58, 62, 63, 68, 76, 78, 81, 86, 87, 92, 94, 95, 98, 101; National Trust (Copyright Reserved): 90; Royal Commission on Historical Monuments (England) (Crown Copyright): 65, 72, 77, 82, 83, 85, 88, 93.

Drawings
Mr R.Bradley: 13 (Knight's Farm), 16 (Rams Hill); Cambridge University Press: 60 (Cottenham); Dr T.Champion: 41 (Chalton); Professor G.Clark: 7 (Hurst Fen); Professor B.Cunliffe: 13 (Chalton); Department of the Environment: 80 (Wawne); Mr B.Dix: 21 (Odell); Mr P.Drewett: 14 (Black Patch); Mr P.Dury: 24 (Little Waltham); Mr P.Fasham: 24 (Winnall Down); Dr P.J.Fowler: 30 (Overton Down); Ms M.Gray: 41 (New Wintles); Mr J.Hurst: 80 (Wawne); Mr D.Jackson: 24 (Twywell); Mr S.Losco-Bradley: 41 (Catholme); Mr D.Longley: 13 (Runnymede); M3 Archaeological Excavation Committee: 24 (Winnall Down); Dr P.Mellors: 5 (Deepcar); Mr R.Mercer: 8 (Carn Brea); Mr D.Neal: 36 (Gadebridge); Oxfordshire Archaeological Unit: 21 (Barton Court and Farmoor); Mr M.O'Malley: 5 (Broom Hill); Dr J.Ravensdale: 60 (Cottenham); Professor P.Rhatz: 16 (Shearplace Hill), 19 (Hog Cliff Hill); Mr H.Thompson: 14 (Mam Tor); Dr P.Wade-Martins: 44 (Longham, Stanfield and Weasenham); Dr G.Wainwright: 7 (Broome Heath), 16 (Shaugh Moor), 21 (Berwick Down); Dr S.West: 41 (West Stow).

Preface

To write a history of rural settlement in England at the present time may seem an impossible task. Certainly in the last few years there has been a revolution in our ideas as new evidence has flooded in from a host of different disciplines. Much of this new work has yet to be examined critically and assimilated, but whatever the final outcome it is already clear that most of the traditional views as to how and when the English countryside was settled and how it changed over time must now be discarded.

In this book I have attempted to draw together some of the new evidence and give it a chronological coherence. Any success that I may have achieved is largely the result of the work of many friends and colleagues in various fields of study. I am grateful to them all.

A number of people and institutions have helped in the writing of this book. Most of them are listed in the Acknowledgements but I would like to mention especially some others. Mick Aston read the book in draft and supported it, perhaps because he too believes in its theme. Moira Hegerty has been a tower of strength in completing the final typescript while Bernard Thomason produced all the line drawings. David Wilson has given me access to the air photograph library at Cambridge and Richard Muir has allowed me complete freedom to choose from his magnificent collection of photographs. Without the kindness and help of all these the book would never have been finished.

The origins of this book lie in the work I have carried out for over 20 years for the Royal Commission on Historical Monuments (England). No one who is interested in the English landscape could have had better training, greater opportunities or more expert and companionable colleagues. To the Commission and all its staff, past and present, go my sincere thanks.

In the end, however, it is my wife who has really made this book possible. She has helped and encouraged me in all I have done, while raising a family, caring for her students and carrying out her own completely unrelated research, all at the same time. It is her book as much as mine and thus it is rightly dedicated to her.

Christopher Taylor

For Angela

Contents

List of Illustrations

Introduction

The English landscape is made up of many interrelated features. Its basic skeleton has been formed from the rocks, moulded by time, etched by rivers and ice, and clothed with a mantle of green vegetation, but superimposed on this is man's work. No part of England is untouched by man's endeavours over thousands of years. The most obvious of these are the great urban and industrial centres which sprawl across so much of the land. Between them lie lesser towns and a myriad of villages while hamlets and farmsteads dot every part of the country.

All these settlements are a vital part of the living landscape. In addition there are other less obvious places where man has lived at some time, but which he has abandoned. Deserted villages lie in almost every part of England. In some counties the remains of farmsteads, founded in medieval times but long since relinquished, exist in their hundreds. All over the country are the sites of prehistoric, Roman, Saxon and later settlements which can be recognized only from the air or from scraps of pottery, flint or bone which are exhumed by the plough. It can safely be said that it is not possible to find anywhere in England that is more than a short distance from a place where man has at some time lived.

This book is concerned with every kind of settlement in the countryside – villages, hamlets and farmsteads – both those that are lived in now and those that have been abandoned. Inevitably, in a work of this length not every aspect of these settlements can be covered. On the whole the details of buildings, their structures and architecture, will not be dealt with to any great extent. It is the more general side of the history of rural settlement we shall be looking at, that is the development of man's habitats from prehistoric times to the present day from the historical and locational point of view: how and why settlements came into being, what form they took and for what reason and how and why they changed through time. Thus our interest is more with the position, size, form and reasons for settlement in the countryside than with whether the buildings were round or square, or of wood, brick or stone.

This aspect of the study of rural settlement is one that has for long been, and indeed still is, largely the prerogative of geographers. They first analyzed settlements in terms of location, morphology and function and they have remained leaders in this field. Nevertheless much geographical writing on settlement has inevitably concentrated on the rather bald concept of spatial relationships and simple morphology, often with little feeling for or appreciation of the complex historical development through time.

Scholars in other disciplines have also worked on many of these aspects of settlements, and archaeologists especially have in the past been greatly concerned with the development of prehistoric and Roman settlements, and more recently with later ones. However, with a few notable exceptions, archaeologists tend to be myopic, perhaps because of their inevitable concentration on the minutiae of human activity that are their basic source of information. Thus, though much information about settlements has been recorded by various archaeological methods, archaeologists have been slow in seeing the overall patterns which cross cultural and period boundaries.

Historians have, in the past, been rightly concerned more with people, their aims, ideas, motives and institutions, than with their physical settlements. In more recent years some of these archaic divisions between the disciplines have been crossed and we are now in a much better position to see how complex the history of rural settlement in England really was. Nevertheless most of the results of the new co-operation have not seen the light of day in a general sense. They remain buried in learned journals, interminable conference reports or expensive academic volumes. This writer, involved as he has been in teaching the history of the English landscape at all levels from primary schools to university and adult education, has constantly been made aware of the lack of communication between those who practise the new co-operative scholarship and the general reader, teacher or student.

In this book the intention is to summarize some of the recent work on the history of rural settlement in England and in particular to bring out three aspects which seem to be of importance, but which do not appear to have been generally recognized. These are, firstly, the largely irrelevant nature of 'geographical determinism', secondly, the incredible complexity of settlement in all its forms as it has developed and changed over the last ten or twelve thousand years, and lastly the importance of mobility of settlement through time.

The concept of geographical determinism has dogged all studies of settlement since the late nineteenth century when geographers first systematically developed the theory. Though most geographers have long since discarded it, it still figures largely in discussion of settlement of any form or date. While there are clearly certain general physical determinants which cannot be ignored, for example a mining village can hardly grow up away from a coalfield, or a port away from access to water, most of the specific determinants of settlement location are probably not concerned with the physical nature of the site at all. With hindsight, some physical determinant may always be identified, but it is doubtful whether it was seen with such clarity by the first occupants of the site. Thus a particular village may be located on a patch of dry gravel, or at a spring line, or near a ford, but it will also probably be clear that there are many other places close by which are just as suitable, if not better, but which have not been used.

In a discussion of the origins of any particular site, of whatever period and function, the physical nature of the site is of far less importance in the decision to settle there than the human factor. Although there are obvious problems involved in identifying the human element it is possible to perceive at least some of the reasons why particular sites were chosen and this aspect of settlement will be looked at specifically.

The complexity of rural settlement is another part of the study which has been often overlooked. For example, until recently most people believed that in Roman times England was a land of towns, splendidly elaborate villas and some vaguely defined villages. Yet we now know that this picture is very oversimplified. Roman towns differed widely in size and layout and there were also huge agglomerations of semi-urbanized settlement covering many square kilometres. Lesser settlements included villas of all kinds, large compact villages, small hamlets, farmsteads and isolated cottages over most of the country. Similarly, in medieval times the typical nucleated village, clustered round a focal point, is usually regarded as the normal form of settlement, except in the more remote regions of the country such as Cornwall and parts of the north. Yet the reality is very different. Even in the midland counties nucleated villages are only one facet of a very complex settlement pattern that also includes hamlets, farmsteads and cottages.

Perhaps the most important aspect of rural settlement history is its mobility. Most of us have been brought up to see the pattern of English rural settlement as very old. Some of us live in 'Saxon' villages, or we travel far to admire the fine open greens of places such as Finchingfield in Essex (Fig. 1), which we are told are the visible remains of the original settlers' clearance of the woodland centuries ago. But again the reality is very different.

1 **Finchingfield, Essex** *The archetypal English village, apparently a haven of stability in a changing world. Thousands of people visit it every year but most of them fail to see that it is itself the result of continuous and profound change.*

Most of our villages are not that old. Few in the form that we see them today are Saxon and many are relatively modern. All have changed their form and their layout over the centuries and many have moved or have been rebuilt on new lines or in different places. This picture of continual change is not a recent phenomenon. Even in prehistoric and Roman times people moved or altered their settlements constantly, as is well seen at Ebsbury, in Wiltshire (Fig. 2). Indeed it is probable that settlement mobility, in the broad historical sense, is normal and that static settlement is an aberration.

These three major concepts – of human rather than physical determinism, of complexity and of mobility – are the themes of this book. They do not constitute a new ideology of rural settlement in England but they do show the complexities and intricacies involved in unravelling the history of our landscape and our homes. It is also clear how little we still know of the history of our forefathers and how difficult it is to make simple and easily understandable generalizations about rural settlement.

There are three terms – village, hamlet and farmstead – which have already been used several times and which need to be discussed at this stage, particularly as the distinctions between them are not clear-cut. A village has been described as a settlement of twenty or more individual homesteads, or families, though, as we shall see, this definition is not always appropriate, particularly in prehistoric times when village-like settlements were rather smaller. A hamlet is usually defined as a settlement housing from three to nineteen families, which means that there is no clear-cut dividing line between village and hamlet but that the ends of the spectrum are easily identified. A farmstead is more satisfactorily defined. This is a single dwelling house and its agricultural appurtenances but these buildings may have been home to more than one family.

2 Ebsbury, Wiltshire *This remarkable site encapsulates much of the history of settlement in England. In the background, surrounding the wood, are the ramparts of an unfinished hillfort. Within the wood, hidden by trees, is a Roman village. In the foreground, on either side of a track leading towards the village, are the banks and ditches surrounding a small Roman hamlet. To the left of the track and just below the rectangular dry pond are the banks around a small medieval farmstead, probably of thirteenth-century date.*

Part I Prehistoric and Roman Settlement

Our ideas of where and how prehistoric, Roman, and indeed later people lived are affected by how we find the evidence for occupation. But the amount and location of the material that we discover are dependent not on the original dwellers but on the events and changes that have taken place since.

The history of archaeology shows this clearly. The first archaeologists who looked for prehistoric remains saw forts, ditches and burial mounds dotted all over England but concentrated in certain areas, notably Wessex, especially around Salisbury Plain, but also, for example, in east Yorkshire, the Peak District and south-west England (Figs. 2, 9, 17). Almost all these concentrations were on light dry soil. Thus there grew up the idea of open light-soiled upland areas being preferred places for prehistoric settlement, and the belief that everywhere else was either clothed in dark, impenetrable forests or was too marshy to be settled. As a result, a myth about prehistoric people developed which has never been eradicated. The basic error of this concept is that the people who developed it forgot or ignored the fact that by the late nineteenth or early twentieth century these light dry areas were marginal land, mainly under grass, and had been for centuries. Thus the sites of prehistoric and Roman settlements, fields, forts and trackways were preserved there better than anywhere else. The fact that people could not find a prehistoric settlement in the centre of, say, the Warwickshire clayland was not because prehistoric people never lived there, but because, unlike the downlands and wolds, later people had lived and farmed there for centuries and had destroyed all obvious trace of earlier settlement.

The next stage of development in the history of settlement archaeology was to compound this basic error even more. For archaeologists realized that outside the presumed chosen areas there was much archaeological material, in the form of chance finds discovered during building work, ploughing and drainage. Hundreds of stone axes, fine flint arrowheads, bronze spears and Roman coins came to light, especially during the extensive engineering, agricultural and urban developments of the late nineteenth century. These activities coincided with an increasing interest in and thus recognition of the material objects of past cultures. When plotted on maps, the location of these objects showed the archaeologists that the prehistoric and Roman people must have at least traversed the primeval dense forest, fen edges and marshy river valleys as well as upland mountain passes in order to have the opportunity for dropping their prized possessions. As a result, 'route ways' were postulated along which people were supposed to have moved from one dry area to another, beating their way through the forests (Fig. 12).

At the time it did not occur to most of the archaeologists involved that at least some of the finds that they were plotting on their maps might indicate the settlements of prehistoric and Roman people and not casual losses. This was probably partly because, owing to the circumstances of discovery and the limited interests of archaeologists of the period, only the fine axes were found, and not the flints or the stone chips that were also with them and which showed that people had lived there. Similarly, when an obvious Bronze Age axe was discovered, fieldworkers would not notice the minute fragments of pottery that lay round about because they were not looking for them.

The concept that prehistoric and Roman settlement was concentrated on the dry upland areas suffered a severe blow with the development of aerial photography from the 1920s onwards. For the aerial camera began to reveal the existence of thousands of archaeological sites that were quite invisible on the ground because they had been flattened by centuries of cultivation, but which could be seen from the air in certain conditions and at certain times of the year as a result of differential crop growth (Fig. 3). In the 1930s, 1940s and 1950s it became obvious that later prehistoric and Roman man in fact had lived, apparently in considerable numbers, in all the major valleys of England. With hindsight it became obvious that this was 'reasonable', for these valleys were floored mainly by large spreads of gravel producing dry soils eminently suited to primitive occupation. Thus, paradoxically, these discoveries were seen as further confirmation of the fact that settlement was confined solely to areas of light soil, even though the areas involved were now seen to be considerably larger than had hitherto been recognized. As more archaeologists took to the air, and cameras and films improved, further areas covered with dense prehistoric and Roman occupation were revealed. The evidence of crop-marks now showed indications of settlement on limestone plateaux, heathlands and sandstone hills. So the areas of apparently preferred prehistoric and Roman settlement again expanded, though the basic hypothesis remained.

Again there was a basic flaw, not only in the original concept, but in the appreciation of what the eye or the camera high above the ground can perceive and what the crops in the ground could show. For, except in exceptionally dry conditions, crop-marks will be visible only on light soils. Heavy

3 Prehistoric Settlement, Rustington, Lincolnshire *These crop-marks, visible only from the air, show part of a complex settlement area. The site has not been excavated but probably represents the result of long-term settlement 'drift' over a period of perhaps two thousand years.*

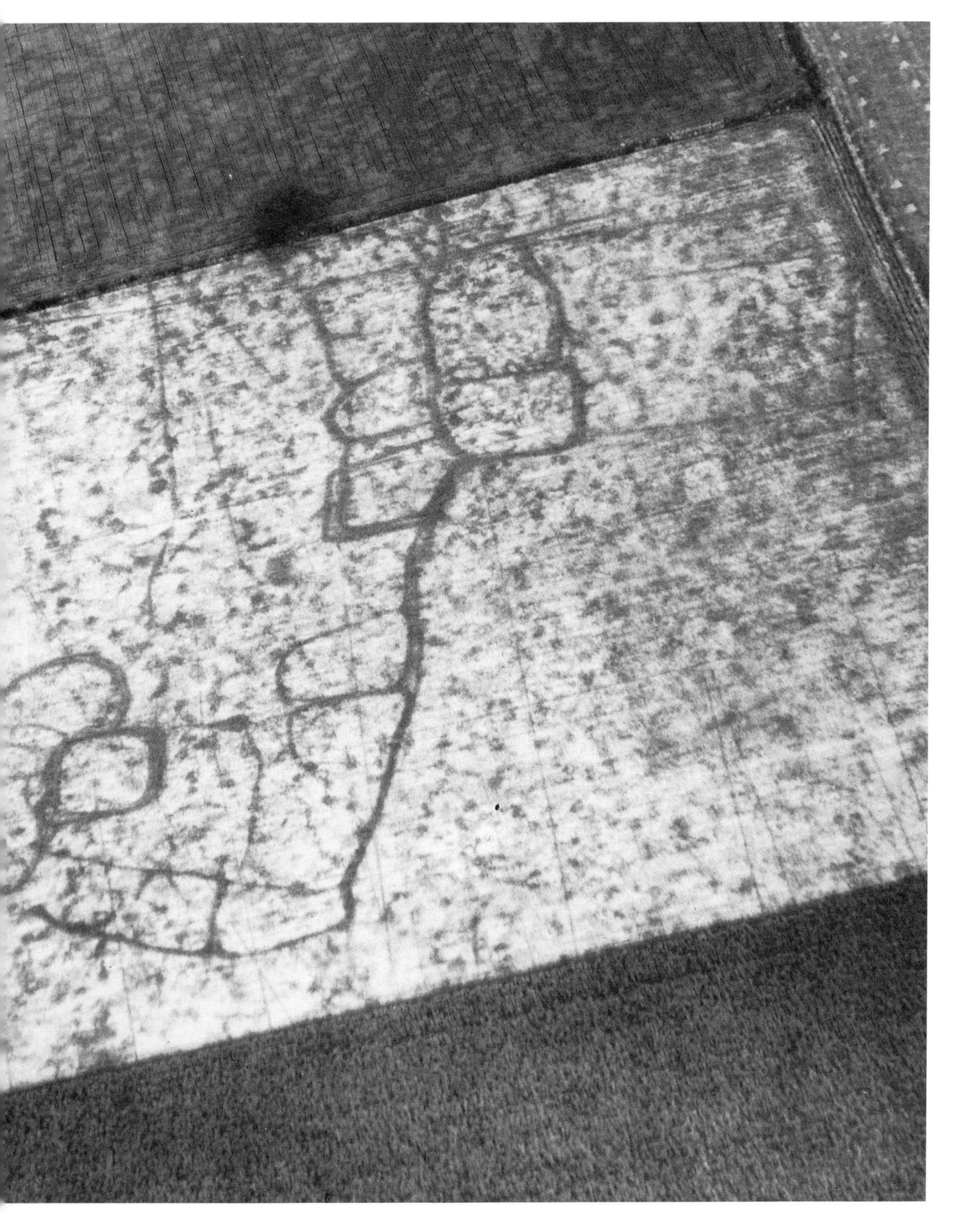

clayland, for example, because of its water-holding characteristics, will not show crop-marks except in times of extreme drought and even then the marks may not be clear. Continued air photography, especially during fine dry summers such as that of 1976, actually proved this when evidence of prehistoric and Roman occupation in some quantity on heavy clayland came to light (Fig. 38). These discoveries finally began to overturn the idea that ancient people lived only on dry soils and that they could not cope with heavy land which, it was assumed, would in any case have been forested in prehistoric and Roman times.

The next stage in disproving the old ideas came from another source with the growth of palaeo-ecological studies, including pollen and soil analysis and work on prehistoric snails and insects which enable archaeologists to understand past climates and environments. Recent work by a new generation of scientists, using highly complex and sophisticated techniques, has shown that, far from there being dense impenetrable forests throughout prehistoric times, the great attack on woodland in England started as early as 5500 BC, and that this continued fairly steadily so that by about 1000 BC there was probably less woodland in England than there is now. Thus the primeval forests that inhibited settlement and movement in prehistoric and Roman times have been removed from our maps.

Soil scientists have also recently produced new information which has perhaps tended to cause further confusion in archaeological minds as to where early prehistoric people lived. They have suggested that the lack of occupation sites in some places, such as in narrow steep-sided valleys, or on the wide flood-plains of major rivers, is the result of the massive amount of erosion and deposition of soil and rocks that has taken place over the last ten thousand years (Fig. 6). Some of this erosion and deposition was, of course, the result of natural processes, but most appears to have been caused by man himself as he removed the forests, ploughed the land and grazed and over-grazed his pastures. The result has been that many, perhaps most, of the earlier prehistoric settlement sites are in fact buried under many metres of silt and soil slips and thus can be found only by chance when deep modern digging takes place.

The final blow to the old ideas of where people lived in the centuries before Christ has come over the last ten or fifteen years as a result of the huge upsurge in interest in the past. This has produced more and better-trained professional archaeologists and, of much greater importance, hundreds of amateur archaeologists who are prepared not only to dig, but to comb the countryside for the minute scraps of pottery, flints, and stone that reveal the whereabouts of the homes of prehistoric and Roman people. These workers have, of course, found much additional evidence of early occupation on chalk downs, river valleys, heaths and sandstone hills. But they have also discovered Mesolithic, or Middle Stone Age, settlement on the Pennine moorlands, Bronze Age occupation on the clay farmlands of the Midlands and Iron Age and Roman farmsteads deep in the present woodlands of the country.

Thus what has finally emerged is the realization that early man lived almost everywhere in England, and that he was not controlled by his environment to anything like the degree that we have always believed. Indeed the reverse is true; prehistoric man actually controlled his environment most of the time. The evidence we now have also shows the great variety and complexity of prehistoric and Roman settlement and its mobility. With these new concepts in mind we can thus look at the detailed results of recent archaeological work and see more clearly than ever before how our remote ancestors lived.

-1-
The Beginning of Settlement

Though man lived in what we now call England during the long periods of warmer conditions in the latter part of the Ice Age, we know almost nothing about his form of settlement. It is not until after the final retreat of the ice, around 11000 BC[1], that the real story of settlement in England begins. Then, as the climate slowly improved, the bare landscape was gradually clothed with vegetation, wild animals moved into the new forests and fish populated the rivers (Fig. 4). These animals were soon followed by the so-called Upper Palaeolithic people. They were succeeded by a more numerous population who produced different types of flint tools and are known as Mesolithic or Middle Stone Age people. In the context of this book the distinction means little, for both groups had a very similar way of life and form of settlement which lasted longer than those of any succeeding people, some 5000 years. During this time there were considerable changes in the climate, and thus in the vegetation and wild animals available, so that over the millennia these people were forced to alter their sources of food.

At first the climate was extremely cold with a sub-arctic vegetation and with reindeer the dominant animal. It became milder and then extremely cold again before finally becoming warmer than today. This warm climate was at first very dry, but then became wet producing an almost country-wide vegetation of mixed oak forest, comprised mainly of oak, alder and elm trees. Within this forest the predominant wild animals were wild cattle, red and roe deer and wild pigs.

For both the Upper Palaeolithic and the Mesolithic people these animals were vital for survival. They were not only a major source of food, but also provided many other important materials, such as hides for clothing and shelter, and bone and antler for tools. So, although the population at this time also caught fish and gathered fruit and nuts, their reliance on the larger animals meant that their way of life, and thus the location and types of their settlements, was based on the feeding habits of these animals. Both reindeer and wild cattle tended to migrate over a considerable distance, the cattle for instance moving seasonally from the rich estuarine marshland pastures to the forested areas. The red and the roe deer moved over shorter distances but they too travelled seasonally from woodland to upland pastures.

The result was that early prehistoric people had a nomadic existence living in temporary structures

[1] All the dates given in the chapters on prehistoric settlements are given as actual years BC. This is to assist the general reader though archaeologists now rarely use this form of dating. They use the dates provided by Carbon-14 dating and usually express them as years bc. This is because Carbon-14 dates are not actual calendar dates and vary from these depending on age. To establish the actual date involves a complex process of recalibration which not all archaeologists are in agreement with. However, for the purpose of this book the Carbon-14 dates have been recalibrated to the generally accepted calendar dates. Roughly speaking a Carbon-14 date of 500 bc has a true date of about 700 BC, a date of 1000 bc a true date of about 1250 BC, 2000 bc a date of 2520 BC, 3000 bc a date of 3785 BC and so on.

4 Walton Common, Norfolk *One of the few surviving examples in England of a genuine prehistoric landscape. Ice lenses that appeared in the ground during the last glaciation have melted to create this pitted surface. It was in a countryside such as this that early Mesolithic man first lived and hunted.*

rather than permanent settlements. Very few traces of such settlements remain for in most cases almost nothing but minute flint and stone tools has survived the changes and the destruction brought about by later peoples in the landscape over the more recent 7000 years. Except in the most exceptional circumstances, the bone tools, the hide coverings of the tents or huts and all traces of where the shelters or bivouacs stood have now disappeared.

However, in spite of this, as a result of the most careful and time-consuming work by archaeologists involving the detailed searching of ground for flint tools, a very large number of settlement sites have been discovered and many have been excavated. The first point to note about these settlement sites, as pointed out in the introduction to this section, is that they are very widespread over the country and are by no means confined to the 'best' areas or types of land. One of the reasons why archaeologists believed that Mesolithic people lived only on such 'good' sites is that early discoveries were very often the result of the ease with which archaeologists found the worked flints on light, sandy soils. It is much more difficult to find such flints on, for example, chalk downland, where the surface of the modern soil is in any case covered with broken-up natural flints. It is almost impossible, except in special cases, to find the same flints on the Pennine moors where they are buried under later peat, which is in turn covered by bracken or heather.

As a result of the detailed work that has been carried out over the last few years we can now safely say that Mesolithic people did roam over every part of England and, for short periods at least, lived almost everywhere. Certainly there is still a concentration of sites on the lighter soils and along the streams and rivers, although this may be a bias from past discoveries. But the realization that a vast number of occupation sites are now known to exist almost everywhere else is far more important in its implications. Sites have been found in profusion on the upland moors of England, especially after accidental fires and the subsequent soil erosion. They have been discovered on heavy glacially-derived clay soils in Northamptonshire and Warwickshire, and on the high downland in Dorset and Wiltshire, as well as on the lower chalklands of south Cambridgeshire and north Essex. They lie along the sea coasts of southern and eastern England and can be found on the dry sandy heaths of East Anglia.

The very profusion of these sites might indicate that the population of England in these remote times was large. This is not so, for the available evidence has to be spread over 5000 years or more and each site may represent no more than a few days, or at the most months, of occupation. Nevertheless, it is important to realize that England, even at this period, was not an empty country with a few family groups ekeing out a miserable existence. There must have been a relatively large number of people in close contact with each other. Though it is, of course, impossible to estimate the population of the country at this time, we should perhaps be thinking of thousands rather than hundreds, people who were constantly on the move, and probably using well-known and well-defined trackways.

There is strong evidence of their ability to move about, or perhaps to trade with each other. For example, in southern England many Mesolithic people acquired a liking for tools made of chert as well as of the more usual flint. But the sources of chert, a sedimentary rock, are fairly limited. The main concentration of good-quality chert is on the Isle of Portland, in Dorset, and while the Mesolithic people of south Dorset clearly used it frequently, it has also been discovered on occupation sites all over southern England in Devon, Gloucestershire, Wiltshire, Hampshire and even in Surrey. Chert tools, of course, are easily recognized and durable and it is important to realize that, if these were traded, then many other objects, perhaps vital necessities of life, were also probably moved about, though by their nature they cannot have survived to have been discovered. Hides and skins, wooden tools and salt come to mind here.

Thus certainly by about 6000 BC there is good evidence that England was occupied by a fairly technologically advanced people, constantly on the move as they followed the herds of wild animals, but with close connections with their neighbours.

From those settlements that have been excavated we can obtain an even clearer picture of how the people of the time lived. For their settlements are not by any means identical, and they show a wide range of size and form which implies a complex way of life. Occasionally, in the few places where they occur, natural caves were used as semi-permanent or temporary dwelling places. More usually, how-

5 **Mesolithic Settlements** *These five excavation plans of Mesolithic settlements illustrate the poverty of settlement evidence in this remote period, as well as the difficulties of interpreting it.*

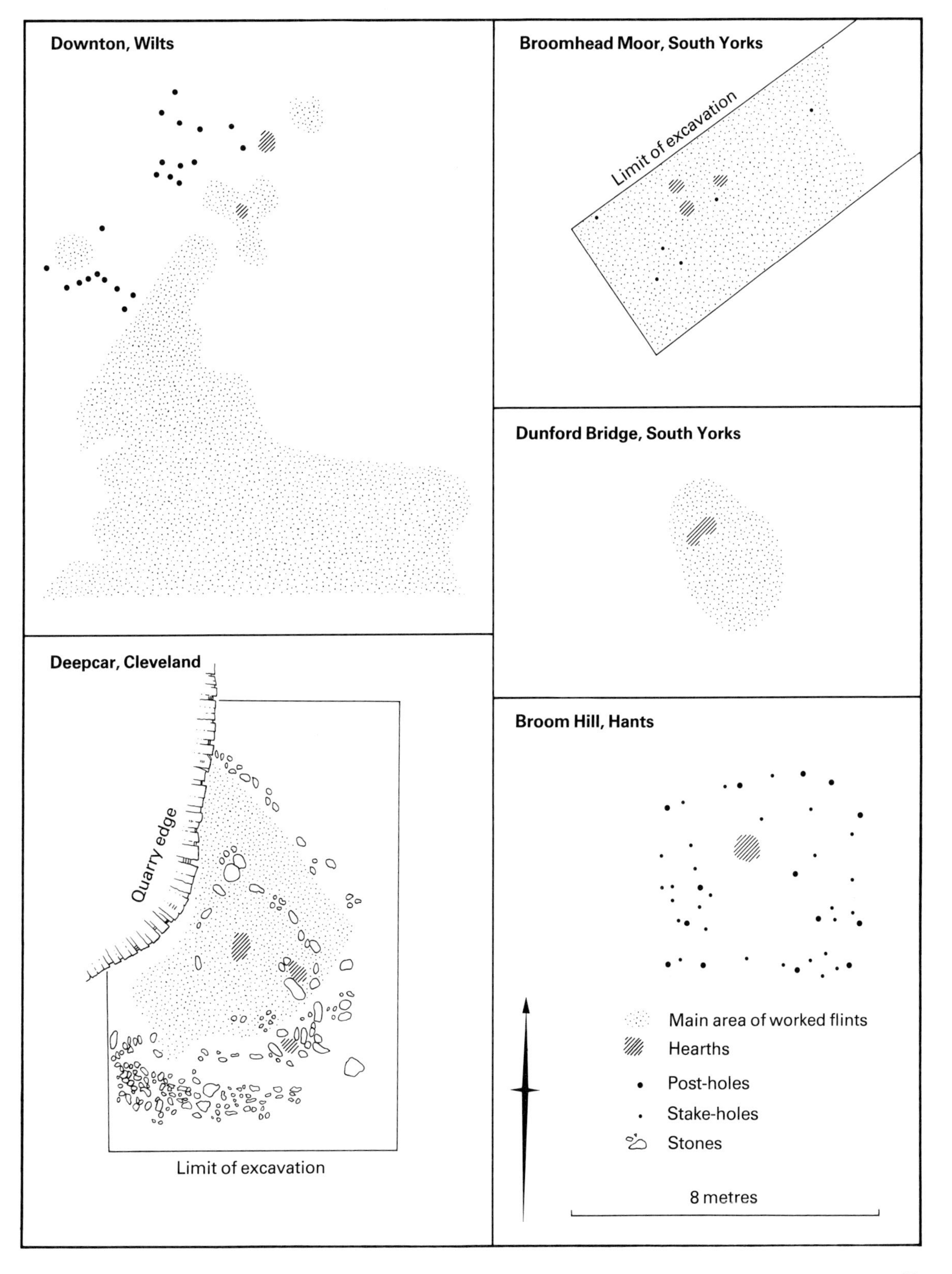
Downton, Wilts
Broomhead Moor, South Yorks
Limit of excavation
Dunford Bridge, South Yorks
Deepcar, Cleveland
Quarry edge
Limit of excavation
Broom Hill, Hants
Main area of worked flints
Hearths
Post-holes
Stake-holes
Stones
8 metres

ever, Mesolithic people lived in huts or shelters and it is the traces of these which enable us to appreciate what they must have been like and to identify different settlement types.

One site was discovered at Downton, Wiltshire, on the dry gravel terraces of the River Avon (Fig. 5). Here, in addition to a very large spread of flint tools and the innumerable waste flakes formed during their manufacture, a series of small holes which had once held both upright and inclined posts was discovered, together with the places where there had been fires, perhaps for cooking food. These post-holes appeared to be the remains of two very light timber structures, only 2.5 metres in diameter and perhaps representing two short-lived wigwam-like tents.

Another, equally temporary, site was excavated by Mr Wymer at Thatcham, Berkshire, in the Kennet valley. This, one of many known along that valley, produced even less evidence for a structure. All that was recovered was a number of concentrations of domestic rubbish, mainly bones and flints, as well as several hearths, each about 7 metres in diameter. The concentrations of rubbish probably represent the areas covered by small tents or shelters of hide-covered branches, and indeed a pile of stones on the edge of one such area was interpreted as possibly being connected with the weighing down of hides.

Of the Mesolithic sites in northern England, a group in the southern Pennines has been examined by Mr J. Radley (Fig. 5). On Broomhead Moor, at a height of over 400 metres, at least ten sites have come to light. One of these has been excavated and consisted only of a number of stake-holes with flint tools around it, associated with some hearths. This site again appears to be no more than where a temporary hut or tent was positioned. Not far away, at Dunford Bridge, two other sites were found, only 20 metres apart, at a height of 500 metres. One was in a sheltered position and consisted of only a hearth and a scatter of flints, the other was on the exposed edge of a steep slope and seemed to have had a rough stone wall protecting it from the elements. Another site situated on a high spur between the Rivers Porter and Don at Deepcar, near Sheffield, produced two roughly concentric circles of stone which may have been the bases of two temporary tents, or possibly just of two windbreaks.

In a very different area, on Hampstead Heath, London, another Mesolithic site also produced holes where upright posts once stood, associated with hearths, while at a site near Havant, Hampshire, the discovery of semi-circular arrangements of stake-holes suggests the existence of simple windbreaks. At Farnham in Surrey and Selmeston in East Sussex only shallow hollows have been found, where people seem to have crouched to prepare meals, make tools or clean hides.

However, once again, the limits of archaeological evidence must be appreciated. Though the traces of structures are slight, we must not fall into the trap of assuming that these structures were primitive and their inhabitants poverty-stricken and permanently close to starvation or hypothermia. One only has to see how comfortable and warm the wigwams of American Indians are and yet how little trace they leave on the ground in order to appreciate that the structures we discover may not reflect the actual standard of living of Mesolithic people. It is quite possible that these people had well-constructed hide-covered tents which were ideal for their nomadic way of life and which provided all the shelter and comfort they wanted.

On rare occasions archaeologists have found quite substantial remains of Mesolithic houses. At Broom Hill, Braishfield, near Romsey in Hampshire, a group of perhaps four huts has been discovered (Fig. 5). One was roughly circular, 4.5 metres by 5 metres, and made of fairly stout timbers driven into the ground, with a hollowed interior containing a hearth. This may have been a much more permanent encampment than the previous examples described and this raises the whole question of the functions of the various forms of Mesolithic settlement.

For while most Mesolithic sites are certainly of a very temporary nature, it would seem that they can be divided into four types on the basis of their function. There are those which appear to have been occupied only once, and then very briefly, while there are others which seem to have been re-occupied on a perhaps seasonal basis over a number of years. Those described from the southern Pennines fall into the first category, while some of the sites in the Kennet valley are of the second type. In addition those of the first type are usually very small and cannot have been used by more than a handful of people while those of the second are sometimes larger. There are also sites, if such they can be called, which have hardly been occupied at all and consist merely of a handful of waste flakes and one or two tools. Such scatters of flint have been located in many places in England but those in north-west Northamptonshire are particularly notable. In this part of the country there are perhaps twenty such sites known from an area of about 26 square kilometres of heavy clayland. In addition there is a fourth form of settlement, which seems to have had a more permanent occupation, perhaps lasting for a number of years. The Broom Hill, Braishfield, site is of this form and another example is at Upleatham, in Cleveland, where a large number of hearths and evidence of extensive food preparation were discovered.

From this evidence, as well as using modern ethnographic parallels, a reconstruction of the possible way of life of Mesolithic people may be suggested. It is likely that in any given area there was a fairly large extended family or 'tribal' group with its own clearly defined territory or hunting area, perhaps loosely based on the territory of migrating animals as well as on the availability of river or coastal fishing and other natural resources. These groups would have had a base camp where the people lived together for certain times of the year, but which was occupied by only a few members of the group, the old and very young, for most of the time. The area around such camps would be extensively exploited for the smaller mammals, such as beaver and roe deer, and thus the camp would have had to be moved after a certain number of years. These base camps are perhaps those which show extensive evidence of semi-permanent occupation, with very large quantities of domestic rubbish. Below these base camps in scale were perhaps gathering camps which were much smaller, possibly used by ten to fifteen people in the autumn and early summer for the gathering of special local resources such as nuts and berries, or for the hunting of certain animals on migration. These are the sites which have evidence for stake-constructed dwellings, but with a relatively small amount of domestic rubbish, indicating repeated visits over a number of years.

The next type of settlement was probably what has been described as a light-exploitation camp. These would have only been occupied by single families of up to about five people during the winter and summer as they moved around collecting specific types of food, such as shellfish on the coast and small mammals in the forest. Such sites may be those of small size with little domestic debris, very few tools and very slight evidence for any shelters at all. Finally there would have been bivouac sites where small hunting parties of perhaps two or three people stayed overnight. These are the sites with no hearths and perhaps only a few waste flakes.

Looking at the distribution of these different types of Mesolithic settlement emphasizes the likely seasonal and temporary occupation of many of the smaller sites. Most of the larger 'base' camps, while not actually in 'good' positions with regard to their precise location, seem to be situated in places where there was easy access to a variety of resources. Thus the base camp at Upleatham, just south of Redcar, in Cleveland, is close to the coast, the estuary of the River Tees and its lower valley, as well as to the Cleveland Hills and the North York Moors. At the same time, many small sites of the same period have been found to the south on the northern edge of the moors, and these are likely to be the gathering camps or light-exploitation camps.

In the Pennines, the picture is the same. The large 'base' camps seem to lie below the 100 metre contour, while the smaller sites are all on the high moor, often above 400 metres. Even in the Midlands the same pattern is detectable. The large site at Elkington, Northamptonshire, perched on a low sandstone hill, is well sited for access to the surrounding clayland, then forested, as well as to the valleys of the Avon and the Welland. The scatters of flints discovered in the surrounding parishes may well be the sites of the light-exploitation or bivouac camps of the hunters and gatherers operating from the main camp. Another area where these exploitation camps may be recognized is on the east side of Dartmoor, where a number of small occupation areas, each set around a spring head, have been found.

Recent work in south-eastern England has indicated that these 'base' camps are approximately 10 kilometres apart and thus the centres of territories some 100 square kilometres in area. If this is indeed so, then we have a landscape, at least in the late Mesolithic, already divided up and perhaps controlled by well organized groups of people in considerable numbers. All this is supposition, but it does explain the variety of Mesolithic settlement sites and may well explain how they functioned in the hunting and gathering economy of the period.

Throughout most of these centuries then, Upper Palaeolithic and Mesolithic man lived a nomadic existence, but towards the end of the Mesolithic period, around 5000 BC, there is some indication of a change in the environment. It is difficult to be sure exactly what was happening for the evidence is slight and not fully understood. Scientists who have studied the changes in vegetation at this time by pollen analysis have detected alterations in the natural vegetation in certain parts of England which cannot be explained away as natural phenomena. For example, there is evidence of some small-scale deforestation accompanied by soil erosion, as well as localized increases in the amount of alder, hazel and ash. In addition, there appear to have been some clearances within the forested areas, although these were not apparently very extensive, and the beginning of blanket bog formation on the uplands following the removal of trees. The interpretation of these observations is disputed, although most experts believe that they were caused by man interfering with his environment for the first time. It is perhaps relevant to note that it is at this same period that there is a massive increase in the number of occupation sites. There are numerous late Mesolithic settlements of relatively small size along the coasts and edges of rivers and especially on the upland moors. It seems very likely that these reflect a rapid increase in population which may have led to pressure on the established pattern of hunting and gathering territories and to a shortage of game.

If this is what happened then the woodland clearances and the creation of pastures may be the result of deliberate action by Mesolithic people to improve grazing land and perhaps reflect early attempts to domesticate deer and cattle instead of merely hunting them. The increased occurrence of alder, hazel and ash, which are all pioneer woodland species, suggests the use of fire to clear land, and the fact that charcoal has been found in association with the evidence for such species supports this idea. Modern experiments in North America show that such firing would have influenced the animal population of an area in three ways: by increasing the total number of animals, by increasing their weight, health and reproduction rate and by controlling their movements and thus restricting them to certain areas. The latter effect alone would have tended to eliminate nomadism and lead to a rather more settled life. However, we shall never know what the end result of these trends would have been for the whole pattern of settlement in England was radically altered around 4500 BC by new developments, new ideas, new techniques and perhaps by new people. These completely disrupted the existing pattern: many Mesolithic people were absorbed into the new cultures, while others were driven out onto the upland marginal land.

-2-
The First Villages and Farmsteads

The impact of the new ideas and perhaps new people who arrived in England around 4500 BC is still marked in the modern landscape by major monuments, many of which can be visited. These include a large number of burial mounds, the great earthen long barrows of southern and eastern England and the chambered 'megalithic' tombs which are even more widespread. The famous West Kennet long barrow in Wiltshire, Kit's Coty House in Kent and Hetty Peglers Tump at Uley, Gloucestershire, are among the best known, but there are many others. In addition there are very obvious major sites which appear to have been the temples or religious monuments of these people. Stonehenge, at least in its early period, was one of these as were the great earthen circles at Avebury in Wiltshire and Arbor Low in Derbyshire. Yet impressive as these sites are, they represent only one part of the culture of these people and arguably the least important part. They tell us very little of the Neolithic way of life and settlements.

Unfortunately, despite the major monuments that do survive from this period, very few traces of Neolithic settlements remain. Reconstructing a picture of them and their distribution involves using all the forms of evidence and techniques that were discussed in the previous chapter, from the pottery fragments and animal bones revealed by the trowel of the archaeologist to the pollen grains found in contemporary soils and peat deposits from which the palaeobotanist can reconstruct the climate and vegetation of the period.

All this material tells us much about the people who lived in England between 4500 and 2500 BC. Unlike their predecessors they certainly made pottery, for pieces of their crude vessels are commonly found. Of greater significance is the fact that it is clear they were not merely hunters and gatherers but were expert farmers growing crops (mainly cereals), herding cattle, sheep and goats, and keeping pigs. They certainly had the use of the plough by 3000 BC. They made fine tools of flint, including instruments for preparing hides, cutting meat, reaping crops and hoeing fields. They had superb axes. These were also usually of flint, capable of cutting down relatively large trees, but some very superior axes were also made, from especially hard rock. These latter axes were produced in 'axe factories' which have been identified in many places in south-west Cornwall, Northumberland, Leicestershire and the Lake District (Fig. 6), as well as further afield in north Wales and in northern Ireland. There were also other tools of bone and wood which were used for more mundane purposes.

The existence of the axe factories and the discovery of their products hundreds of kilometres away from them indicates a complex trading system and it is known that pottery was among other objects regularly traded. Such trade, which probably included commodities such as hides, salt, and animals, whose transfer is not recorded in the archaeological record, suggests well-defined trade routes and perhaps trackways. Indeed a whole series of deliberately constructed trackways of this period has been found in the Somerset Levels. In addition to this, the very existence of the burial mounds and the great temples noted earlier implies a complex ritual or religious life and probably a highly developed social structure with chieftains, priests and peasants.

All this evidence indicates that in Neolithic times, probably from 4500 BC to around 2500 BC, England was occupied by a group of people who were technically advanced, with a complex social structure and religious organization, apparently very different from the earlier Mesolithic groups. Where did these people come from? They seem to appear in the archaeological record, fully fledged, with all their techniques and organizations well developed, around 4500 BC. Until recently it was confidently assumed that Neolithic people arrived with all their new ideas from the continent, where the various techniques were already in being, and drove out the older Mesolithic people to the remoter areas of England. Now we are not so sure. The changes in the landscape that have been detected in the late Mesolithic, coupled with the evidence of changes in how people lived, support the view that Mesolithic people themselves may have acquired the ideas and techniques from abroad and slowly developed them, without a massive influx of new people. This is a difficult and almost insoluble problem, for by the very nature of archaeological work it is very difficult to find the actual beginning of a new idea, technique or social change. It is only when such ideas, methods of manufacture or ways of life are widely used or practised that they become recognizable in the archaeological record. It may be that the development of the Neolithic life-style commenced as early as 5000 BC, but it is only when it was widely accepted, at about 4500 BC, that we can be sure of its existence.

What were the settlements of these people like? As in the Mesolithic period, it is not easy to find them, even though the advanced methods of agriculture practised at the time tended to ensure that settlements were now more permanent than they had ever been before. The many religious monuments show clearly that Neolithic people were capable of erecting considerable structures in wood or stone. In the chambered tombs, for example, the burial chambers themselves and the long passages that connect them with the outside world, all lying concealed beneath the earthen mounds, are usually constructed either of massive upright slabs, with cap stones to form a ceiling, or of beautifully laid dry-stone walling with corbelled roofs. Similarly, when some of the unchambered earthen long barrows have been excavated, the remains of massive timber structures have been discovered, usually in the form of deep post-holes where large timber uprights once stood. A large timber building of this type, measuring 12 metres by 6 metres, was found at the long barrow at Nutbane, Hampshire. It may have had a ridged roof and was probably used as a 'mortuary house'. This lay inside a rectangular enclosure surrounded by a wooden fence. When its use as a place of burial was ended the structure was burnt down and a long mound erected over it. Similar buildings have been found beneath many other long barrows.

Even more impressive are the traces of circular timber buildings that have come to light during excavations of some of the great Neolithic temples, or 'henges' as they are usually called. For example, in 1967 excavations were carried out by Dr G. Wainwright within the henge known as Durrington Walls, near Amesbury, Wiltshire. The site is bounded, as with most henges, by a large bank with an internal ditch. Within this enclosure were at least two circular structures, whose plans were revealed by concentric rings of post-holes. One, 14.5 metres in diameter, was interpreted as having been a circular roofed building, perhaps with a central raised lantern. Another 'temple' or henge at Marden, near Pewsey, also in Wiltshire, produced a circular ring of post-holes 10.5 metres in diameter, while at a similar site at Mount Pleasant near Dorchester, Dorset, five concentric rings of post-holes, 38 metres in diameter, were discovered.

Neolithic people may have based the layouts of their domestic dwellings on the structures erected for religious purposes. Indeed the rectangular 'mortuary houses' under the earthen long barrows have been regarded as 'houses of the dead', directly modelled on the normal houses of the living. However, when we turn to the actual settlements of Neolithic times we find that archaeologists are faced with considerable difficulties and that, up to now, settlements showing good evidence of structure and plan have been very hard to find.

There are two reasons why this should be so. First, the preservation of the stone chambers within, and the post-hole structures under, the long barrows or burial mounds is the result of the protection afforded by the mounds themselves. The covering of earth has protected the structures from subsequent destruction and thus saved them for modern archaeologists. Equally, the existence of the mounds today, easily identifiable as burial places, enables the archaeologist to pinpoint and excavate the site without any difficulty. The domestic settlements, which have no diagnostic boundaries, cannot be identified so easily and thus have been discovered only by chance, or more often because they were lying below later occupation which drew the archaeologists there in the first place.

The second and more important reason lies in the subsequent history of any site. This, of course, applies equally to the Mesolithic settlements, and even to later prehistoric, Roman and indeed medieval settlements, but is particularly valid in the Neolithic period. It is now over 4000 years since these Neolithic settlements were occupied. During those years much has happened to the sites, in terms of both human and natural events, to alter, destroy or obscure the traces of the original occupation. To take the effect of natural agencies first, it is not usually recognized how much erosion has taken and still is taking place in the landscape. For example, it is estimated that the surface of the chalk downlands in southern England is now up to one metre lower than it was in Neolithic times as a result of the dissolving of the chalk ground surface and the subsequent removal of the acid insoluble residue. Thus the remains of Neolithic farmsteads, hamlets, or even villages which once existed on chalk downlands will have been entirely removed, except for the lower parts of exceptionally deep pits or post-holes. The details of small structures, hearths, floors or any other activity which took place on the then existing ground surface will have disappeared long ago. And the material removed from the downlands has, inevitably, found its way downhill into the adjacent valleys in vast quantities. This means that any Neolithic settlement that lay in a valley may be buried under a considerable depth of hill-wash or river and stream deposits and thus will never be discovered except by the merest chance.

The role of chance in finding burial sites was demonstrated when a Neolithic site was found on the edge of the River Thames at Runnymede, west of London. This site was discovered some 2 metres below the present ground surface only because a bridge for the M25 was being built across the river and this needed deep concrete footings to support it. It was during the excavation for the bridge abutments that the remains of the Neolithic occupation came to light. Even then the site had been largely removed by the action of the river itself at some time between 2500 and 800 BC leaving little for the modern archaeologist to discover.

The same processes of erosion and deposition have occurred all over the country to a greater or lesser extent. Thus, even in the high uplands and deep valleys of northern England, such as Langdale in Cumbria (Fig. 6), the chances of finding the sites of Neolithic settlements in anything like a complete form are remote. On the upland moors yet another factor comes into play to hide any possible remains: the development of blanket peat bogs. Most of these were formed in the early Neolithic period or later and successfully covered up earlier occupation debris. The development of these peat areas is in fact the result not of a natural process but of interference by man, and follows the clearance of woodland from the uplands. Man's actions elsewhere have speeded up the true natural processes of erosion and deposition, leading to increased destruction of Neolithic and other prehistoric settlements. Arable farming on sandy heaths, limestone plateaux or chalk downland produces much faster rates of erosion than if the land had remained under forest or pasture.

As we noted in the introduction, one of the main features of all settlement in England is its mobility. Few people lived on the same spot for very long, not more than a couple of centuries at the most, especially in the prehistoric period. After relatively short periods of time the original sites were abandoned completely or at least the settlements were shifted a short distance away. The old dwelling places were then incorporated into the fields of the immediate descendants of the first occupiers of the site and these people and later generations removed the stones, ploughed the ground, grazed it, built their own settlements on top of it, and then ploughed it again many, many times.

With all these factors playing a part in the destruction or concealment of Neolithic settlements, it is difficult to believe that any traces of them could be discovered. Yet many hundreds of sites are known and, though most of them tell us little about the detailed appearance of the houses and the arrangement of the settlements, they are very important for our understanding of the overall distribution of Neolithic occupation. Most of these occupation areas can be recognized by scatters of minute pottery fragments, flint tools and the numerous waste flakes produced during their manufacture. More substantial evidence is provided by the pits found during excavations. These are

6 Great Langdale, Cumbria *The scattered farmsteads are assumed to be medieval in origin and no traces of any earlier settlement are visible. Yet on the hillside to the left are Neolithic axe factories which were being exploited as early as 4000* BC. *Where did the workers live? It is likely that their homes were either where the present farmsteads stand, or they are buried beneath the screes and valley-bottom alluvial deposits formed in the last six thousand years.*

actually only the lower parts of deeper pits, which may have been dug for the storage of grain around and within most Neolithic settlements. The rest of the occupation areas have usually been destroyed, ploughed away or removed by erosion. Nevertheless, fragmentary though they are, these pits can tell us much. After their use as grain stores, they were usually back-filled with domestic rubbish and thus when they are excavated they are found to contain pottery, bones, flint tools and apparently less important objects which are vital in understanding the way of life of Neolithic people as well as the nature of their environment. For example, cereal grains indicate what crops were grown, and snail shells and beetle cases what the climate and natural vegetation may have been like.

But the pits tell us much more. First, by their overall distribution they show that Neolithic people lived everywhere and were not restricted to 'good' places or 'light' dry soils as the old textbooks would have us believe. Of course, many have been found on the familiar chalk downlands, such as those near Avebury and Amesbury in Wiltshire, at Maiden Castle, Dorset, and at Dunstable, Bedfordshire. But they are also known from the valleys of the major rivers of England. They have been found on the edge of the Great Ouse at Eaton Socon, Bedfordshire, close to the River Cherwell at Cassington and Stanton Harcourt in Oxfordshire, and near the River Stour at Wimborne, Dorset. They lie on the seashores, as at Clacton and Walton-on-the-Naze in Essex, on limestone hills, such as Charmy Down, near Bath, on heavy clayland in Suffolk and heathland in Norfolk and Surrey. They have been found in Devon and Yorkshire, Northamptonshire and Kent, Gloucestershire and Berkshire. They are known from such varied places as Cambridge and Bournemouth, and were discovered under what is now the main runway at Heathrow Airport. Other evidence of Neolithic settlement has been found in the Eden Valley in Cumbria, which seems to have been particularly densely occupied, as well as all along the Cumbrian coast. The general pattern is of total occupation by a large number of Neolithic people in all parts of England, with little indication of restrictions imposed by environmental considerations.

While the distribution of pits and scatters of pottery and flints are of value in showing the widespread nature of Neolithic settlement, it is more difficult to see the size and layout of the actual settlements themselves. Do the pits and scatters of pottery represent single farmsteads or hamlets, or did large villages exist? Although six or eight pits might represent a single farm in use over five to ten years, do twenty or thirty pits mean that the site was occupied by one farmstead for twenty odd years or by a small hamlet for only five years? This sort of question is almost impossible to answer, especially as it is only on very rare occasions that the total number of pits which must have existed has been discovered by archaeologists. Chance discoveries or the limitations of time and money often mean the archaeologist can examine only a small part of what may have been a very large site.

However, while bearing these difficulties in mind, it is possible to draw some general conclusions. First, it is likely that the commonest form of Neolithic settlement was indeed a single farmstead, or a hamlet, perhaps occupied by a single or extended family. On the other hand there certainly were larger settlements of village-like proportions. At Hurst Fen, Mildenhall, Suffolk, over 200 pits were discovered by Professor Clark and this was certainly not the full extent of the site (Fig. 7). Such a number surely indicates a considerable settlement, probably in being for more than a few years. Yet on the other hand there is good evidence that many of the smaller farmsteads and hamlets were very short-lived and were abandoned perhaps after only two or three years. Indeed, there is also evidence that a certain proportion of the Neolithic population, like their Mesolithic predecessors, were still nomadic, at least at certain times of the year.

At Walney Island, on the Cumbrian coast, semi-circular rings of very slight stake-holes have been discovered, perhaps the remains of temporary tents. The obvious explanation is that the site was the seasonal camp of hunters who were still preying on the wild animals coming to the coastal pastures. On the other hand it could have been the home of Neolithic farmers practising transhumance with their domesticated herds of cattle, bringing them down to the rich pastures for the summer season before returning to the sheltered valleys in the winter. Another temporary site was found at

7 Neolithic Settlements *Here the excavation plans of three Neolithic settlements indicate both the variety of form and the complexity of occupation at this period, and the limits of archaeological evidence. None of the excavations, large and expensive though they were, established the full extent of the settlement.*

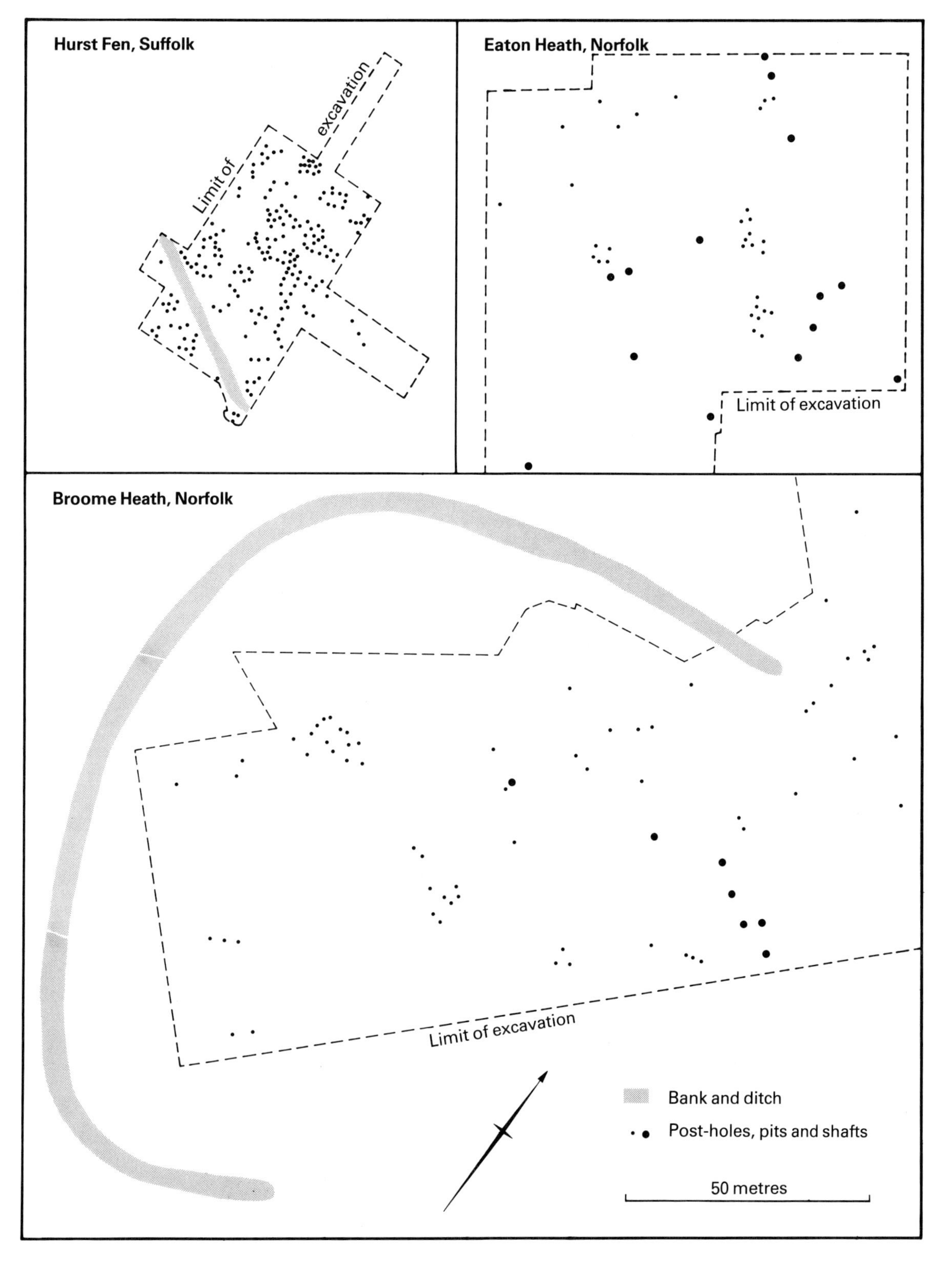
Hurst Fen, Suffolk
Limit of excavation
Eaton Heath, Norfolk
Limit of excavation
Broome Heath, Norfolk
Limit of excavation
Bank and ditch
Post-holes, pits and shafts
50 metres

Rackham in the Sussex Weald near Pulborough. Again a series of stake-holes and a hearth were found, lying within what was at that time a small clearing in the forest. This too may have been a temporary camp for swineherds bringing their pigs into the forests for autumn foraging, just as their descendants did until relatively recent times. One more equally short-lived site has been excavated on the heavy clayland within the new city of Milton Keynes, Buckinghamshire. There again there was no evidence of permanent buildings and the signs of deliberate attempts at drainage indicated to the excavator that it was only used in winter, perhaps for hunting as well as for grazing domesticated animals.

This mention of actual structures, temporary though they were, brings us back to the evidence for more substantial buildings which can be related to those found in and under burial mounds and within the temples of the Neolithic period. In spite of the problems connected with preservation and discovery discussed earlier, such structures have been found in a few places. What appear to have been, admittedly, fairly flimsy circular huts have been noted on the chalk downlands at Winterbourne Dauntsey, near Salisbury, Wiltshire, and at Stonea, on a gravel island in the Cambridgeshire fens.

Much more substantial was the rectangular timber house at Haldon Hill, near Exeter, Devon. It was approximately 9 metres long and 5 to 6 metres wide, with upright timbers set into the stone footings of what was probably a turf or wattle wall. Two central posts may have supported a ridge pole. Another house at Fengate, near Peterborough, Cambridgeshire, the only one excavated in a vast area which has produced extensive Neolithic occupation debris, was almost square. It measured 7 metres by 6 metres and was defined by a shallow trench or ditch which probably held a wattle and daub wall. There was also evidence for a central post supporting the roof. Another possible Neolithic house has been excavated at Aldwincle, Thrapston, Northamptonshire. Though the site was later used for burials, the earliest timber structure, again about 6 metres by 7 metres, is likely to have been a domestic dwelling.

This kind of evidence, limited though it is, does give an insight into the type of house which was perhaps common in Neolithic times. But, just as important, as a result of the meticulous excavation methods, particularly at Aldwincle and Fengate, it is also possible to suggest that the structures that have been found were relatively temporary and that the sites were not occupied for long. The houses were clearly not rebuilt after their original timber had rotted away and, by analogy with similar wooden structures of medieval date, are unlikely to have lasted for more than twenty-five years at the most. Thus again we have evidence of a short-lived pattern of settlement which is so characteristic of much of the history of man's occupation of England.

However, though individual houses, farmsteads, hamlets and even villages may have had short lives, the subsequent abandonment may not have meant the total desertion of the site. For even in this remote period there is evidence for a feature of settlement that recurs throughout all the later periods and which is usually described as 'settlement drift'. This is the process whereby over a period of time a settlement, of whatever size, will gradually move – perhaps up or down a hill-slope, or round in a circle. Why this should happen is not totally understood. Certainly, the fact that a site occupied for any length of time will become 'sour', strewn with domestic debris, covered with abandoned pits and generally unwholesome, and thus may be abandoned in favour of a new area nearby, is a possible explanation. However, as always when dealing with the remote prehistoric period and with somewhat slight evidence, it is easy to accept over-simplistic and deterministic explanations. In the historic period, where the evidence is much more complete, the same phenomenon of settlement drift is apparent and can usually be explained by changing patterns of communications, the pressures of economic events, or as the result of the whim of the landowner. It may well be that the whims of fiercely independent tribal chiefs could have had as great an effect on the movement of Neolithic settlements as those of medieval lords certainly had on medieval villages.

Whatever the reasons for Neolithic settlement drift, it appears to have taken place, though naturally it is not always easy to document clearly. One site which gives some indication of the process over a very long period indeed is that excavated on Broome Heath in Norfolk (Fig. 7). Some sixty-seven of the usual pits were discovered, spread over a wide area, together with a few post-holes of some possible wooden buildings. These post-holes were all that could be found – the normal erosional processes had presumably destroyed many others. Perhaps the most interesting discovery was that, although the structures and pits found on the site could not

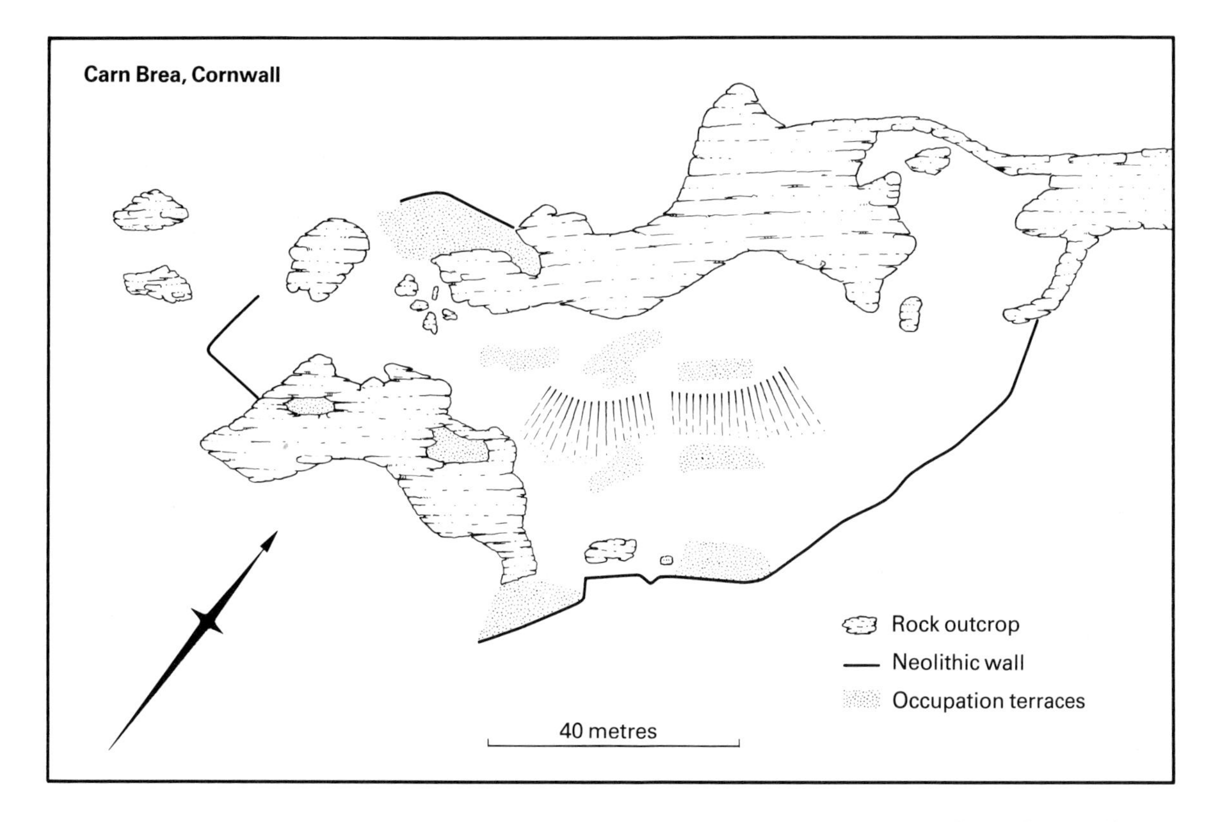

8 Neolithic Settlement, Carn Brea, Cornwall
Though this is the only known example of a semi-fortified Neolithic village, with houses set within a walled enclosure, it may be that it was a very common form of settlement at this period.

represent anything more than a small village, the dates obtained by Carbon-14 methods seem to indicate that the site had been occupied for at least 1200 years. Given the relatively few pits and the short life of timber structures, as noted earlier, this is plainly impossible. A better interpretation is that this site, which was at least 180 metres across, contained one or two farmsteads which, over many centuries, moved around the general area. In addition, although there is no way of proving it, there might well have been long periods when the site was abandoned and farmers returned to it only sporadically. Towards the end of its life, the later inhabitants constructed a large curving bank and ditch around part of the site, and fronted the bank with a timber revetment. This must have given it a fortified appearance, but it certainly was not defensive as the bank only formed a C-shape in plan. Its purpose is unknown and it indicates yet another variable in the catalogue of Neolithic settlement types.

Another variant, this time a village enclosed by a continuous stone wall, perhaps defensive in intention, has been excavated by Mr R. Mercer on Carn Brea, a high granite massif between Redruth and Camborne in Cornwall (Fig. 8). Its high eastern peak is surrounded by a dry stone wall which thus encloses an irregular area some 116 metres by 80 metres. Within it, tucked into spaces between the bare granite rock, were ten deliberately levelled platforms or terraces. On these terraces the excavator discovered numerous post- and stake-holes, indicating a number of successive buildings, as well as hearths, pits and domestic refuse, including pottery, flint arrowheads and axes. The site appears to have had a relatively short life, perhaps of just under 400 years. Here we seem to have a genuine protected Neolithic village of a unique form. On the other hand, this site has survived so well probably simply because it is situated in a granitic area where it was either impossible or unnecessary for later people to destroy the remains. The same form of encircling wall may have existed elsewhere in England, but in stoneless areas, where these walls

would be built of earth, they would not have survived later mutilation. In any case there are at least two more such sites in Cornwall which, though they have not been excavated, appear to have a very similar form. It may be that the Carn Brea site is more typical than we suspect. Indeed, recent excavations at Crickley Hill, Gloucestershire, have led to the discovery of what may be another fortified settlement protected by a surrounding bank and ditch.

LEFT **9 Knap Hill, Wiltshire** *The circular earthen enclosure on the hilltop is a Neolithic causewayed camp. The small rectangular enclosure, attached to it at the bottom right, is a Roman farmstead.*

BELOW **10 Neolithic Causewayed Camp, Mavesyn Ridware, Staffordshire** *On the very edge of the River Trent, which is visible in the top right-hand corner, the aerial camera picks out the interrupted ditches of this early prehistoric enclosure. It was perhaps a meeting place for hundreds of Neolithic farming communities who lived in the surrounding area around 3000* BC.

The temporary encampments, farmsteads, hamlets and villages discussed so far are not the only type of settlement of the Neolithic period. There are many very curious enclosed sites, widespread in England, usually known as causewayed camps. Some, such as those at Knap Hill, Wiltshire (Fig. 9), and Hambledon Hill near Blandford, Dorset, have remained as earthworks for us to see today because of their positions on high downland which has not been cultivated since they were constructed. They usually consist of one or more circular banks, with external ditches, and with a number of causeways crossing the ditches giving many points of access into the interior. Aerial photography over the last twenty years has revealed many more similar sites on lower ground, which have been completely flattened by later cultivation and are now only visible from the air as soil- or crop-marks. These include one at Staines in Surrey, near the River Thames, another at Orsett, north of Tilbury in south Essex, one at Mavesyn Ridware close to the River Trent, Staffordshire (Fig. 10), and one at Briar Hill above the River Nene at Northampton.

These causewayed camps have for long presented problems of interpretation. Few of them have any evidence of contemporary occupation *within* them, though their ditches are usually filled with domestic refuse, especially animal bones, as well as burials of both humans and animals. They have been variously interpreted in the past as seasonal meeting places, trading posts or fair grounds, religious sites or enclosures for over-wintering cattle. None of these explanations is entirely satisfactory although the last seems the most plausible.

There are three other important points about these camps. At some of them, notably at Windmill Hill, near Avebury, Wiltshire, the excavators found evidence of 'normal' occupation in the form of the ubiquitous pits, pre-dating the construction of the enclosure. That indicates that the site was occupied by farmers somewhat earlier in Neolithic times. At others, as at Hambledon Hill, there is evidence of contemporary occupation, even though the inevitable erosion has removed most of it. At Briar Hill at least one rectangular timber structure 5 metres by 2.5 metres has been discovered within the camp. Finally, most excavators have concentrated on digging through the banks and ditches, and, to a lesser extent, parts of the interior. Hardly any have excavated the areas *outside* the camp. At Windmill Hill, dense concentrations of flint tools and waste materials from their manufacture have been noted on the hillside south of the camp and it may be that these represent the sites of contemporary occupation which surrounded the camp. The same is true of Briar Hill, where there is some evidence of contemporary occupation in the area around the camp. Whatever the purpose of causewayed camps, they and their implied surrounding occupation areas add one more facet to the picture of settlement in England in Neolithic times.

So far we have stressed the complexity of Neolithic settlement, as well as its density and its mobility. But these settlements did not exist in a territorial vacuum. As was discussed earlier, even in Mesolithic times there is some evidence that Mesolithic people actually occupied some form of tribal land units or economic territories. Thus changes of settlement which occurred at that time were already taking place within the no-doubt flexible and fought-over boundaries of these territories. By the Neolithic period, when the population had increased and the land was used much more intensively, the need for defined territories in which individual families or tribal groups lived and produced their food must have been stronger.

Though one of the great myths concerning so-called primitive people is their alleged freedom to move about untroubled by restrictions of boundaries or territorial limits, all the evidence of history and anthropology suggests otherwise. Human society, at whatever stage of development, appears to have or have had clearly defined areas of land in which groups of people operate, whether they be hunters, pastoralists, farmers or a modern industrial nation. It is unlikely that Neolithic farmers were any different, and thus there must have been forms of territorial or tribal areas at that time.

It is difficult to prove that this was in fact so but there are some supporting indications. Whether the causewayed camps were connected to occupation areas or not, their use as meeting places, for cattle penning or trade fairs, might mean that they were also the centres of large tribal areas where people from the surrounding land met seasonally for a host of social or economic purposes. In this sense the camps might have operated in a fashion not unlike the hillforts of the Iron Age which we shall examine later. At the moment the number of known causewayed camps is much smaller than that of the later forts and they must have always been relatively few. But from the examples we do have it could be suggested that they may have significance in terms of territory. For example, some of the hilltop camps seem to be sited to overlook and dominate the land below them. This is especially true of Knap Hill (Fig. 9) and Rybury in Wiltshire, which lie close together on the chalk escarpment overlooking the Vale of Pewsey. The territory that they appear to control mirrors very closely the medieval parishes of Alton Priors and All Cannings, and while it is not suggested that these parishes have any exact relationship with Neolithic land-divisions, the apparent coincidence may be significant. Indeed a large and important Iron Age settlement lies just below Rybury at All Cannings Cross and the causewayed camp itself is overlain by an Iron Age fort. It is just possible that the territory of Rybury Camp continued as a recognizable unit into the Iron Age at least.

This picture of a close relationship between Neolithic camps and later forts and their possible territories is seen elsewhere. The great Iron Age fort at Hambledon Hill, Dorset, lies cheek by jowl with the earlier causewayed camp there. Even more significant perhaps is that Maiden Castle, Dorset, the greatest hillfort in England, which was eventually replaced by the Roman town of Dorchester, lies on top of a causewayed camp. Likewise the camp at Briar Hill, Northampton, has the Iron Age fort of Hunsbury a little to the south and the major Roman settlement of Duston to the north. With medieval Northampton to the north-east, this may represent an example of the settlement drift of a major territorial centre over millennia rather than centuries.

One of the few serious attempts at reconstructing Neolithic territories has been carried out by Mr P. Drewitt in Sussex. There the distribution of the known causewayed camps has been combined with the evidence of other settlements and burial mounds. The work suggests that there could well have been a series of major territories some 4 kilometres across on the South Downs. This 4 kilometre size is, of course, a somewhat crude abstract model and cannot be correlated with any real boundaries on the ground. Nevertheless, the exercise has a real validity in that it does suggest a form of organized territorial unit at this period, a feature that recurs in later times.

Up to now in this discussion we have perhaps quite wrongly implied a picture of a very varied and intensive pattern of settlement existing in a stable landscape. But in fact nothing could be further from the truth. The Neolithic period lasted for almost 2000 years and during that time there were immense changes in the landscape, partly caused by natural variations in climate, but mainly by the activities of man himself. At the end of the Mesolithic, there was a fairly large population of hunters and gatherers, living in a variety of temporary and more permanent camps all over England, with somewhat slight evidence of small-scale forest clearances and other man-induced vegetational changes taking place by about 5000 BC. Then, perhaps around 4500 BC, the whole pattern of settlement and land use was radically changed, either because new ideas were adopted or because new people arrived in England. In the remoter parts, some Mesolithic people lived on in the traditional way, but elsewhere they either rapidly acquired the new techniques of agriculture, domestication of animals, pottery manufacture, etc., or were pushed out by the new people who brought these techniques with them. Detailed work by palaeobotanists, using the evidence of pollen found in buried soils or in peat deposits, indicates that there was widespread if localized removal of the forests between 4500 BC and 4000 BC, presumably carried out by means of the new stone and flint axes, but also by firing the woodland to produce rich, if short-lived, nutrients in the soils. Judging by the pollen evidence most of these clearances were for arable land.

The actual settlements associated with these generally small-scale woodland clearances are as yet fairly rare and it is this lack of settlement evidence that makes it difficult to ascertain accurately exactly when and how the Neolithic period begins. But, from 4000 BC onwards, there is evidence of widespread forest removal on a huge scale. Tens of thousands of hectares of land were cleared on downs, heaths, upland moors and river valleys and the new land was cultivated and grazed intensively. Small hamlets and farms appear and even villages in ever increasing numbers. There is evidence of large-scale and long-distance trade, the first causewayed camps appear and the great burial mounds and temples are constructed. The resulting picture is of a very widespread dispersed settlement pattern over much of England with perhaps a large population which had developed strong social, economic and religious ties.

By 3800 BC, or a little before, it is clear that a stable society had developed, living in an equally stable landscape. There is some evidence of regional specialism developing with an increase in pasture-land on the chalk downlands of southern England at the expense of earlier arable and a similar extension of grazing on the Pennines and the North York Moors. However, this pattern was not to last. Around or just before 3200 BC changes occurred. First, there was a considerable rejuvenation of woodland as a result of large areas of earlier clearances being abandoned. This process has been noted in southern England, in Somerset, East Anglia and in the extreme north-west of England. In places, notably on the chalklands of Wessex, though grazing by animals continued, it was on scrubland and not on open grassland. Not all the older cleared land was abandoned for, in the very same areas that there is evidence of regeneration of forest, there are also clear indications that in some places arable farming and pastoralism continued unabated. Certainly long-distance trade still flourished, but many of the temples were either abandoned or used only on a restricted basis and the large communal tombs were given up and replaced by small round burial mounds or by flat cemeteries (burials without mounds). There is also some indication that settlements decreased in number and became smaller.

In essence there appears to have been a reduction of population, an abandonment of land, and less social and religious activity that involved large-scale communal work. Why this change occurred is unclear. It may be that disease was rife, or that there had been over-exploitation of the land to cope with the rising population, resulting in soil erosion, depletion of soil nutrients and thus famine and starvation. We do not know. All we can be sure of at the moment is that around 3000 BC there was a general contraction of settlement.

However, within a short time, the process of expansion was restarted. Well before 2500 BC there was a renewed attack on the forests, and many new settlements appeared. These were even more widespread than before, and extended into all the major river valleys, along the coasts, around the edges of the fens and into the relatively high upland areas. The temples were used again, and burial mounds and cemeteries became common. Though over most of the country a mixed arable/pastoral farming economy was practised, in southern England, and especially on the chalklands, pastoral farming was dominant and even elsewhere transhumance was widely practised. What seems to have emerged by 2500 BC was a society that was much better organized than before, with a better balanced pattern of land use after the excesses of the initial expansion. Further, by 2500 BC new techniques arrived in this country, which brought its inhabitants into what archaeologists usually call the early Bronze Age.

-3-
The Outlines Established

In the archaeological record, there is an important change just before 2500 BC. A new and very different form of pottery appears, highly decorated and usually known as Beaker pottery. Associated with this pottery are the earliest metal tools, first of copper, then of bronze. These objects were until fairly recently seen as being the result of a wave of invaders from the continent of Europe, the Beaker People. But, as with the changes that marked the beginning of the Neolithic period, we are now no longer so sure. It is equally possible that the existing population acquired the expertise for the new pottery and tools by trade and contact with Europe. Whatever the truth of the matter, the new ideas or people were quickly absorbed into the older culture, other pottery types, a mixture of old and new, emerged and the use of bronze gradually became widespread.

In terms of the history of settlement the arrival of the Beakers and the technology of bronze had little effect and there is no evidence of any new type of dwelling or form of occupation. The problems of discovering and interpreting settlements of this period are almost identical to those discussed earlier for the Neolithic, and the picture that finally emerges is much the same. Thus, at Risby Warren, in Lincolnshire, a settlement of the Beaker period was examined by Mr D.N.Riley. It comprised the by now familiar pits, containing pottery and other refuse, but no structures were found. This led to the assumption that the site was that of nomadic hunters or herdsmen. However, it is now realized that on the same heathland subsequent erosion, both natural and man-induced, has removed all but the deep pits and thus the remains of the permanent houses that once stood there have been totally erased. Far from the site being a temporary encampment on the grassy heath, it was probably the centre of a small arable farm.

In sharp contrast is the Beaker settlement found in the valley of the River Avon at Downton, Wiltshire. Here the site was completely sealed by later deposits of valley drift. Its very existence was unknown until Professor Rhatz, while excavating a Roman villa, discovered it below the Roman levels. Here there had clearly been well-built timber houses of which only the post-holes survived. Similarly, at Swarkestone, on the River Trent in Derbyshire, the massive post-holes of a circular Beaker house were found partially under the protective mound of a later barrow. Yet another Beaker settlement has been discovered in the middle of the modern village of Fladbury near Evesham in Hereford and Worcester, close to the River Avon, while the excavators were engaged in revealing Saxon occupation.

The recent meticulous examinations by Mr R.Bradley at Belle Tout, near Beachy Head in East Sussex, have revealed a more complete picture than elsewhere. Several successive and short-lived occupation sites were discovered, which included one circular hut and three which were rectangular or trapezoidal. It was also shown that two of the houses were within a small close, or paddock, bounded by a bank. The work at Belle Tout is also important in that it shows the process of settlement drift very clearly. The earlier Beaker occupation was confined to a small area on the valley floor. The settlement then appears to have moved up the valley a short distance, at which stage the surrounding enclosure was constructed. Then some time later the settlement moved further up the valley again, before finally being abandoned.

Though the number of Beaker and early Bronze Age settlements which have been excavated on a large scale is relatively small, there is other evidence, at least in some areas, to indicate their whereabouts. This is the discovery by chance of unstratified material in other excavations or by close examination of modern ploughed fields. One important result of such finds is the indication that in certain places early Bronze Age settlements were often located not far from the burial places of their inhabitants. While this is true to some extent in the Neolithic period as well, by the early Bronze Age the very large number of burial mounds of the period in some areas allows us to use them as indicators of the total pattern of settlement. One such study has been carried out along the valley of the River Great Ouse between Milton Keynes in Buckinghamshire and St Neots in Cambridgeshire by Dr H.S.Green. Here a number of important results emerged. Firstly, settlements appear to be located on all types of soils with only a slight preference for what is now grade one agricultural land. Secondly, there may have been as many as a thousand settlements in the area roughly covering a time-span of, at the maximum, nine hundred years. If each settlement lasted a minimum of twenty-five years, there must have been at least twenty-seven to twenty-eight settlements along the river at any one time and perhaps considerably more. Though the majority of these may well have been single farmsteads or hamlets, it is of interest that along this same length of river in medieval times there were almost sixty villages. Thus it is possible that in early Bronze Age times the spacing between settlements may have been little more than twice the distance between the villages in medieval times. Such calculations are based on a number of unprovable assumptions and may be regarded as highly speculative. Nevertheless, even at the crudest level, they do show the widespread nature and relative density of settlement in this period.

The distribution of the early Bronze Age settlements in the Ouse valley has also been analyzed to see if probable territories or economic units can be postulated for the period as they have been for Mesolithic and Neolithic times. It has been estimated that during the Bronze Age there were perhaps eighteen separate territories along the river with their centres about 5 kilometres apart. In north Dorset, an almost identical figure has been calculated for early Bronze Age territories there. This spacing is very little wider than the 4 kilometre intervals estimated for the Neolithic territories in Sussex. On the other hand, Mr A. Fleming, using similar techniques for a small area of Salisbury Plain, found that the presumed territories were only just over 2 kilometres across. Whatever these differences may mean in terms of population, settlement density and land-use, the existence of some form of territorial division of land in the early Bronze Age seems to be certain. Exactly what these territories looked like and how they were defined is, of course, not known, but it was presumably within such units that the settlements moved as they were rebuilt and re-sited over the centuries.

Once more it must be stressed that such territories may not have been exactly like our modern or indeed medieval parishes or townships, though on the North York Moors possible early Bronze Age territorial units have been recognized that seem to be almost exactly the same as those of medieval townships. Other work on early Bronze Age territories in Wessex has suggested that certain areas were used only seasonally by pastoral farmers practising transhumance on the downland. At first sight this may seem to indicate that the territories were very different from medieval parishes. Yet it is worth remembering that in many parts of England medieval parishes often had portions of land detached from the main areas, which were originally used for seasonal activities and special agricultural purposes. Thus the medieval parishes in north Kent had detached parts in the Weald which were used for keeping swine, while in east Dorset medieval parishes on the chalklands had detached portions on the heathland to the east, apparently for grazing animals. Other complex territorial arrangements, known to have existed in medieval and later periods, such as the rights of access to the estuarine

11 Bronze Age Hut Circle, Challacombe, Devon *The remains of one of the many isolated huts on Dartmoor that may date from the early part of the Bronze Age. It can only have housed a single family.*

marshes of the Humber held by parishes in North Humberside, and the inter-communal land divided between numerous parishes on high moorland such as that which still remains on Fylingdale's Moor in North Yorkshire, could already have existed in the early Bronze Age. The evidence, weak though it is, suggests that this was so.

As with the earlier discussion on Neolithic times, it is important to realize that these early Bronze Age settlements and their assumed territories did not exist in a stable landscape. The renewed clearance of the forest and the expansion of population and thus habitation which we noted as beginning in the later Neolithic, just before 2500 BC, was accelerated in the centuries after 2000 BC. The evidence deduced by the palaeobotanists shows that continued colonization of the remaining wastes took place far beyond the even remotely 'attractive' areas and extended well into the upland moors and lowland heaths. Indeed many of the isolated hut sites which dot the lower slopes of Dartmoor may date from this period and may be the temporary homes of farmers extending their activities on to near marginal land (Fig. 11).

Most coastal areas came under pressure and areas of sand-dunes, as at Gwithian in west Cornwall, were exploited, occupied and cultivated. The basis of this activity was a diverse and rich society in which there were resources to indulge in massive non-material activities. Many of the older temples continued in use and great cemeteries with burial mounds of elaborate form, stone circles and stone rows appear. In certain areas, notably Wessex, the production surplus led to the brief emergence of an incredibly rich and probably aristocratic group whose wealth is perhaps only hinted at by the richness of the gold and bronze objects discovered in their tombs.

Once more, however, such expansion could not last. Towards the end of the early Bronze Age, there are again indications of over-exploitation. On large areas of the upland moors blanket peat formed, and on the chalk downlands of southern England massive soil erosion occurred, both probably as a result of continuous arable cultivation and/or overgrazing. There is even evidence of wind erosion from bare fields and the degeneration of soils, and of areas of poor land being cleared and cropped, producing even further degradation.

There is some evidence of a return to an older, more primitive method of living as the resources of the country began to run dry. For example, small settlements have been found in remote areas that seem to be the sites of temporary hunting parties as they are associated with large numbers of arrowheads and tools for preparing skins. The fact that there was a deterioration in the climate at about the same time made matters even worse, but the real reason for the problems at the end of the early Bronze Age was that the land had been over-exploited by man. Thus, as at the end of the Neolithic, at about 1500 BC, there was another period of retraction and reorganization.

-4-
The Countryside Fills Up

Until recently the Bronze Age was divided by archaeologists into early, middle and late periods. Now there is a tendency only to have an earlier and later Bronze Age. For the purpose of this book this is convenient, for in terms of the history of settlement the latter part of the Bronze Age has a coherent development, even though it can be subdivided according to distinct pottery styles and types of metalwork. This late Bronze Age seems to have begun around 1500 BC and was at once marked by a massive change in the pattern of settlement and land-use.

The most important visual effect of this change was what appears to have been a huge reorganization of the countryside. This is not easy to document, for as always with these remote periods later activity has largely erased all the evidence in what were perhaps the most favoured areas. But the indications that we do have are very striking. First, palaeobotanical evidence shows that there was a renewed attack on the remaining primeval woodland as well as on those areas already cleared and allowed to regenerate. This process began around 1400 BC and continued on an ever-increasing scale right through this period and indeed beyond. Even more striking is the physical evidence of landscape change. From the beginning of Neolithic times up to the early Bronze Age, the settlements that we have discussed so far were usually surrounded by small fields. Sometimes the actual fields survive. Elsewhere only plough marks cut into the ground surface and then sealed by later burial mounds remain, while in most places only the evidence of cereal pollen and grains of carbonized wheat or barley indicates the existence of fields. But this evidence, together with the palaeobotanical indications of the clearing of woodland, suggests that the field systems surrounding Neolithic and early Bronze Age settlements were the result of continuous piecemeal expansion, and abandonment, with an untidy appearance as a result of slow growth. This is the type of pattern that would perhaps be expected from a society engaged in slow colonization of land.

In contrast, the evidence from the later Bronze Age appears to show a planned landscape that has been totally reorganized and laid out on a large scale. The places where this is most obvious are in those areas which were never used again for intensive arable or only rarely so and where the remains of this activity are therefore still clearly visible. Perhaps the best examples of this planned landscape are to be found on the downs of Wiltshire, Hampshire, Dorset and Berkshire. There the traces of very large field systems can still be seen over many square kilometres, laid off from clearly defined base-lines. These blocks appear to have been imposed on the landscape, and to have a considerable element of planning in them. The base-lines run for many kilometres and the fields themselves ignore local details of topography.

In other places in Wessex there is evidence for an alternative form of land-use. Long linear boundaries, marked by banks and ditches, run for considerable distances across the downs and enclose vast areas of downland, often having central focal points from which the boundaries radiate. Some of these linear banks run across, and so put out of use, earlier field systems. These huge territories, enclosed by linear ditches, were almost certainly used as animal grazing grounds and thus, in Wessex at least, there appears to have been planned agricultural specialization of arable and pasture.

Elsewhere on the upland areas of England there is similar evidence for landscape planning on a large scale. On the lower slopes of Dartmoor, for example, many banks, or 'reaves', have been discovered forming extensive enclosures for arable and pasture and with field systems laid out inside them. Other areas where large-scale boundary banks and ditches enclosing huge areas of land for both arable and pasture have been recognized include the chalklands of east Yorkshire and central Lincolnshire, large sections of the North York Moors and parts of upland Northumberland. If this kind of landscape reorganization took place in the upland areas, there is every reason to suppose that it was also going on in the more fertile valleys and lowlands. Though it is difficult to find evidence to support this theory, some recent work does confirm this conclusion. At Fengate near Peterborough, on the edge of the fenland, large-scale excavations by Mr F. Pryor have shown a set of parallel drove-ways running back from the fen edge and bounding long blocks of land, each sub-divided into fields and closes (small paddocks).

The lack of evidence of lowland reorganization in the later Bronze Age is misleading and when we turn to the evidence for settlement types of the period the picture is equally distorted. Most of the settlements that are known and which have been excavated also lie in the upland areas, where they have been preserved and can be identified. In the valleys and the lowlands, later destruction has removed all but the vaguest traces. Yet these must be taken into consideration, for, as we shall see, it is very likely that the most densely exploited and settled areas of England were in the broad river valleys and the deep claylands.

This point is clear if we look at one form of late Bronze Age activity that is apparently unrelated to settlement. Our major sources of information on later Bronze Age technology, wealth and warfare are the isolated finds of single bronze tools and the great hoards of tools and weapons which continue to be found quite by chance from time to time. These have, in the main, been discovered not on the uplands but in the lowlands. It has usually been said that such hoards and other objects were just buried and 'lost' by peripatetic bronze-smiths on their way around the countryside. More recent work has indicated that they, like the barrows of the earlier Bronze Age, may well indicate the places where richer settlements were located. If this is so, and it seems very likely, we should look for the major settlements in the lowlands, and not on the uplands which were, even by then, probably marginal land. To take specific examples, the great Wilburton Hoard was found on an island in the Cambridgeshire fenlands while the similar New Bradwell Hoard came from the edge of the Great Ouse in Buckinghamshire, both lowland sites. Just outside Brigg, in the Ancholme Valley, north Lincolnshire, a late Bronze Age spearhead and bronze pin came from deposits which also contained the remains of a timber trackway. Indeed a study of the distribution of later Bronze Age tools in Lincolnshire has demonstrated an apparent concentration of wealth on the lower ground near the rivers, which probably means that there were settlements there as well. This is brought out even more clearly along the edge of the fens in south-east Cambridgeshire (Fig. 12). Almost all the known Bronze Age burial mounds lie on the hill-slopes of the chalk downland well away from the fen. The great majority of the contemporary Bronze Age tools and weapons, discovered by chance over the years, have been found along the fen edge itself.

However, we can go much further than merely to infer the existence of lowland later Bronze Age settlements, for many are actually known. The problem, as always, is that they are usually discovered by chance and thus the subsequent excavations rarely involve the totality of the site. This problem is compounded by the fact that later destruction, erosion, or deposition has always removed or obscured much of the material. But even so what is known is impressive. Perhaps the most important of these lowland settlements is that which

12 Bronze Age Settlement in South-East Cambridgeshire *Though no actual settlement sites of the period are known from this area, the distribution of bronze tools and weapons surely indicates that Bronze Age people lived and worked along the fen edges in exactly the same places as Roman and medieval people lived. The burial mounds, mainly on the high downland, are known only because they lie on land which has not been ploughed until recent times.*

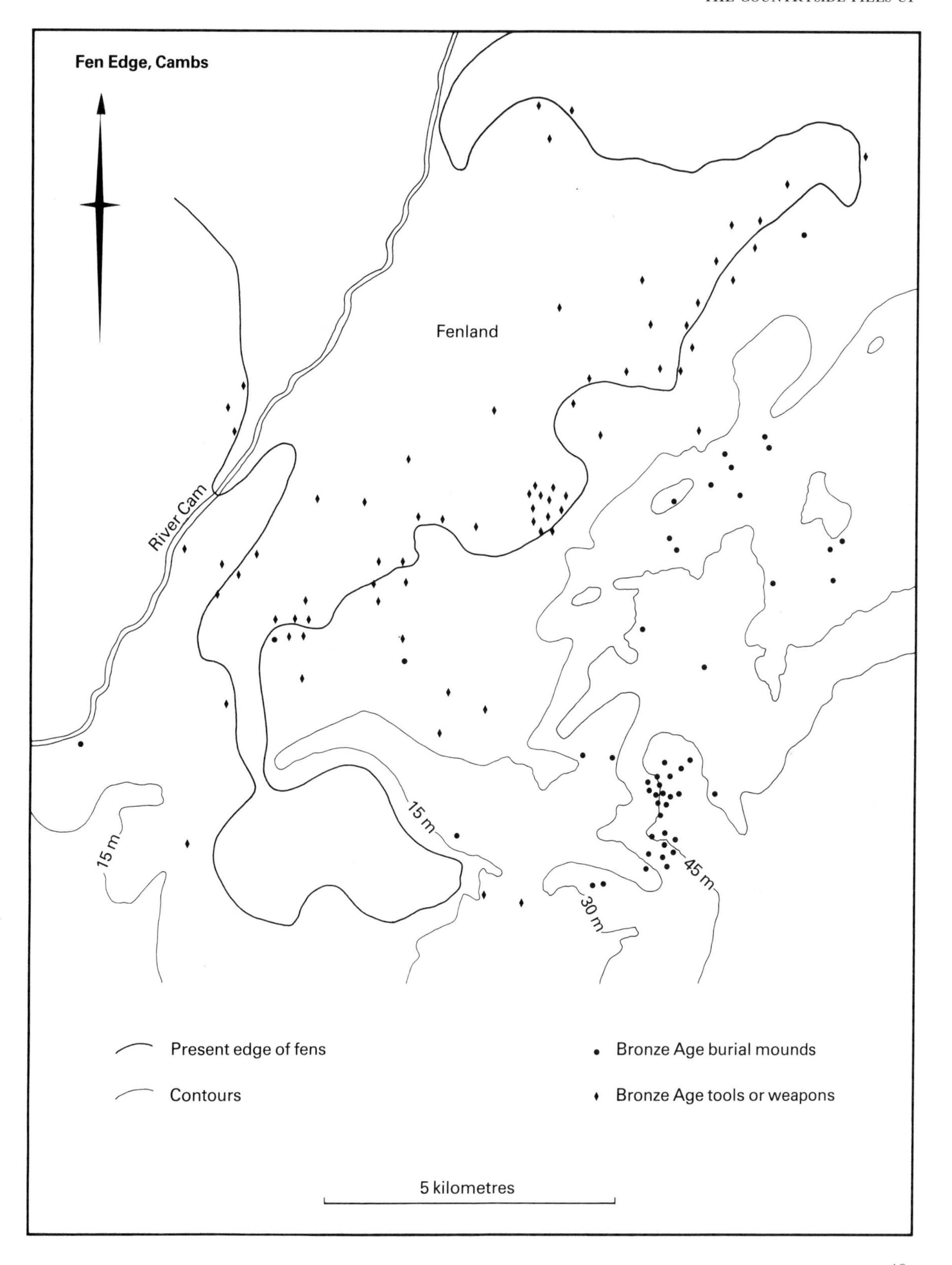
Fen Edge, Cambs
Fenland
River Cam
15 m
15 m
30 m
45 m
Present edge of fens
Contours
Bronze Age burial mounds
Bronze Age tools or weapons
5 kilometres

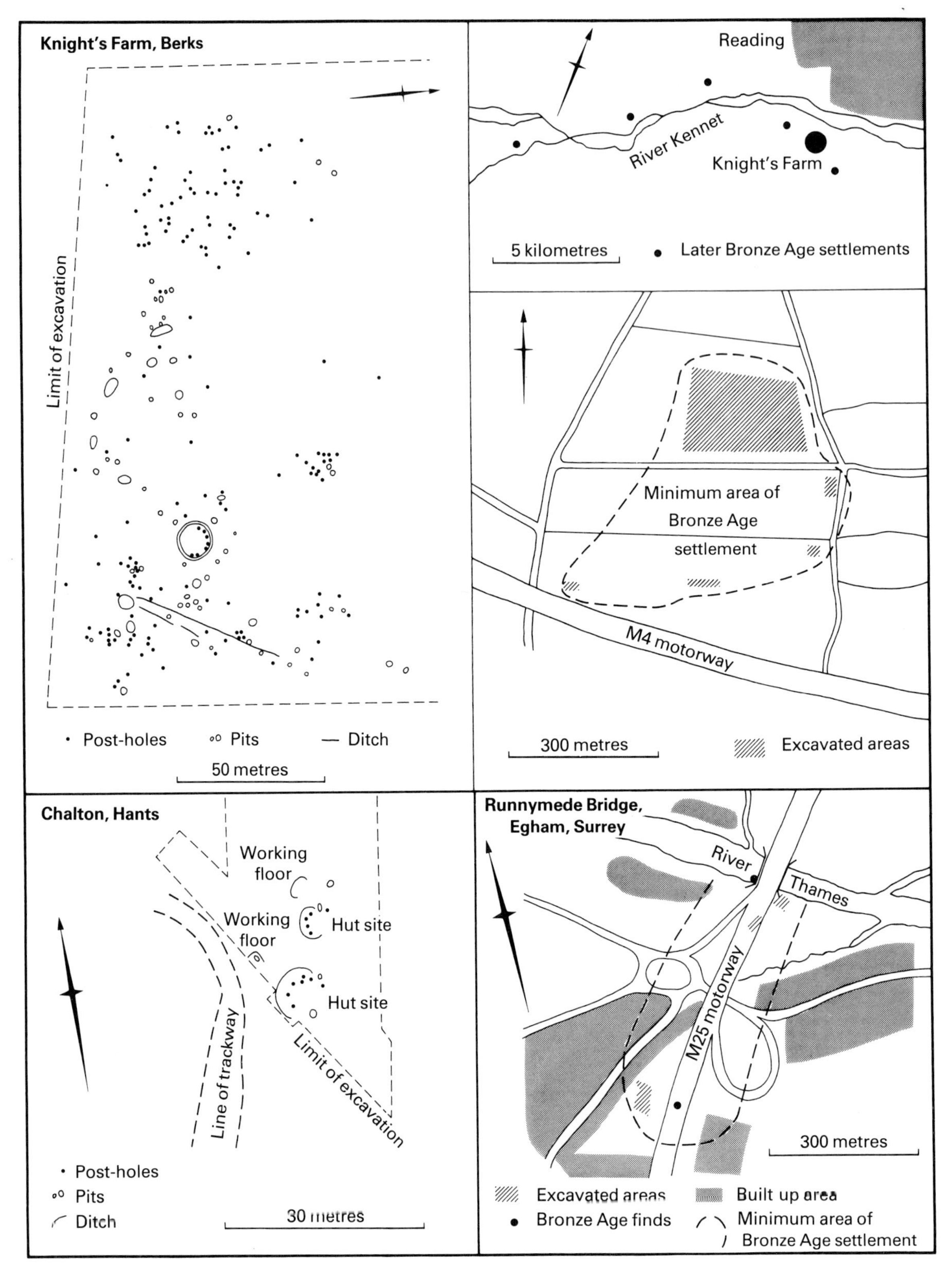
Knight's Farm, Berks
Limit of excavation
Post-holes
Pits
Ditch
50 metres
Reading
River Kennet
Knight's Farm
5 kilometres
Later Bronze Age settlements
Minimum area of Bronze Age settlement
M4 motorway
300 metres
Excavated areas
Chalton, Hants
Working floor
Working floor
Hut site
Hut site
Line of trackway
Limit of excavation
Post-holes
Pits
Ditch
30 metres
Runnymede Bridge, Egham, Surrey
River
Thames
M25 motorway
300 metres
Excavated areas
Built up area
Bronze Age finds
Minimum area of Bronze Age settlement

was found at Runnymede Bridge, Egham, in Surrey on the side of the River Thames, already discussed as the site of Neolithic occupation (Fig. 13). The later Bronze Age remains were much more extensive and included part of a wharf or quay on the river bank, which in itself suggests large-scale water-borne traffic and perhaps trade. More important was that the discovery, made during the construction of a bridge on the M25, together with other material found during the building of the motorway itself, indicated that this late Bronze Age settlement was very extensive, perhaps as much as 450 metres across. As usual, apart from the wharf, no clearly identifiable structures were discovered and only the inevitable pits and post-holes appeared. The evidence of slightly different dates for the material found also suggested that the settlement moved about its overall area, yet another example of settlement drift over a time span of probably two hundred years or so. Another important feature of the site was the discovery of a major hoard of bronze objects within the occupied area. This supports the idea, noted above, that in general such hoards do indicate settlement.

The Egham site is large and complex and, apart from the earlier Neolithic material, entirely of the late Bronze Age. A very different late Bronze Age settlement is that which was found at Billingborough, near Spalding in Lincolnshire, close to the fen edge. This is perhaps far more typical of the prehistoric occupation in the lowlands of England and is a good example of the problems involved in attempting to understand the settlements of these periods. As is often the case in modern excavation, although the area dug was relatively large, covering some 100 metres by 60 metres after four years work, the whole site as revealed by air photographs was at least 1 kilometre long and 400 metres across. The relatively small area excavated revealed an early Bronze Age settlement consisting of wooden structures set within a rectangular enclosure, 70 metres by 40 metres, defined by a ditch on three sides. In the later Bronze Age the occupation moved slightly south-west and was confined to a smaller rectangular ditched enclosure about 30 metres across. Then later still, in the Iron Age, the occupation moved south-west again to yet another rectangular enclosure, for the original site was abandoned and cultivated in the later Iron Age.

Important and interesting though this evidence is, and though it is possible that the enclosures represent a small farmstead that 'drifted' over a period of perhaps a thousand years, because of the small area of excavation in relation to the whole site there are other explanations that are equally probable. The overall site is so large that it may not be a single farm but a village, perhaps quite a large one. Also, though at first sight it appears to show slow 'drift', the evidence for this is just as likely to be the result of successive re-occupations of a suitable site at widely spaced intervals. Thus the early Bronze Age occupation is datable to around 1500 BC, the late Bronze Age occupation to between 1000 to 900 BC, and the Iron Age to possibly 300 to 200 BC.

A similar problem may be seen at another lowland late Bronze Age site at Heathrow, near London. There a site was excavated at the end of the last war when London airport was being constructed. A group of about a dozen circular wooden huts set inside a substantial defensive ditch was discovered with a curious rectangular timber building over-lying them. At the time, though the excavator had his doubts, he finally assigned the whole settlement to the Iron Age, and dated it to about 400 BC. However, in the light of more recent knowledge it looks as if the defensive enclosure and the huts are late Bronze Age and are separated by some five hundred years from the later Iron Age occupation.

The complex nature of later Bronze Age settlement in lowland England has been well revealed by recent excavations and other work carried out along the River Kennet, west of Reading. Two settlements of the period were found, excavated and shown to be of very different types. One, at Aldermaston, was

13 Later Bronze Age Lowland Settlements *These diagrams show the distribution and size of, and evidence for, lowland settlement of the later Bronze Age. The site at Knight's Farm is only one of a number of settlements of this period which lie along the edge of the River Kennet in much the same way as modern villages. The spread of occupation debris suggests that it was of considerable size, though the actual archaeological evidence of pits and post-holes shows the difficulty of understanding its actual form. The upper right-hand diagram shows the position of Knight's Farm in relation to other later Bronze Age settlements along the River Kennet; the lower right-hand diagram shows the overall size of the settlement, while the left-hand diagram indicates the features revealed by excavation of part of the site. The discoveries at Runnymede Bridge also indicate a large area of settlement. At Chalton the settlement seems to have been tiny and perhaps no more than a single farmstead.*

relatively small, as most of the site was excavated and its limits on at least three sides ascertained. It covered an area of about 50 metres by 30 metres and thus was possibly never more than the site of a single farmstead. Only a few pits, probably used for storage, and numerous post-holes were found. The latter suggested that there had been at least two oval wooden structures, about 15 metres and 11 metres across, and possibly one more. They appear to have been rebuilt or repaired on more than one occasion, but it is unlikely that the site was occupied for more than a century at the most. The second excavation was at Knight's Farm, south-west of Reading (Fig. 13). Here only part of the area could be examined and the excavators estimated that the settlement had originally extended over a minimum of 10 hectares, giving it a size far in excess of most medieval villages. No clear structures were found, but plentiful evidence of dense occupation in the form of pits and post-holes was discovered. The settlement was occupied for a relatively long period of time, perhaps from 1400 BC to about 400 BC, and so spanned at least part of the Iron Age.

One notable feature of both these sites is that they were both discovered purely by chance as the land was being worked for gravel. Neither site was visible from the air, and there was no trace of either on the surface in the form of pottery or flints. Worse, because of subsequent destruction, even the deepest feature found was less than 50 centimetres deep. Without the dedication and skill of highly professional excavators, working under the most difficult conditions, nothing would have been found at all. How many more thousands of such sites in similar positions, as well as those of earlier and later periods, must there be which will never be recognized or which have already been destroyed without trace? It is, of course, impossible to answer that question but we can now begin to envisage a lowland Bronze Age landscape packed with settlements.

In this same area, along the Kennet valley, other workers have found evidence for a further four settlements, forming a string of sites 1 kilometre to 4 kilometres apart. If we ignore the modern urban centres in the area and assume that we know of only about a quarter of the settlements that actually existed in the Bronze Age, the scatter of farmsteads, hamlets and villages along the Kennet valley appears to be very close to that of say AD 1500. This is the measure of the later Bronze Age settlement in England.

A site that may perhaps be regarded as intermediate between upland and lowland has been found at Chalton, Hampshire (Fig. 13), on a spur on the side of a valley cut into the chalk downs. It is of interest for a number of reasons, but perhaps the most important is how it came to be discovered and what this implies where other sites are concerned. It was totally unknown until road works in 1968 led to three short exploratory trenches for a re-routed water-pipe. One was watched by a local archaeologist and the site was noted and then excavated by Professor Cunliffe. It proved to be a small open later Bronze Age settlement, comprising two circular huts, 8 metres and 5 metres in diameter, together with pits and two working floors or small areas within which some unknown activity took place. It was interpreted as the dwelling of a single family and the fact that the huts had never been repaired or rebuilt suggested that it had had a very short life. However, it is possible that only a very small part of a much larger occupation area was actually discovered.

Two other features of the site are worth noting. Firstly, it was completely sealed by half a metre of later soil, partly the result of Roman cultivation, but mainly hill-wash from the slope above. It is thus interesting to speculate, as we did with the river valley sites, how many more such sites, similarly sealed and thus invisible either from the air or on the ground, still remain to be discovered. The answer must be many thousands. The second notable feature of the site was the discovery of a bronze axe, a disc and a knife, all found inside one of the huts where they had been abandoned. Again it may be worth considering whether the almost countless similar tools and bronze objects found by chance all over England may also have come from similar settlements. In the present state of our knowledge it is impossible to be certain exactly how large these lowland later Bronze Age settlements were. On the whole all that can be said is that they appear to have

14 Later Bronze Age Upland Settlement Types *Three very different kinds of upland later Bronze Age settlement. At Black Patch, the individual farmsteads lie widely scattered amongst fragments of contemporary fields and trackways. At Mam Tor the occupation is closely packed within the encircling ramparts of the fort. Borough Hill, one of the largest hillforts in England, is probably also late Bronze Age in date judging from the finds made there. The difference in size between the huge Bronze Age fort and the relatively tiny later Iron Age one is remarkable.*

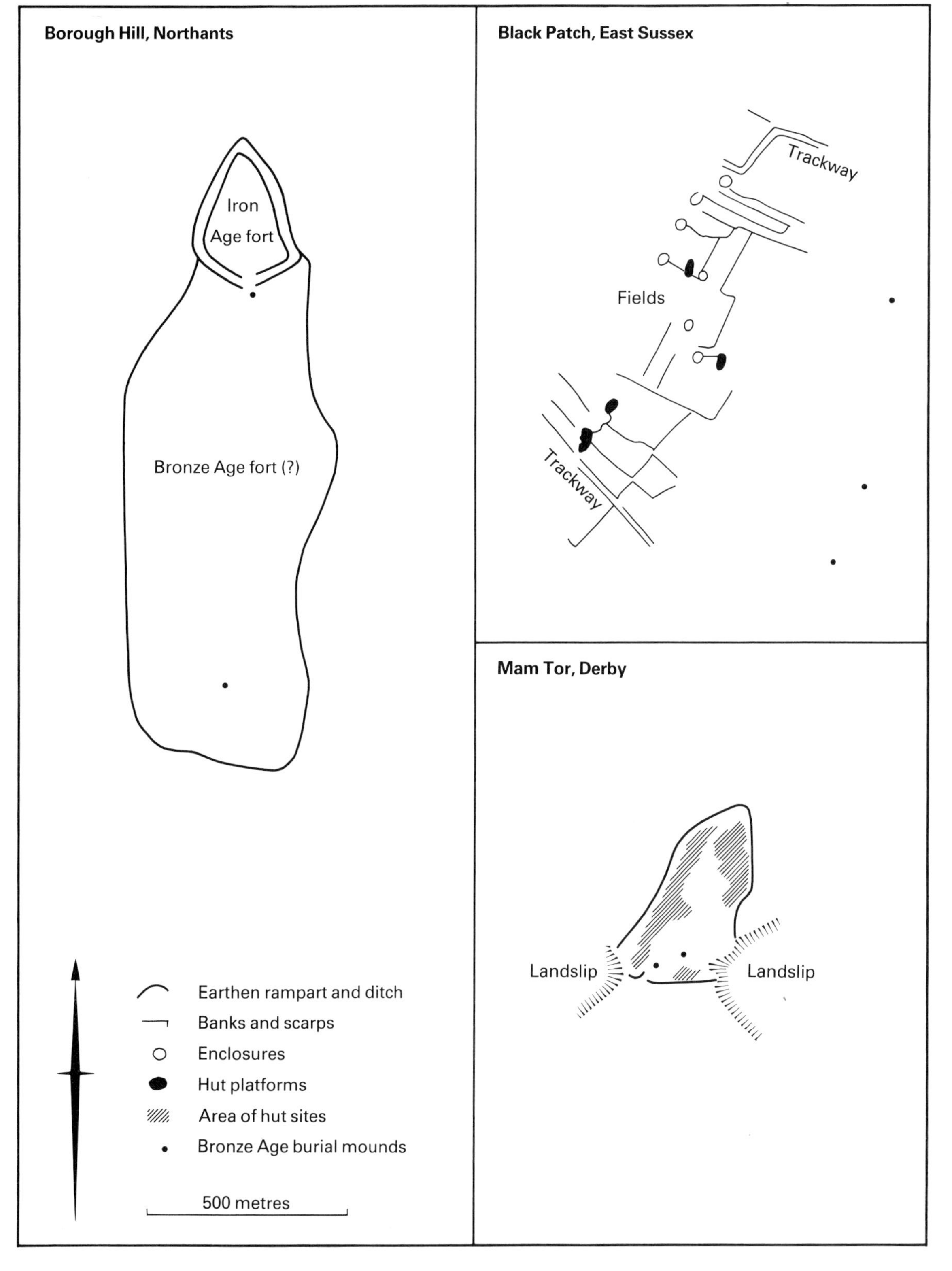
Borough Hill, Northants
Iron
Age fort
Bronze Age fort (?)
Black Patch, East Sussex
Trackway
Fields
Trackway
Mam Tor, Derby
Landslip
Landslip
Earthen rampart and ditch
Banks and scarps
Enclosures
Hut platforms
Area of hut sites
Bronze Age burial mounds
500 metres

been bigger and more wealthy than the contemporary sites on the uplands.

The upland settlements have received more attention from archaeologists than they perhaps deserve. This is of course partly because they can often still be recognized from their upstanding remains and are sometimes integrated with contemporary field systems. But the immediate result of work on them indicates that they are poorer and much smaller than the lowland sites. Thus though we know much more about them it must be stressed that they are probably unrepresentative of late Bronze Age settlements as a whole and so the information obtained from excavations of upland sites should not be applied to all settlements of the period. Such places may only be settlements on what was already marginal land, only occupied because of overpopulation and possibly lived in on a temporary or seasonal basis.

Even so, while accepting the limitations of the evidence, these sites cannot be ignored and indeed can, if treated with circumspection, tell us much about human occupation at this time. Perhaps the most interesting fact which emerges is how diverse these settlements were. An example of one type was discovered at a place known as Black Patch, on the downs near Lewes, East Sussex (Fig. 14). Even here only part of a very large site was excavated. The overall picture was of an area, 1 kilometre long and 400 metres across, of surviving late Bronze Age

15 Prehistoric Settlement, Dean Moor, Devon *A typical example of groups of huts set within stone-walled enclosures that occur in many places on Dartmoor. Excavations on similar sites indicate that they date from the Bronze Age, though whether they were permanent settlements or merely seasonally occupied by cattle farmers is not known.*

fields, trackways and small enclosures or paddocks. Within these fields were four clearly defined platforms cut into the hillside, at the corners or on the sides of the contemporary fields. Only one of the platforms was examined and was found to be made up of five terraces, each of which was the site of a circular wooden hut, on average 6 metres in diameter. The excavator, Mr P. Drewett, identified one house, which had its own enclosed yard and pond and which yielded richer finds, as that of the head of the household or extended family, and one house as that for his wife. He interpreted another as being for dependent relatives and two others as probably used for storage.

Valuable as this excavation was, it still poses considerable problems of interpretation. The hut-group certainly had a short life, as usual, perhaps of only twenty to thirty years, and was occupied by only one family. But what of the other hut-platforms higher up the hill? Do they represent successive moves by the same family, or are they all contemporary and thus form a rather straggling 'hamlet' lived in by four extended families comprising perhaps thirty to forty people? We do not know.

A related form of late Bronze Age settlement is that found on Dartmoor, associated with the great linear boundaries, or 'reaves', and field systems. There we find beautifully preserved isolated huts with granite stone walls, either lying within great enclosures, as on Dean Moor, on Dartmoor (Fig. 15), or with no signs of paddocks or stockyards around them. One of the latter type, on Holme Moor, has been excavated and immediately produced unexpected results. It was found to have been preceded by a circular wooden hut, 6 metres in diameter. It was later rebuilt with an earthen bank faced with stone. What does such an isolated moorland house represent? Can it have been a permanently occupied house or was it merely a hut in which lived the herdsman who attended the stock corralled in the great stone-walled enclosures on the surrounding land? The excavator, Dr G. Wainwright, thought that the latter explanation was more likely. But if this is so then where are the permanent dwellings of the period? Some may be the tightly-packed groups of hut-circles which can be found in all the river valleys around the edge of Dartmoor. These, on the better soils and in more sheltered positions, are the most obvious potential late Bronze Age sites. However, few have been excavated, and when they are some appear to be of Iron Age or later date. Another possibility is that permanent late Bronze Age settlements are marked today by the almost countless existing farmsteads which are scattered all over the softer lowlands in Devon and in east Cornwall, below the Dartmoor massif. As we shall see in Chapter 10 these are very old places indeed. Can they be as old as the late Bronze Age? Again we do not know.

If we accept that it is likely that in the late Bronze Age people lived in the lowlands in considerable numbers and that, for example, the farmsteads of Devon and Cornwall do mark sites of settlements of this period, then it is possible that we can overturn the interpretation of sites such as Black Patch on its Sussex downland. It could perhaps more easily be interpreted as a seasonal settlement of pastoral or arable farmers, the latter working the out-field of an in-field and out-field system on the high downlands. The main areas of arable and, most significantly, the main permanent settlements may have been below the downs on the rich coastal plains and river valleys around Lewes, where all trace of occupation in the Bronze Age has long since been destroyed or obscured.

There are numerous other later Bronze Age settlements known from the upland areas. Many of them can be recognized by the surrounding banks and ditches which still survive, and which, in contrast to those at Black Patch, enclosed the settlements. This feature has enabled archaeologists to identify them and a number have been excavated in recent years. As a result they have been afforded an importance in late Bronze Age terms which is probably quite spurious. An example of this type of site is that called South Lodge Camp on the downlands of Cranborne Chase in Dorset (Fig. 16). It is a rectangular ditched enclosure some 50 metres across, laid on top of earlier Bronze Age fields. Inside the enclosure a whole series of circular wooden structures (not shown on plan), as well as pits, was discovered. The site is still perhaps no more than a large farmstead which housed an extended family and is unlikely to have had a life of more than a century or so.

A variant of this form of settlement, in a very different environment, has been excavated on Shaugh Moor on Dartmoor (Fig. 16). It consisted of a stone-walled oval enclosure, set in an isolated position on the side of a broad moorland valley. It contained five small stone huts and the remains of some wooden structures (not shown on plan). Though it appears to have been occupied for almost a thousand years, and certainly the individual houses were altered and rebuilt during that time, it is very doubtful that it was a permanent settlement. It is equally likely to have been a temporary seasonal place where a family of some ten to twelve people lived while tending animals. Again the limited importance of such sites in terms of total Bronze Age settlement, as well as the problem of knowing where the permanent settlements of this period lay, are obvious.

Another relatively short-lived settlement with no evidence of 'drift', which belonged to the earlier part of this period, was excavated at Shearplace Hill, Sydling St Nicholas, Dorset (Fig. 16). This is an important site for a number of reasons. One is that it has survived into this century as an upstanding earthwork with banks, ditches and platforms marking the enclosures and hut-sites which made up the settlement. Also, although there are many sites similar to this in southern England, none of them has been excavated and all have usually been assigned to the Iron Age or Roman period. It may be that the Shearplace Hill site is an example of a relatively common type of late Bronze Age upland farmstead, so far unrecognized elsewhere.

The farmstead consisted of two circular huts lying side by side with a yard in front of them and two small enclosures or paddocks to the north and south. A hollowed trackway passed the site with a short 'drive' off it leading into the farmyard and with another track passing the north side of the farm. In addition, fragments of the contemporary field system were also traced in the surrounding area. This site appears to have been a late Bronze Age upland farmstead, occupied for about three hundred years by no more than a single family.

A very similar site, that on Itford Hill, near Lewes in East Sussex, shows many of the same features. It was recognized because the circular embanked depressions of its hut-sites still existed on the close-cropped downland. It proved to be only a small site, perhaps slightly larger than Shearplace Hill, with three or four families living there and with a relatively short life of perhaps only twenty-five years.

There is one more type of late Bronze Age site which is perhaps of more significance and which has been recognized only in the last few years. This is the relatively well defended or fortified site. The best example of this type of site is probably that of Rams Hill on the Berkshire Downs (Fig. 16). Again, the site was well known and protected by virtue of the fact that it lay inside an Iron Age fortress. It covered about one hectare of land on the summit of a hill and started life, probably in the earlier Bronze Age, with the construction of a flat-bottomed ditch with vertical sides, of no real defensive proportions, surrounding the site. Within it was one sub-rectangular wooden structure. After an interval of time, at a date in the early part of the late Bronze Age, the perimeter ditch was altered by the construction of what appears to be a defensive rampart inside it. Later still stout fences or palisades were built on either side of the ditch, again apparently for defence. Then, finally, the defences were abandoned and the settlement became an open one. During the defensive phase and the later one there was certainly one large circular wooden house and one other circular structure. Detailed analysis of the animal bones, soils and pottery found there suggested that the site was occupied only seasonally, probably only in the autumn and then not on a regular basis. A temporary pastoral encampment is the most likely explanation and thus its importance has probably been overrated by archaeologists, some of whom have seen it as a major communal centre for social, economic and religious interchange. Its real significance would seem to lie in the fact that it was a defended site unlike anything found in the earlier period.

Another defended site is that at Norton Fitzwarren, in Somerset, situated on a low hill. There an area of about 2 hectares was apparently bounded by a V-shaped ditch with banks on both sides. Ivinghoe Beacon in Buckinghamshire and Mam Tor in Derbyshire (Figs. 14, 17) also seem to have been defended sites in the later Bronze Age. At the latter a small excavation led to the discovery of three circular huts inside the defences and later work has indicated that these were only a few of a very large number covering much of the interior.

Two examples of other forms of late Bronze Age defended sites have been found at Thwing, on the wolds of North Yorkshire, and at Mucking in Essex on the northern edge of the Thames estuary. At Thwing, the excavator, Mr Manby, discovered an

16 Later Bronze Age Upland Settlements *All these settlements date from the latter part of the Bronze Age and all are situated on high moorland or downland, perhaps marginal areas even then. Even though they probably represent the smaller and relatively poorer farmsteads and hamlets of the period, they still display considerable variety of form.*

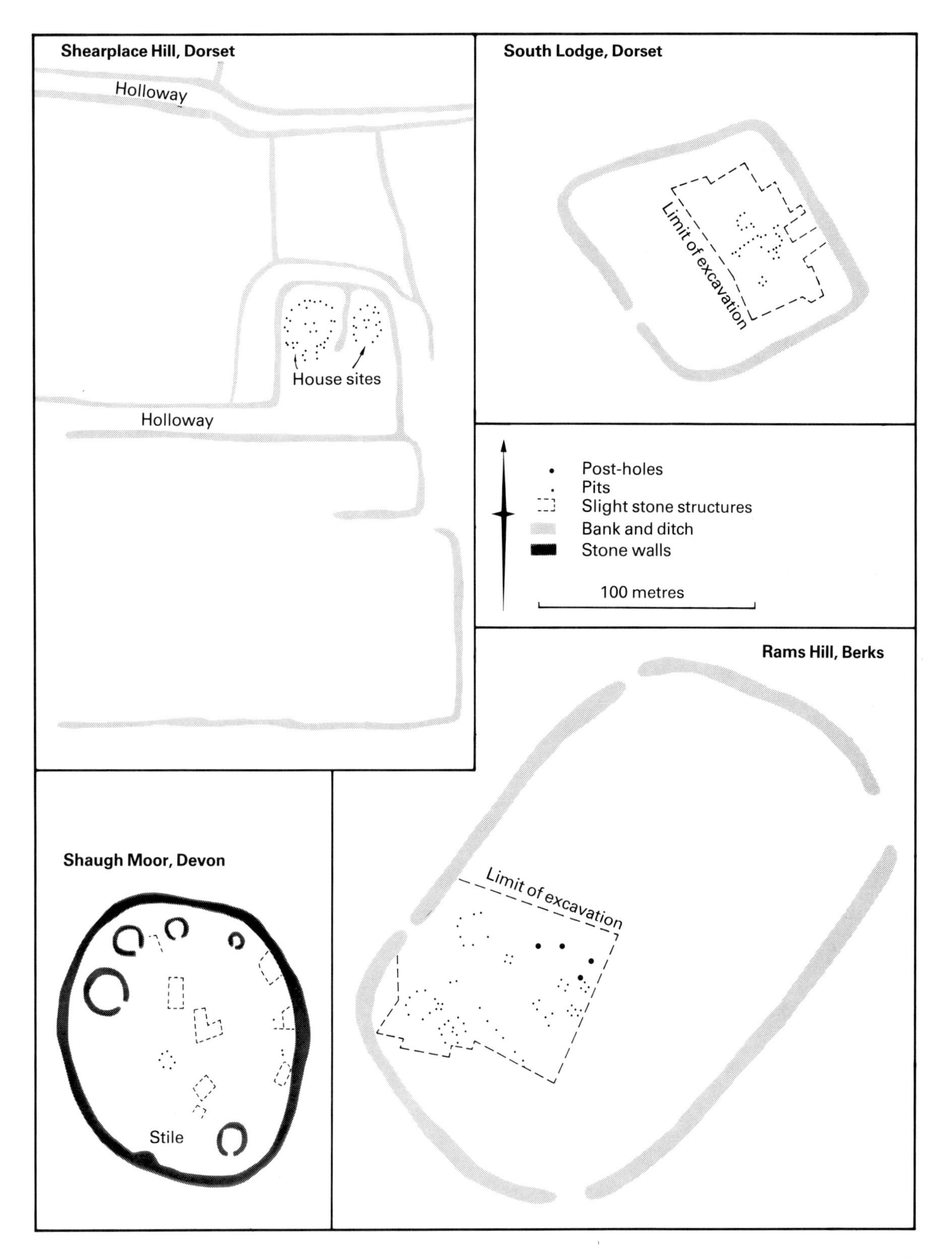
Shearplace Hill, Dorset
Holloway
House sites
Holloway
South Lodge, Dorset
Limit of excavation
Post-holes
Pits
Slight stone structures
Bank and ditch
Stone walls
100 metres
Rams Hill, Berks
Limit of excavation
Shaugh Moor, Devon
Stile

17 Mam Tor, Derbyshire
This massively defended hillfort, set high on the Peakland hills, has usually been assigned to the Iron Age. Recent excavations have shown that in fact it is of later Bronze Age date. The dimpled effect inside is the result of landslips, for the ground here is very unstable. In the right foreground the whole hillside has collapsed taking part of the fort with it.

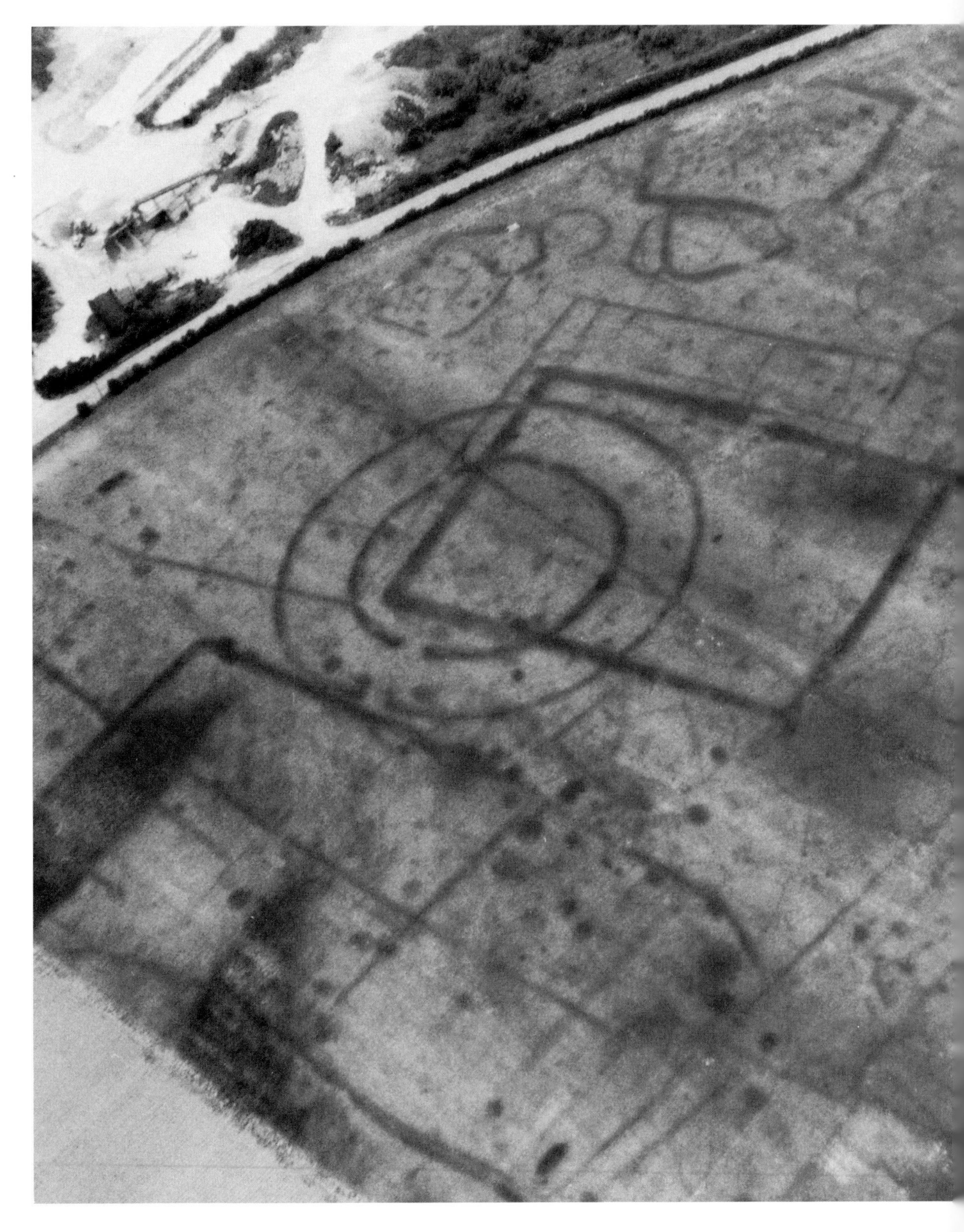

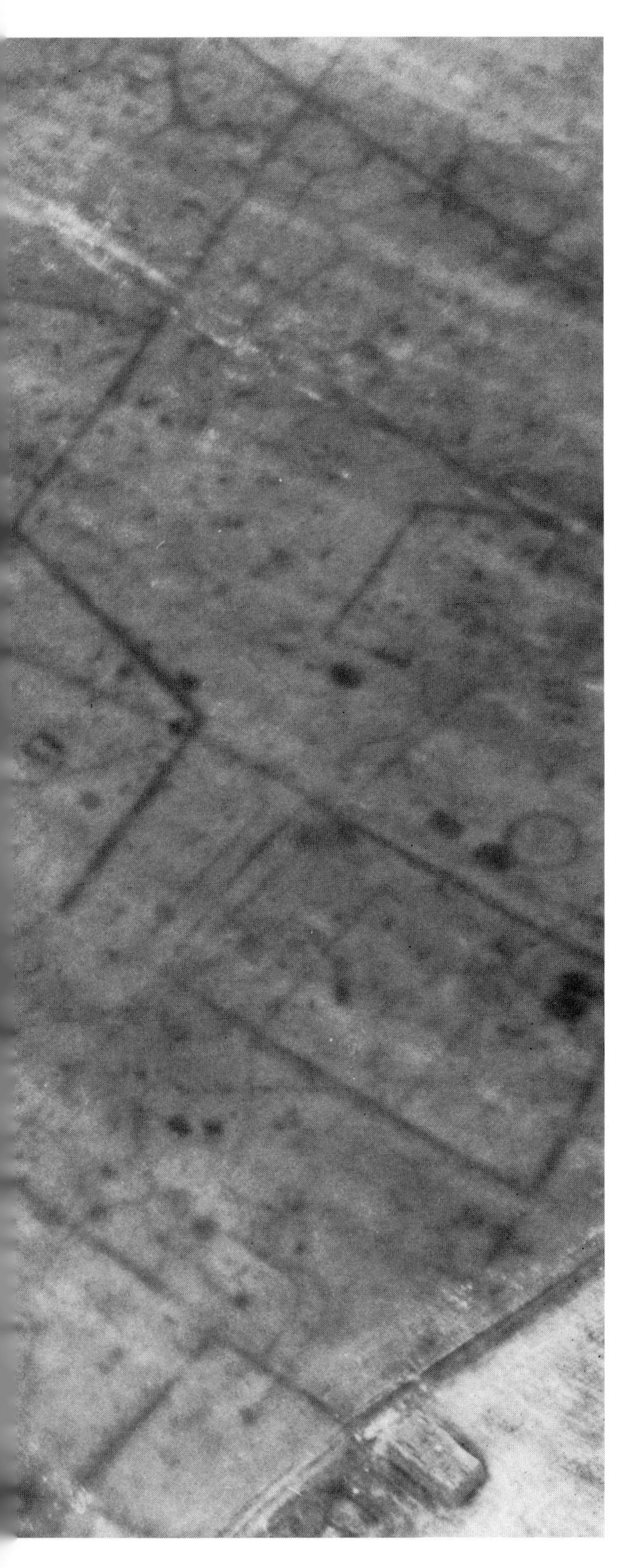

almost perfectly circular ditch, up to 3 metres deep, with an inner rampart originally enclosed in timber uprights, surrounding an area about 90 metres in diameter. Exactly in the centre was a huge circular building 25 metres in diameter, so large that it is doubtful if it could have been roofed. There was evidence of some semi-permanent occupation and quantities of animal bones, and the close proximity of great dykes or ranch boundaries may mean that it was a settlement based on pastoralism but with a very strong element of defence. At Mucking, two sites 1 kilometre apart have been discovered (Fig. 18). There the evidence was far less clear than at Thwing, but both sites consisted of two concentric rings formed by ditches 1.5 metres deep. One site was 85 metres in diameter and the other 43 metres.

All this evidence suggests that there was a well-defined type of defensive site in the later Bronze Age, which was very often, as at Rams Hill, Norton Fitzwarren and Ivinghoe Beacon, the precursor of later Iron Age forts. Finds from other unexcavated hillforts also support the idea that quite massively fortified sites may have existed well back in the Bronze Age and are not necessarily just an Iron Age phenomenon. One particularly good example is Borough Hill near Daventry in Northamptonshire (Fig. 14). The undoubted Iron Age fort there is quite small, covering only 5 hectares at one end of the massive hilltop. At an earlier period, and conceivably in the later Bronze Age, the whole hilltop was bounded by a much slighter defence work enclosing no less than 54 hectares. Certainly the site was occupied in the later Bronze Age, as a number of finds of bronze tools and weapons testify, though how densely settled it may have been is not known. It is worth noting that the total area of Borough Hill is much the same as that of the open settlement at Black Patch which seemed to have comprised the homes of only four families. We have

18 Prehistoric and Later Settlements, Mucking, Essex *Since this photograph was taken the area has been excavated prior to its destruction for gravel quarrying. As a result, the date and purpose of most of the visible features are understood. The concentric rings are in fact a small fort of later Bronze Age date, probably of around 1000* BC. *Many of the enclosures marked by narrow ditches are part of an earlier field system dating from about 1300 to 1400* BC, *while the large rectangular feature is Roman. Many of the dark 'blobs' or pits are early Saxon huts and part of the scattered 'village' at Mucking.*

to be very careful when we attempt to link the population of a site to its physical size.

Though these defended sites of the later Bronze Age were not suspected until a few years ago, their existence is explicable and is almost certainly related to the mass of evidence of spears and swords at this time. These weapons and defensive sites, when put together with the evidence for a planned landscape of fields and ranches and with well-defined territorial systems, imply inter-tribal or at least inter-family warfare. This must have taken place on an extensive scale as the landscape filled up and pressures of relative overpopulation and over-exploitation forced people to protect what they held or to take what they needed. Thus, a picture emerges of a tightly packed landscape in the later Bronze Age with a growing population that was needing to fight for the increasingly limited resources. A wide variety of settlement forms shifted slowly in well-defined estates, whose available land was used in the best possible manner, whether for arable or pasture, depending on soil type or pressure of population. More important, in contrast to earlier periods when settlements of similar size were generally evenly distributed, now for the first time larger, richer, and more permanent settlements tended to be concentrated in the major river valleys and on the lowland clays. The upland moors, the downlands and the heaths were left for seasonal, shifting settlement and the necessary defensive sites.

But the really significant features of the later Bronze Age landscape were the territorial divisions. Once these had been fixed it was difficult to remove them. They could be incorporated into larger units by conquest and divided again by inheritance, but because these units were related to a firm and largely unchanging economic basis they were the most stable part of the landscape, both then and later. This is what makes the late Bronze Age so important.

-5-
A Crowded Country

The later prehistoric period known to archaeologists as the Iron Age extends roughly from about 800 BC to the Roman invasions in AD 43. It takes its name from the appearance of iron tools in the archaeological record, but from the point of view of the history of settlement in England, it is really only a time during which all the trends we have seen developing in the later Bronze Age were intensified.

Firstly, there is considerable evidence that indicates an intensification of arable farming and the production of a much greater supply of food than before. Very large grain-storage pits have been found in settlement sites but of perhaps greater significance is the fact that some areas of former pasture were ploughed up and there was continuing clearance of the remaining woodland. Indeed, by the late Iron Age there may well have been a serious shortage of timber. Certainly the hillforts of the period do not have the elaborate wooden-faced ramparts that characterize those of the earlier Iron Age; domestic houses became smaller and, in the north and south-west of England at least, stone replaced timber as the major building material. It could well be that by the first century BC there was less woodland in England than there is now. This has important implications for interpreting the history of Iron Age and subsequent settlement.

There is also evidence of a further extension of agriculture into the richer, but heavier claylands, and of a marked push into the high moorlands and mountains where complex pastoralism and transhumance practices became widespread. Linear ditches of considerable complexity continued to be constructed in parts of Wessex and east Yorkshire in order to further define and intensify the use of limited areas of pastureland.

It is clear that the exploitation of the English countryside for agriculture was too intensive in some places and that the natural balance of nature was being upset. In the Weald of south-eastern England scientists have recognized the break-down of soils on arable land at this time, while over large parts of southern England plough-soil washed down by erosion from the downs accumulated in the valleys and was spread over the flood plains of the major rivers. The same processes have also been recognized in the Midlands.

All these features imply one thing, a greatly increased population and thus many more settlements. And this is precisely what the archaeological record shows. Far more Iron Age settlements are known than from all the rest of the prehistoric period together. They have been found on all types of soils, in almost every position and in every part of England except on the highest moors of the Pennines and in the undrained marshlands. Most significant of all, they appear to reach their greatest density on some of the heaviest soils, indicating that the later Bronze Age trend towards a marked concentration of settlement in such areas was now fully established.

A number of detailed studies have been carried out which show both the density and the location of Iron Age settlements in England. For example, it has been estimated that 22 per cent of all the early or middle Iron Age sites in south-east England were situated on heavy soils and that only 34 per cent lay on chalk, despite the long-held belief that most settlements lay in the latter areas. It is also significant that many of the chalk downland sites were not only small but were abandoned, apparently in favour of lowland sites, later on in the Iron Age. Other studies indicate how closely packed Iron Age settlements were in the landscape (Fig. 19). In south Hampshire they are, on average, only 0.8 kilometre apart, on the boulder clay areas of north-east England they lie roughly 1.0 kilometre apart, in Cornwall 1.3 kilometres apart and in south-east Northamptonshire and north Bedfordshire, on a variety of soils varying from light limestone to heavy clay, there is an average spacing of 1.5 kilometres. In north Essex Iron Age settlements are about 1.0 kilometre apart on the boulder clay areas, but are very rarely found on the chalklands. Even on the uplands of north-eastern England, settlements of this date seem to be spaced at an average distance of 2.0 to 3.0 kilometres. As in the case of Bronze Age settlement, it is certain that at least half of the sites that once existed have not yet been discovered, so these figures indicate that settlement at this period was incredibly dense.

Other features which are characteristic of Iron Age settlements include a general increase in size compared with those of the later Bronze Age, especially in the lowland areas. This is again a reflection of a growing population and the continuing exploitation and development of these lowland areas. Settlements also tend to be rather more permanent than those of earlier date. While there is still considerable settlement 'drift' and movement on to new sites, many more places than before appear to be occupied for two or three centuries before obvious movement takes place. There is also evidence of consciously planned settlements, perhaps reflecting the impact of major landlords controlling the size and layout of settlements under their jurisdiction, something which was to become increasingly common in later times.

All this evidence of continued woodland clearances, increased arable, vast numbers of new settlements, a growing population and over-exploitation of resources indicates that the strains on the environment and thus within Iron Age society were even greater than those noted in the later Bronze Age. Weapons of iron became common, elaborate shields, swords and spears have been discovered and light-weight war-chariots have been found. Other evidence, for example of slavery and of ritual cannibalism, also supports the theory of a society under pressure, becoming increasingly short of land and being forced to organize itself into powerful groups in clearly defined territories in order to survive. Most important of all, the Iron Age is marked by a growing number of defensive structures or hillforts, scattered all over England. These show a desperate need for defendable sites, either as permanently occupied protected places or as temporary refuges in times of danger. The spacing of these forts also shows the consolidation of the older pattern of territories into a hierarchy of local estates, tribal areas, and finally kingdoms.

The variety and complexity of Iron Age settlement is such that only a relatively few examples can be given in a book of this length. Nevertheless, these can give some idea of what the Iron Age landscape looked like. At the simplest level there were the isolated farmsteads (Fig. 20), usually found on high downland or moorland, where perhaps a single family or possibly an extended family lived, cultivating the surrounding land and grazing the outlying pastures.

The most famous of these was that excavated by Professor G. Bersu just before World War Two at Little Woodbury on the downland just south of Salisbury, Wiltshire (Fig. 19). It consisted of a circular enclosure or farmyard bounded by a bank and ditch and with curving 'antennae'-like ditches extending outwards from its entrance, probably to act as a droveway when animals were being brought in. Within the enclosure was a single large circular wooden house, probably the home of an extended family group. This farm at Little Woodbury had a relatively short life, perhaps no more than two hundred years or so before it was abandoned for ever.

A slightly different site, but also that of a single farmstead, was excavated by Dr G. Wainwright on Berwick Down, also in Wiltshire and also on a high

19 Iron Age Settlements *The detailed plans show the wide variety in size and form of enclosed Iron Age settlements, ranging from single farmsteads to hamlets to large villages. The inset map indicates the density of Iron Age settlements over a small part of Northamptonshire and Bedfordshire when compared with medieval villages there. It should be contrasted with the map of Roman settlements in the same area (see Fig. 30).*

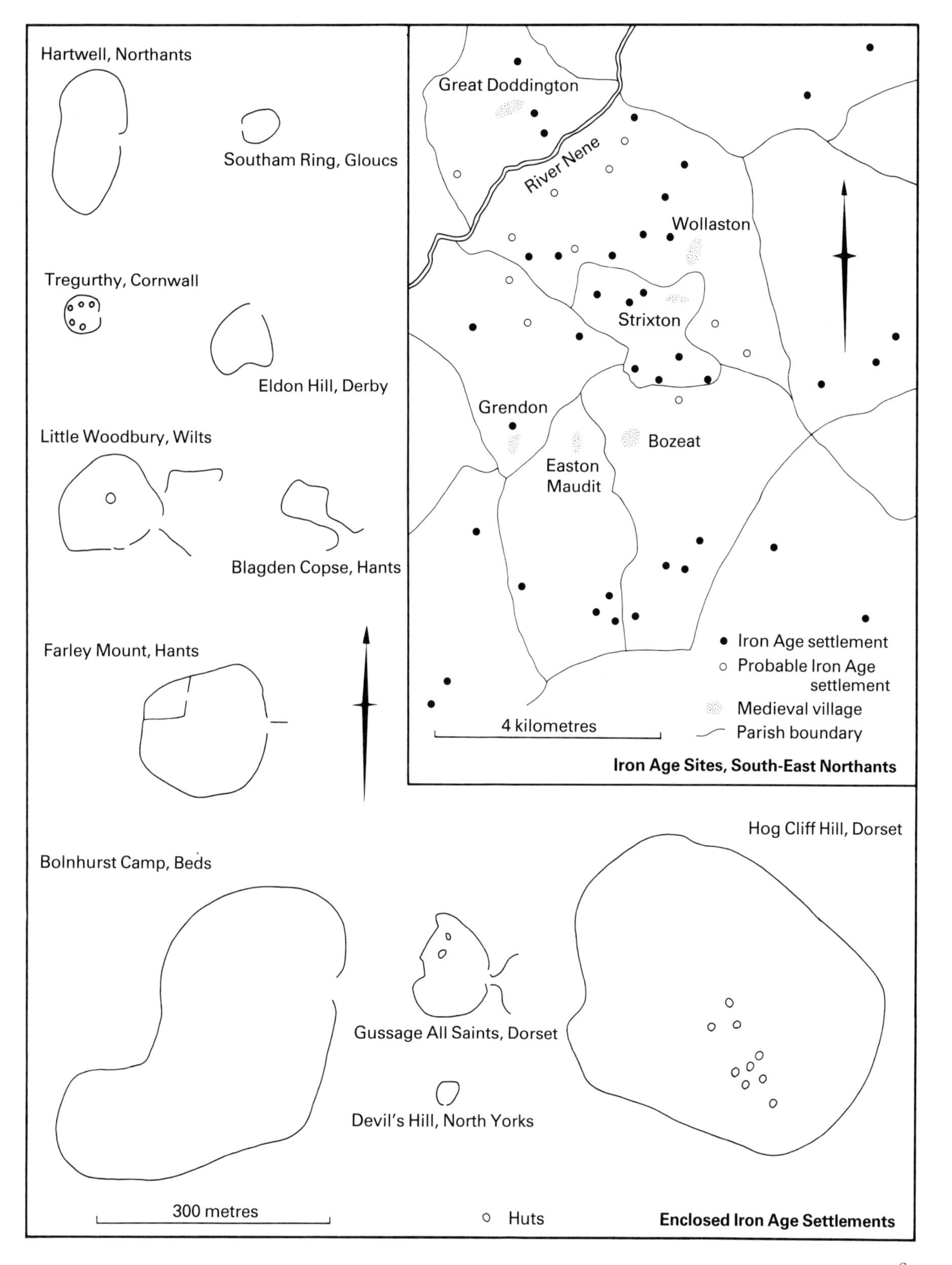
Hartwell, Northants
Southam Ring, Gloucs
Tregurthy, Cornwall
Eldon Hill, Derby
Little Woodbury, Wilts
Blagden Copse, Hants
Farley Mount, Hants
Great Doddington
River Nene
Wollaston
Strixton
Grendon
Bozeat
Easton Maudit
Iron Age settlement
Probable Iron Age settlement
Medieval village
Parish boundary
4 kilometres
Iron Age Sites, South-East Northants
Hog Cliff Hill, Dorset
Bolnhurst Camp, Beds
Gussage All Saints, Dorset
Devil's Hill, North Yorks
300 metres
Huts
Enclosed Iron Age Settlements

20 Iron Age Farmstead, Queen Elizabeth Country Park, Petersfield, Hampshire *This modern reconstruction of a farmstead excavated at Pimperne, Dorset, shows what a typical small Iron Age settlement may have looked like, though perhaps rather neater than the original.*

downland spur (Fig. 21). Here the enclosure was kite-shaped, less than 0.5 hectares in area, and bounded by a low bank and shallow ditch set in an outer and larger enclosure. As at Little Woodbury the enclosure contained a single circular wooden hut, here 4 metres in diameter, together with storage pits and other evidence of agriculture. However, the evidence for the length of occupation indicated that it was much shorter than at Little Woodbury, perhaps less than fifty years. On the other hand, within 300 metres of the site is another Iron Age settlement and a Roman one. These have not been excavated but they may well represent the earlier and later occupation of the same spur and thus the excavated site may be only one phase of a much longer period of settlement here during which normal 'drift' occurred.

A more complex Iron Age site has been found in the same general area of chalk downland, at Gussage All Saints in Dorset (Fig. 19), and this was also examined by Dr Wainwright. There the excavations revealed occupation spread over some five hundred years or so, though within that period there were considerable changes in the settlement's form. It began around 500 BC as an irregular enclosure bounded by a shallow ditch and with a single entrance protected by a timber gateway. No clear evidence of any houses in it was recovered, though these must certainly have existed. After about a century the enclosure ditch was recut and deepened, the gateway rebuilt and made more

21 Movement in Iron Age and Roman Settlements *All these sites exemplify, in different ways, how Iron Age, Roman and even Saxon settlements were continually being moved and changed.*

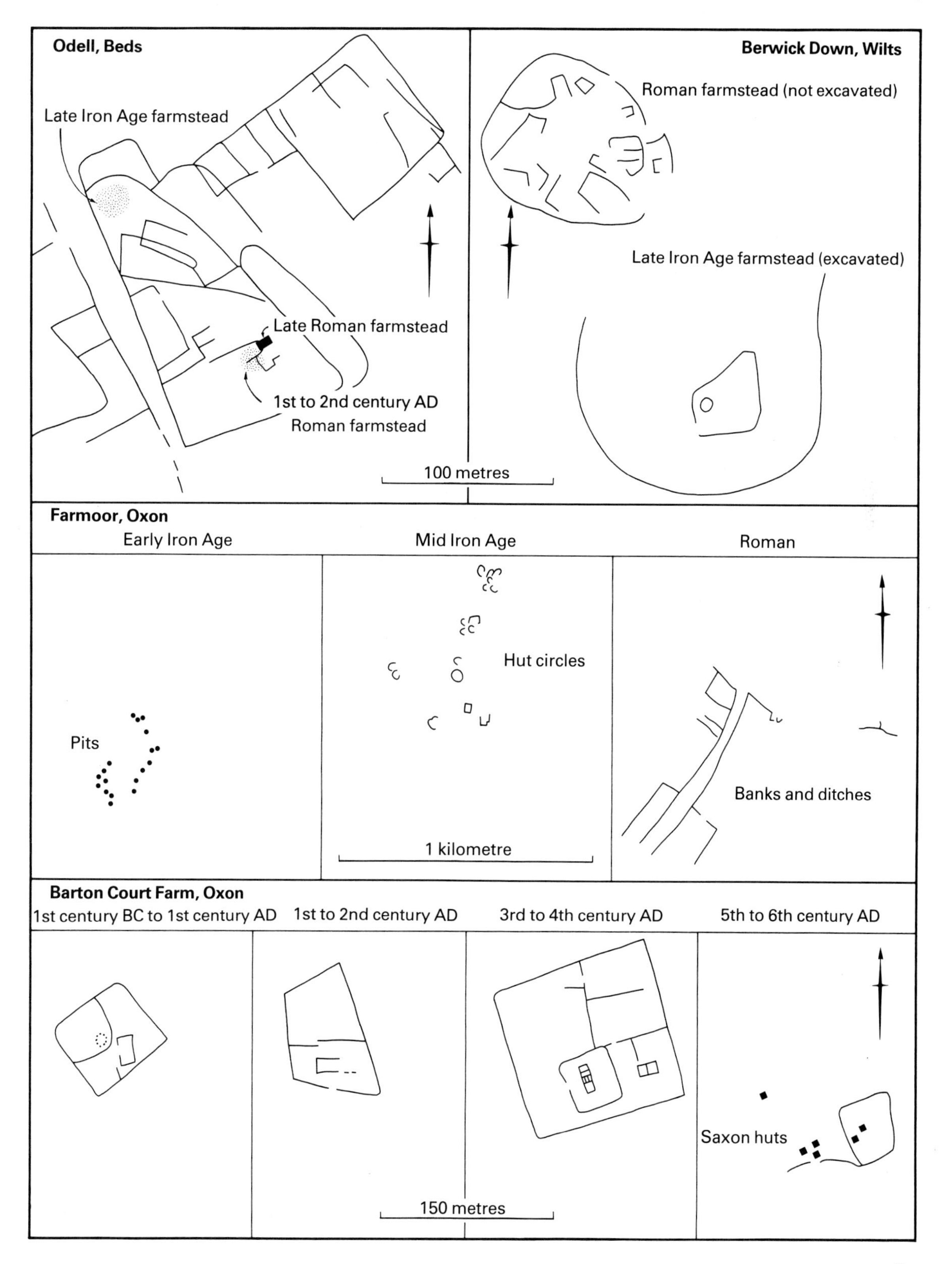

Odell, Beds
Late Iron Age farmstead
Late Roman farmstead
1st to 2nd century AD
Roman farmstead
100 metres
Berwick Down, Wilts
Roman farmstead (not excavated)
Late Iron Age farmstead (excavated)
Farmoor, Oxon
Early Iron Age
Mid Iron Age
Roman
Pits
Hut circles
Banks and ditches
1 kilometre
Barton Court Farm, Oxon
1st century BC to 1st century AD
1st to 2nd century AD
3rd to 4th century AD
5th to 6th century AD
Saxon huts
150 metres

elaborate and a complex 'antenna' ditch dug outside it. Within the enclosure were at least two small circular huts, up to 9 metres in diameter. This farmstead lasted for around 250 years, after which the outer enclosure was then virtually abandoned and replaced by a single circular 'yard' only 13 metres across, inside which was a single hut. In addition a small ditched stockyard was constructed nearby. In this final stage the settlement must have again been a single farming unit and as such it remained in use until just after the beginning of the Roman period, when it was finally abandoned.

The history of settlement at Owslebury near Winchester, Hampshire, examined by Dr J. Collis, is even more complex. Like the sites already discussed Owslebury lies on high downland soils. It began as a roughly circular enclosure about 1 hectare in area and enclosed by a substantial ditch 1.5 metres deep, approached by a ditch-edged trackway. Within it the excavator postulated the home of a single wealthy farmer. This farmstead lasted a century or so, after which it was completely abandoned for well over a hundred years. Its successor was very different. It consisted of a much bigger enclosure more than twice the size of the earlier one, approached by ditched trackways leading into four or five different entrances. The excavator suggested that this was the result of a growing population and the need for a large enclosure. However, this may not necessarily be so and the discovery of a small cemetery suggests that the site was occupied by a single if rich farmstead throughout its life. The site continued to be occupied into the Roman period. Other variants on enclosed Iron Age farmsteads in Wessex may be seen at Farley Mount and Blagden Copse, both in Hampshire (Fig. 19).

Not all Iron Age settlement sites on the southern downlands were single farmsteads. A very different settlement was excavated by Professor P. Rhatz, on Hog Cliff Hill, near Dorchester in Dorset (Fig. 19). The inevitable enclosure here covered 10 hectares, as large as a hillfort, and curiously the surrounding ditch had a large external bank. This latter feature is most unusual as it is common for the ditch to encircle the bank. Within the enclosure were at least nine small circular huts and possibly more. This settlement, which again probably lasted less than a century, was certainly more than a single farmstead and was perhaps a large hamlet or small village. Yet another variation has been recorded at Boscombe Down near Salisbury, Wiltshire. Here an area of at least 7 hectares was covered with storage pits and evidence of occupation but there was no encircling enclosure of any kind. This site seems to have been a large open 'village'.

So far we have concentrated on rural settlements on the higher downlands of Wessex. If we look at other parts of England we see sites of the same variety and complexity. For example, in Cornwall the main Iron Age and indeed Roman settlement appears to be a type of site usually called a 'round'. These are usually circular enclosures, often under 1 hectare in area, bounded by a stone wall and outer ditch and in many cases occupying hill-slope positions, as at Breage in Cornwall (Fig. 22). Inside there are usually between two and six circular stone houses, set around a courtyard, and they are clearly to be interpreted as small agricultural hamlets. Those which have been excavated, such as the ones at Tregurthy (Fig. 19), Trevisker and Crane Godrevy, were all occupied in the later Iron Age and into the Roman period, while others are late Roman in date. Yet, in spite of the apparent longevity of rounds, they are by no means the only type of Iron Age settlement in that part of England. There is also a series of well-defined villages, of which those at Carn Euny and Chysauster are good examples. Carn Euny lies on the lower slopes of the moorland, close to the limits of modern agriculture. It is uncertain how large the village originally was for ancient and modern destruction has obliterated part of it. Excavations there by Mrs P. Christie uncovered at least ten houses and an unknown number of others once existed. Three of the houses were large, 9 metres in diameter, while the rest were much smaller, 5 metres to 6 metres across. All the houses were clustered together in a compact mass sharing communal walls and completely interlocked. The differences in house size and the existence of separate 'rooms' in the larger ones suggest differences in social standing amongst the inhabitants. These stone houses had clearly been rebuilt and repaired many times, indicating a relatively long period of occupation, and this was confirmed by the dating of material from the site and the evidence of earlier pre-stone building

22 Hillfort and Round, Breage, Cornwall *On the summit of the rounded moorland hill is a small hillfort, probably of the early Iron Age. Below it, in the foreground, is a typical Cornish 'round' or enclosed hamlet. The latter is probably also Iron Age in origin but was no doubt occupied in the Roman period as well.*

structures. The earlier occupation may have begun in the fifth century BC and from then until the first century BC the houses were of timber. Then the existing stone houses were erected and these lasted into the Roman period. A large number of similar sites, all at least of the late Iron Age, exist in west Cornwall and on the Isles of Scilly.

Other areas of England present the same picture of a variety of settlement. In Avon, on a hillside in the Vale of Brington, excavations have revealed a small 'open' or unenclosed farmstead, while in Gloucestershire, at Southam Ring (Fig. 19), field-work has led to the discovery of a very small embanked settlement, presumably a single farm-stead. Further north-east at Draughton, on the high uplands of Northamptonshire, an equally small farmstead was found to consist of a single hut 10 metres in diameter and two semi-circular structures only 6 metres across. The former was apparently the main house, and may have been the only one, while the latter were perhaps sheds. All lay within an encircling ditch 30 metres in diameter.

On the upland moors of the Pennines there are numerous small farmsteads, most still easily visible on the ground by virtue of their stone-walled enclosures and huts, as at Eldon Hill, Derbyshire (Fig. 19). Few of these have been excavated and some that have belong to the Roman period. It is thus difficult to be sure on form alone which are of Iron Age date and which are Roman. Clearly the impact of the Roman invaders had little effect on the form of rural settlement on these moorlands. However, a number of excavations have shown that a large proportion of these sites began in the Iron Age or in some cases in the late Bronze Age and lasted well into the Roman period, almost always as small farmsteads but with important changes of form. In northern England the earliest Iron Age sites of fifth- or sixth-century date seem to have been semi-fortified. They are what are known as pal-

isaded enclosures, that is, small groups of timber houses surrounded by a wooden stockade. Later the stockades were replaced by well-built stone or earthern ramparts. This sequence was first noticed in England at Huckhoe, west of Morpeth in Northumberland, but has since been confirmed elsewhere, notably at West Brandon, near Durham. In the north-east of England there are also many examples of small farmsteads of very rectangular form. Some of these are undoubtedly of Roman date and many, as we shall see later, are the result of deliberate rural settlement planning. However, not all can be neatly classified. For example, at Burradon, north-east of Newcastle, on the flat clay coastal plain, one of forty rectangular enclosures known in the area has been excavated. The work revealed that the site had started life in the early part of the Iron Age as a large rectangular ditched enclosure with a series of small wooden circular huts inside it. Later a new enclosure, equally rectangular but smaller, was constructed and a single very large round timber hut built within it.

With the exception of the last example, almost all the Iron Age settlements described so far lie on upland sites rather than lowland ones and most can be regarded as lying on what was relatively marginal land. It is now time to turn to the richer lowlands of England and see what archaeologists have discovered about the rural settlements there. As with the later Bronze Age and perhaps even the earlier periods, there are considerable problems connected with the interpretation of these lowland sites. Most of the upland sites either remain as earthworks or as crop-marks or soil-marks which can be readily identified and thus delimited. The excavators can therefore usually be sure of the limits of the original occupation area, and of the overall size of the site, and are thus able to interpret the remains as a single farmstead, hamlet or small village according to the size and number of dwellings. In contrast, in the lowlands the Iron Age settlements are often of two types, based on the circumstances of their discovery. They are either parts of huge and very complex areas of crop-marks or they are just scatters of pottery spread over many hectares. Given that only a limited amount of excavation can be carried out, such sites are rarely totally excavated and thus the exact nature, size and form of the settlement is not often recovered.

However, despite these limitations it is clear that Iron Age settlements in the lowlands were of a different order from those on the uplands. Certainly

the small enclosed or open single farmsteads occur. At Great Shelford, near Cambridge on the gravel terrace of the River Cam, a small late Iron Age settlement was discovered and excavated. It consisted of a ditched and embanked enclosure containing a single large timber hut, together with pits and hearths. Likewise, at Hartwell in Northamptonshire (Fig. 19), there is still a small enclosure bounded by a low bank and ditch, just large enough for a single house. Two other enclosures, this time rectangular in form, existed until recently a few

kilometres away. Interestingly all survived as earthworks until this century because they lay inside woodland which was part of a medieval forest. They illustrate well the extension of late prehistoric settlement into areas which were neither occupied nor cultivated by people of more recent centuries.

Not far away in the same county, at Bozeat and Great Doddington (Fig. 23), two D-shaped enclosures, only 100 metres across and visible as crop-marks, have both turned out to be small farmsteads whose encircling ditches were so massive as to

23 Iron Age Farmstead, Great Doddington, Northamptonshire *This D-shaped enclosure, visible only from the air, lies close to the River Nene. Excavations on the site have indicated that the surrounding ditch was of defensive proportions.*

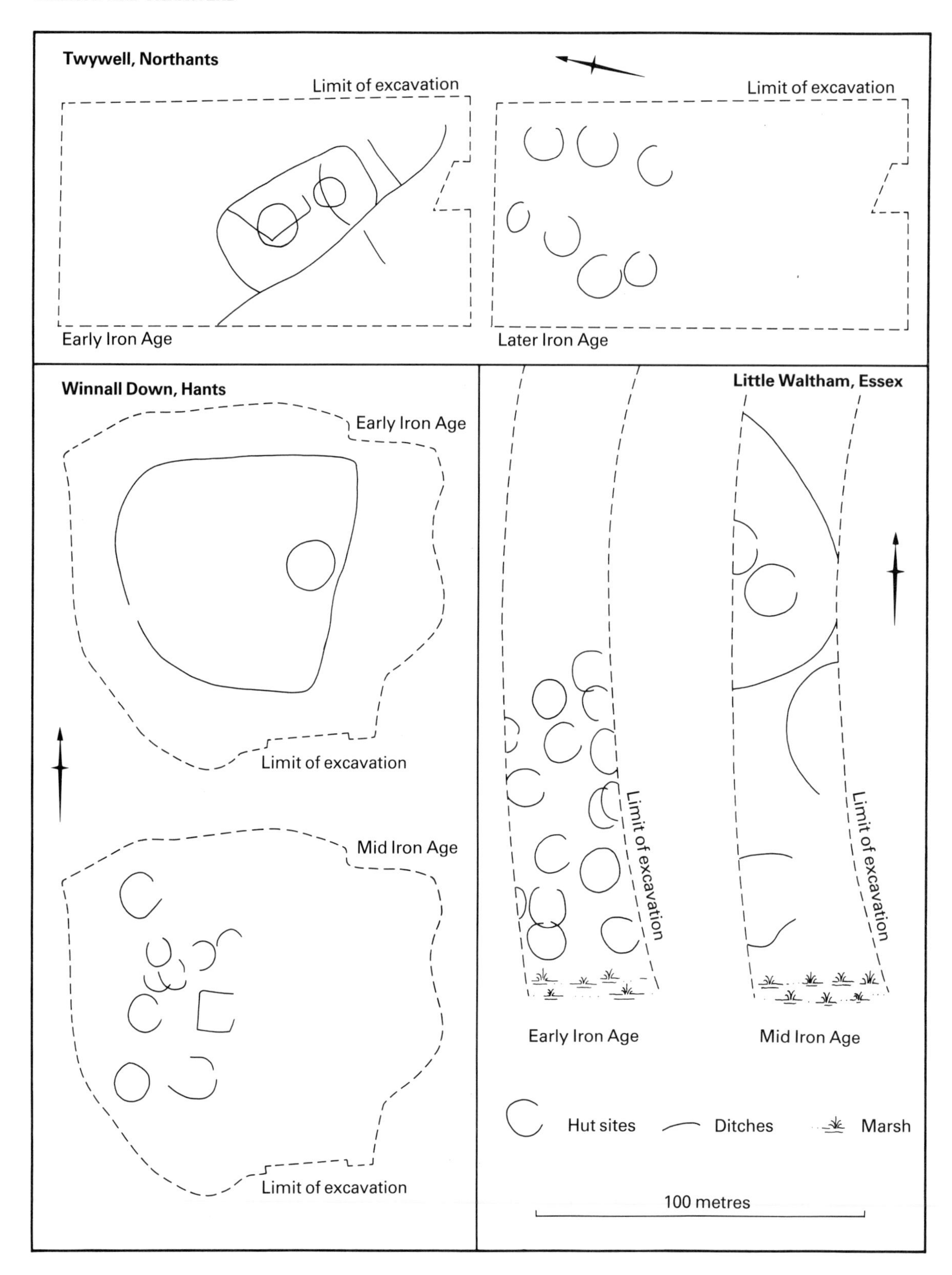
Twywell, Northants
Limit of excavation
Limit of excavation
Early Iron Age
Later Iron Age
Winnall Down, Hants
Early Iron Age
Limit of excavation
Mid Iron Age
Limit of excavation
Little Waltham, Essex
Limit of excavation
Limit of excavation
Early Iron Age
Mid Iron Age
Hut sites
Ditches
Marsh
100 metres

suggest that they were defensive in function. One lay on heavy boulder clay, the other on dry sandstone soil.

In addition to sites such as these which are not very different from the upland ones, there are also what can only be described as extensive villages. One such site has been discovered at Dragonby in north Lincolnshire, situated on a broad sandy shelf between the valleys of the Rivers Trent and Ancholme. Much of the site was destroyed as a result of ironstone mining and was thus obliterated without record, while another part of it must lie under the modern village to the north. The actual interpretation of the remains excavated is difficult for the site was also inhabited in the Roman period and this occupation has destroyed much of the Iron Age detail. Nevertheless, pits, ditches, trackways and hut circles seem to be packed together. Because of the area of land already worked for ironstone and thus not available for excavation, it is impossible to ascertain the true extent of this Iron Age village but it cannot have been less than 16 hectares in area and was probably much larger. This would make it considerably larger than most medieval villages and bigger than most modern ones.

Another, perhaps even larger, Iron Age village which again illustrates the problems of interpretation of such sites is Little Waltham in Essex, in the valley of the River Chelmer (Fig. 24). The land available for excavation by Mr P. Drury was the line of a new bypass, covering some 7 to 8 hectares, and it appeared to be cutting a swath across a huge area of occupation. Within this swath the earliest settlement, beginning in the third century BC, was an open or unenclosed occupation area with fifteen circular huts 10 metres to 13.7 metres in diameter, though no more than seven were occupied at any one time. After some two hundred years this settlement was replaced by one surrounded by a timber palisade in which at least two huts stood. However, as less than a quarter of the enclosure was examined there were probably other houses within it. This enclosed settlement probably lasted only a hundred years and was in turn replaced by a new settlement, not excavated, a little further away. Despite the problems of limited excavation, the evidence from Little Waltham indicates that it was occupied by a large Iron Age village whose form was changed on at least one occasion, and also that this site is an example of the now familiar settlement drift.

Another lowland site which also poses problems of interpretation but which provides equally good evidence of large-scale occupation is that of Twywell on the side of the Cranford Brook in Northamptonshire (Fig. 24). Here again ironstone mining led to the discovery of the remains and had already destroyed an unknown part of the site before it was excavated. What remained to be examined, by Mr D. Jackson, proved to be an Iron Age village which had drifted from south to north across the site and had changed its basic form considerably. It began in the fourth century BC as a small settlement enclosed by a ditch. This enclosure was altered and other enclosures added to it later on. These later enclosures may represent a group of farmsteads, but subsequently they were abandoned and replaced by a new settlement to the north which had the character of an open or unenclosed village. At least seven circular huts were discovered, not all contemporary, and this village lasted until the first century BC. It is interesting to note that while the village at Little Waltham changed from an open one to an enclosed one, the Twywell sequence is the opposite, as is the site excavated at Winnall Down, Hampshire (Fig. 24). There are many other examples of both types of site and they all show how complex Iron Age settlement was and how difficult it is to attempt neat classifications and patterns for the period.

A further example of a large Iron Age village in a very different area is that excavated at Ledston, east of Leeds on the north side of the River Aire in West Yorkshire. The site was discovered by aerial photography and from the air a vast complex of ditches and pits was visible, covering some 7 hectares. The initial excavation was limited to an area only 80 metres by 20 metres, yet from it came the remains of several huts, storage pits and ditches, suggesting that this was only a fragment of a very large settlement area.

Air photography also led to the discovery of a large Iron Age village at Beckford in the Severn valley, near Tewkesbury, Gloucestershire. The air photographs showed a whole series of conjoined ditched enclosures. When some of these were excavated they were found to be crammed with large storage pits set around cobbled yards and associated with round huts. Each enclosure ap-

24 Change in Iron Age Settlements *All of these excavated sites show how Iron Age settlements could radically change their form within a relatively short time.*

peared to be a simple farmstead but they were so grouped as to form a compact village – yet another variation in Iron Age settlement. The village only lasted 150 to 200 years, though further excavation may well reveal a longer period of occupation and internal drift.

Another large Iron Age site, more akin to that already noted in the chalk downlands at Hog Cliff Hill, Dorset, is that at Bolnhurst, Bedfordshire (Fig. 19). The remains consist of a large irregular enclosure covering some 7 hectares and bounded by a slight bank and ditch. Fieldwork by Mr A. E. Brown has indicated that it is of late Iron Age date and was probably occupied by a large number of people. Yet here are no light chalk soils, so beloved of another generation of archaeologists. The site lies in the centre of an area of extremely heavy clay land. It probably represents the sole survivor of what was once a common type of semi-fortified lowland Iron Age village.

Finally in this consideration of the variety and complexity of Iron Age settlements, the excavations carried out in recent years in the Thames valley are especially worth noting. Sterling work by the Oxfordshire Archaeological Unit has been concentrated on five sites, all within 12 kilometres of Oxford itself, and all close to the River Thames. One at Ashville, west of Abingdon, was an open 'hamlet', probably with a maximum size of seven houses. It was occupied in the second and third centuries BC after which the site was abandoned and the area divided up into fields and cultivated. Not far away, on the other side of Abingdon, a late Iron Age settlement at Barton Court Farm could not have been more different (Fig. 21). Here was a simple farm set up in the first century BC and continuing right through the Roman period. In the Iron Age the farmyard consisted of a rigidly geometric trapezoidal enclosure with a single round hut set in one corner within its own subsidiary ditched enclosure. Further west again, at Mount Farm, near Dorchester, another simple farmstead has been excavated. This had a much longer occupation than Abingdon, perhaps as much as 400 or 500 years, and though it certainly consisted of a simple hut in the middle of its life, it experienced many changes of plan.

Well upstream, along the Thames above Oxford, the site at Farmoor has been excavated (Fig. 21). The early Iron Age occupation appears to have been an open 'hamlet' on the dry gravel terrace above the river. But after two hundred years or so it was moved north on to the flood-plain itself where a group of huts was erected together with a stockyard (partly shown at the south-west end of the Roman site). This site had a very short life and may have been a temporary one connected with grazing cattle on the meadows. The final site in the Oxford area is near Hardwick, actually in the valley of the River Windrush, and within its flood-plain. Here two concentric ditches 50 metres and 65 metres in diameter were discovered with 'antennae' ditches leading out from the entrance. Within the inner enclosure were six circular huts. Yet the site appears to have been occupied only seasonally and for a relatively short time in the middle of the Iron Age. It has been interpreted, as has that at Farmoor, as a pastoral summer encampment.

These sites in the Oxford region are important for they show the variety of settlements within a small area. Villages, hamlets and single farmsteads all exist of varying social status and with very different purposes. Of course in a very real sense we should not be surprised at this. The same is true of all the succeeding periods, and indeed probably of the earlier ones too, if we did but have the same detailed evidence. In a similar area of land in Roman, medieval or even modern times we find a similar variety of settlement form and status, all reflecting the complex society that uses or used it.

There are two other forms of Iron Age rural settlement which reflected exceptional conditions and which should also be brought in here. One such is the 'lake' village of the Somerset Levels where the houses were erected on marshy islands, supported by timber piles, and the other is the occupation of caves, as in the Cheddar Gorge, curiously also in the same general area as the Somerset Levels.

There is one type of Iron Age settlement that we have not yet looked at and which is the best known of all, by virtue of the fact that we can still see the remains clearly in many parts of the country. For while few of the multitude of farmsteads, villages and hamlets discussed so far are visible on the ground, the great hillforts are not only marked on all modern maps but their substantial ramparts are still clearly evident enclosing countless hilltops and spurs. They have been relegated to the end of this section on Iron Age settlement for, common as they are, it has to be emphasized that they form only a very small proportion of the total Iron Age settlement pattern. The less obvious sites are much more important for it is in those that by far the greatest proportion of the population lived.

Nevertheless, the hillforts are important for they too show great variety of form and usage and also demonstrate the growing instability of Iron Age society and the emphasis on warfare which we referred to earlier. Although the first forts, as we have seen, appear in the late Bronze Age, it is in the Iron Age that they are most numerous and reach their full range of complexity and size. Although many people are familiar with the great forts of southern England, such as Maiden Castle, Ham Hill, Hod Hill and Yarnbury (Fig. 26), there are hundreds more less spectacular examples all over the country, not always on dominating hilltops and very often quite small. Woolsbarrow in Dorset, in the centre of the heathland, is hardly noticeable. Badbury in the same county, while much more obvious, is sited on little more than a swelling in the downland. In south-west England the rocky coasts are dotted with promontory forts, such as the Rumps, Cornwall, where only a rampart across the neck of the headland formed the artificial defences (Fig. 25). Similar promontory forts, often of considerable size, occur inland where there is suitable topography. One of the best examples, though little known, is that at Nottingham Hill, Gloucestershire (Fig. 25).

There is also considerable variety in the size of hillforts. Some of the largest are in Wessex, but even there Maiden Castle, with its 20 hectares, is dwarfed by Walbury in Berkshire, which covers 34 hectares, and by Casterly Camp in Wiltshire, covering 25 hectares, while at Bindon Hill, Dorset, the apparently unfinished fort there encloses no less than 166 hectares. Yet in the same area there are also much smaller forts, such as Blewburton in Berkshire (3 hectares), Abbotsbury in Dorset (1.8 hectares), Small Down Knoll (Fig. 27) in Somerset (3 hectares), and Knook Down in Wiltshire (1.4 hectares). Between these extremes there are many others of all sizes. Outside Wessex the same variation occurs. In the north of England the hillforts tend to be much smaller than in the south and many are under 1 hectare in area, that at Titlington, in Co Durham, being a typical example (Fig. 28). Even so there are some relatively large ones, usually in the 4 to 8 hectare range.

Hillforts vary in form as well as in size. Many are bounded only by a simple rampart and ditch. Others have multiple defences of great size. And it is obvious that many have grown or have been developed from one form to another. Thus Hambledon Hill, Dorset (Fig. 25), though never excavated, seems to have started as a small univallate fort of 5 hectares. It was then increased in size to 8 hectares, still with a single rampart and ditch, and finally expanded to no less than 13 hectares and enclosed by double ramparts and ditches with extensive scarping of the slopes below. Hillfort entrances are equally varied – some are simple gaps through the ramparts but others are of great complexity with in-turned or out-turned banks and ditches, outer enclosures, double or triple gates and 'barbican'-like features (outer defensive systems protecting the gates).

A further important variation lies in the apparent use of hillforts. Some have little visible ground evidence of being occupied at all. The fort on Ingleborough Hill, North Yorkshire, has no more than half a dozen hut circles inside its defences. Yet Yeavering Bell in Northumberland has 130 platforms visible within its 5 hectares, while at Hambledon, Dorset (Fig. 25), there are 207 hut-platforms in the 13 hectare enclosure. At nearby Hod Hill the 22 hectare fort has just 3 hectares of its interior unploughed. Within this small area there are 65 hut-circles and it has been estimated that there must have been well over 200 there once.

All the evidence discussed so far is based on ground observation only. This alone shows a great variety of form, size and usage and suggests a complex hierarchy of status. The evidence from excavations shows all this even more clearly. Most excavations show that the earlier Iron Age forts were defended by ramparts enclosed in timber with walk-ways on the top. Later these 'box ramparts' were replaced by simpler 'dump'-constructed banks with no timber work. These were usually associated with the building of multiple ramparts giving considerable defence in depth. The entrances, too, usually turn out to be well fortified in forts of this type. Even simple 'gap' entrances reveal massive post-holes for towers, 'flying walk-ways' over the gates and evidence for the huge timber gates themselves.

However, it is excavations of the interiors of hillforts which are perhaps the most interesting for it is here that we can find evidence for their usage and status. Just a few examples can be used to indicate how different hillforts were. Thus at Grimthorpe, a small 3 hectare univallate hillfort in North Yorkshire, there appeared to be only one short period of limited occupation early in the Iron Age. At Winklebury, near Basingstoke in Hampshire, a very different story was revealed during excavations by

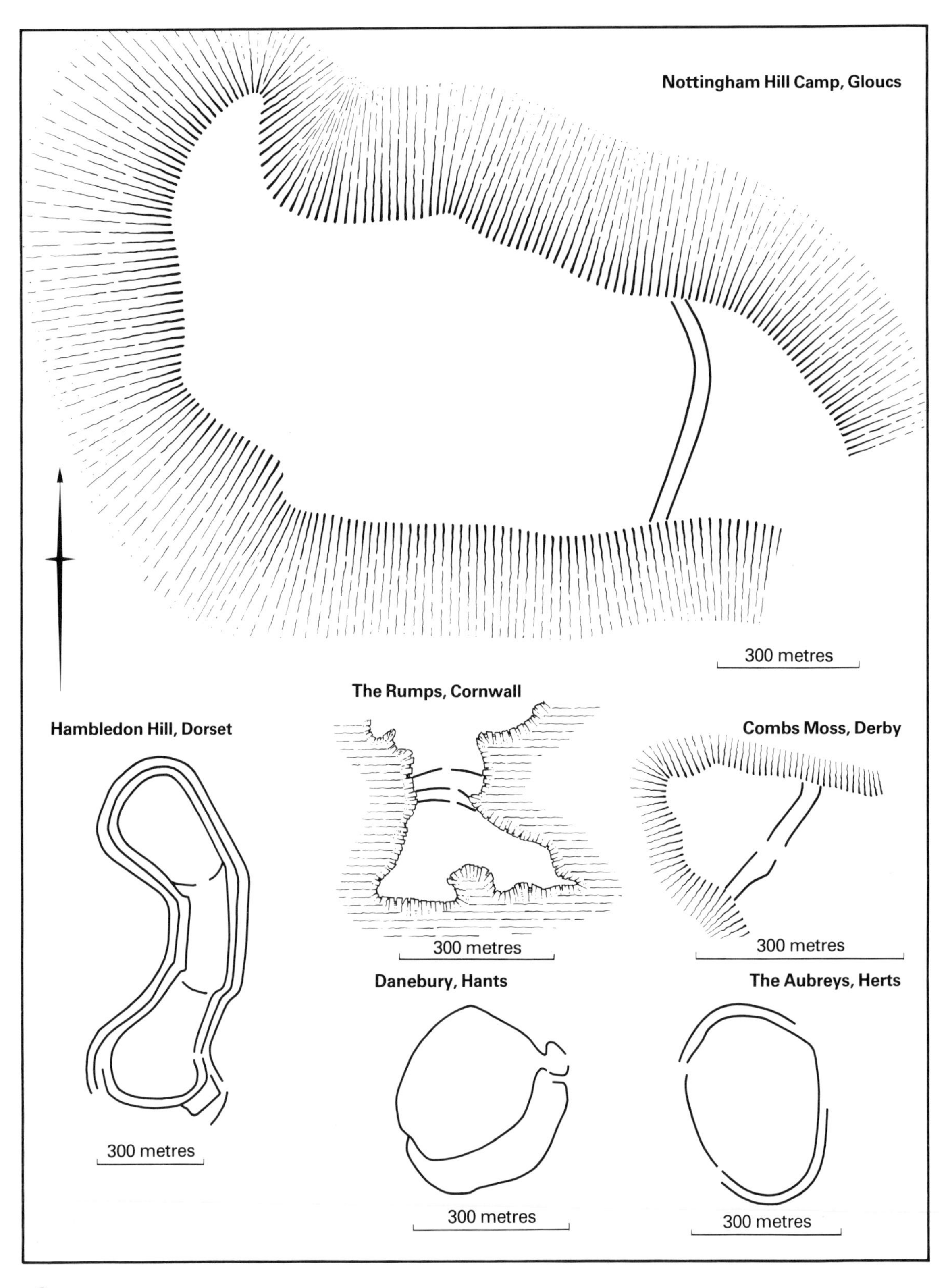
Nottingham Hill Camp, Gloucs
300 metres
The Rumps, Cornwall
Hambledon Hill, Dorset
Combs Moss, Derby
300 metres
300 metres
Danebury, Hants
The Aubreys, Herts
300 metres
300 metres
300 metres

25 Iron Age Forts *These plans illustrate how widely Iron Age forts differ in form and size. Hambledon is a complex multivallate hillfort with a long sequence of development. Danebury and The Aubreys are simpler, but they also show a number of different phases. The Rumps and Combs Moss represent, in two different ways, the very common use of fortified promontories. Nottingham Hill Camp is a superb example of the huge, but slightly defended settlements, about which little is known.*

Mr K. Smith. In the fifth to sixth centuries BC the 7.6 hectare fort was defined by a single rampart of 'box' construction. The interior appears to have been occupied by a small number of people living in a few circular huts, though with an unusually large number of storage pits. The fort was then abandoned until the third century BC when it was refurbished and the rampart rebuilt in a 'dump' construction form. As in the earlier period a limited number of people seem to have lived there.

In contrast to these two sites is Danebury, near Stockbridge in Hampshire, excavated by Professor B. Cunliffe (Fig. 25). The fort, covering 5.4 hectares, was first occupied in the fifth century BC, again with a simple 'box' rampart and with limited occupation. Then, around 400 BC, the interior of the fort was totally reorganized on new lines which were to last for three hundred years. This work involved the deliberate laying out of streets, which were lined with rectangular timber houses measuring 3 metres by 3.5 metres, a pattern which can be explained only as conscious planning. A complex and impressive double gateway was erected, which also suggests some major authority in control of the fort. This authority remained, for the houses, though often rebuilt, were always on the old alignments and the ditches were cleaned out regularly. This situation lasted until about 100 BC when the entrance was rebuilt in a very complicated way, perhaps because of a serious military threat. Shortly afterwards the whole fort was abandoned. The final phase was on the eve of the Roman invasion when the fort was repaired and given a new outer rampart and wide ditch on one side. There was no permanent occupation and presumably it was taken over by the Roman army.

The great variation in hillforts indicated by these few examples forces us to rethink our ideas of the place of these forts in Iron Age society. The simplistic pattern of distribution, which many archaeologists have produced in working out neat tribal territories and centres of political control and trade, is clearly unacceptable. Some forts, such as Danebury, Maiden Castle or perhaps Hambledon (Fig. 25), are obviously major political centres and perhaps the nearest thing to towns that prehistoric society ever produced, with all that that implies for trade and social organization. Others, such as Winklebury, may have been local centres where a few people lived permanently but whose main purpose was as a refuge for the inhabitants of the surrounding land in times of danger. Yet other forts may have been used only at the times when danger threatened. On the other hand, many small hillforts, especially those in the north of England, seemed to have been the semi-permanent homes of minor chieftains. Thus hillforts, like the farmsteads, villages and hamlets of the period, cover the whole spectrum of a complex society, and, as with the other types of settlement, changed their form, size and purpose over time.

The overall distribution of hillforts may, towards the end of the Iron Age at least, have some validity in terms of reflecting variations in social and political organization, if looked at carefully. In Wiltshire, for example, the very large multivallate forts are spaced roughly 15 kilometres apart and may be semi-urban political centres of tribal subunits, but with smaller forts between them suggesting a lower level of chieftains or similar political organization. In the north of England the picture is different. There are far more small forts, suggesting a larger substratum of local chieftains than in the south, with fewer great forts and in some areas none at all. Even more important is the relative lack of forts in the Midlands and the east of England which other evidence suggests were occupied by larger and perhaps richer rural settlements. Does this mean that these areas were differently organized politically or that there was less pressure on the Iron Age society there? We do not know at the moment. All we can see are the barest hints of a complex Iron Age society and we may misunderstand the true picture completely if we attempt to order this complexity. To discuss hillforts as if they represent a single type of settlement is as mistaken as if we grouped fourteenth-century York, a thirteenth-century great baron's castle, a temporary eleventh-century motte and bailey castle and a small twelfth-century moated site together and called them all medieval fortified sites without any thought as to their purpose, date, function or status.

Towards the end of the Iron Age, certain clearly defined tribal areas are identifiable in England for

26 Yarnbury, Wiltshire
One of the larger Wessex Iron Age hillforts set on an unprepossessing site in the centre of the downs. What we see is only the end of a long period of development. Within the main ramparts are faint traces of an earlier fort, perhaps of late Bronze Age or earlier Iron Age date.

ABOVE **27 Small Down Knoll, Evercreech, Somerset** *One of the many small Iron Age forts that dot the landscape of southern England. Here was no great political power base, but merely the defended centre of a small tribal territory packed with countless small farmsteads.*

RIGHT **28 Prehistoric Settlements, Titlington, Co Durham** *On the edge of modern and medieval arable land, the cultivation of which has doubtlessly destroyed much else, lies a group of settlements of much earlier periods. At the top of the picture is a small Iron Age fortress. Below it, to the left, is an enclosed farmstead, probably of Roman date. Further down again are slight traces of isolated huts which may be of the Bronze Age.*

their names have come down to us from classical authors. Thus in central southern England there were the Durotriges, in the south-east Midlands the Catuvellauni, and in south-west England the Dumnonii. In the century or so before the Roman conquest these tribes certainly had some political existence as is indicated by a crude coinage, imitating that of the Roman Empire. Yet to what extent these units were welded into a coherent, cohesive social structure is unknown.

One final type of Iron Age settlement is that said to be the result of the non-existent Belgic invasions in the first century BC. These Belgic peoples have bedevilled the understanding of the late Iron Age. Because they were mentioned by Julius Caesar it is assumed that their arrival must have had a considerable impact although it has proved impossible to identify them in archaeological terms. There are indeed a number of complex systems of dykes or linear ditches and banks in south-east England, such as those round Colchester, St Albans and Silchester, within which are areas of extensive and rich settlement. These are not necessarily related to any late invasions of Belgic warriors but are merely, in the most productive areas of England, the final achievement of a prehistoric society.

Here, at the termination of the prehistoric period, we see the end of the long process of development of settlement which started in 10,000 BC. As must be now obvious, it is not a simple story of steady expansion by primitive people but a highly complex picture of ebbs and flows, expansion and contraction, and above all of incredible variety in the way in which people lived. By the first century AD the outlines of England were fixed after millennia of trial and error. Everywhere man cultivated the land, grazed his beasts and, most importantly, lived in great numbers, all within clearly defined economic and political territories. Indeed, as we have already suggested, England was an over-exploited country, perhaps on the verge of a major political, social and technological collapse. Then suddenly, in AD 43, England was drawn into the Roman Empire and a new and even more complex pattern of settlement developed on the foundations already long established.

-6-
The Impact of Rome

The period during which England lay within the bounds of the Roman Empire was, compared to the prehistoric period, very short, slightly less than 400 years, from AD 43 to about AD 410. Yet during that time there were many profound changes in settlement patterns and forms.

As we have seen, by the end of the Iron Age England was an almost totally exploited land, with a large population living in a wide variety of settlement types, and occupying all kinds of soils and positions. At the same time there is evidence of actual overpopulation and over-exploitation, potentially leading towards the collapse of Iron Age society itself. We have no idea whether this would have occurred eventually, for the arrival of the Roman army in AD 43 and the subsequent incorporation of the country into the Roman Empire resulted in three important changes: first, the Romans introduced improvements in agricultural technology, which allowed more land to be cultivated; secondly, England was drawn into the economic sphere of the Empire; thirdly, a relatively stable government, protected from external pressures by military might, was established. These three factors alone allowed the trends in rural settlement which had become apparent in Iron Age times to be intensified.

New and better ploughs, an internal military market for food, considerable export potential for agricultural produce and freedom from internal warfare all led to a population explosion accompanied by a further extension of arable land, intensification of pastoral farming in those areas most suited to it, and, of course, to even more settlements of every size and form. It is the sheer number of rural settlement sites that is perhaps the most remarkable feature of the Roman period. In eastern Northamptonshire, for example, it has been estimated that there was a *minimum* of one settlement every 0.4 to 0.5 square kilometres (Fig. 30). In more prosaic terms, within the writer's own small Cambridgeshire parish, Whittlesford, after ten years of careful observation, it is now possible to say that there were once five and possibly six separate Roman settlements, two of considerable size, each covering more than 3 hectares.

In some areas of Bedfordshire, Roman settlements turn up with almost monotonous regularity, 500 metres apart, regardless of soil or situation. A similarly dense pattern of settlement is evident in the north of England. On the lowland glacially-derived soils of north-eastern England, Roman farmsteads lie, on average, about 2 kilometres apart. Along the higher moorland edges, close to the Cheviot Hills, they are grouped in small clusters of two or three farmsteads, each cluster being 2 to 3 kilometres from its neighbours. Most remarkably, on the silt fenlands of south Lincolnshire and north Cambridgeshire, Roman occupation sites were only a few hundred metres apart (Fig. 29).

In fact, apart from on the higher moorlands above the 300 metre contour and on the undrained marshlands, Roman settlements existed everywhere in England, often in places which in later centuries were abandoned to the forests and wastes. For example, a number of settlements, including a large villa, are known within Wychwood Forest in Oxfordshire. In Northamptonshire, in the area of the great medieval Rockingham Forest, Roman settlements are common. In an area of 300 hectares in Stanion parish, near Corby, which is known from documentary evidence to have been woodland until the eighteenth century, no less than ten small Roman settlements have been recorded.

The number of rural settlements is the most important feature of Roman times in this country although, as we shall see, by no means all these places were occupied at the same time. Even so, the figures suggest a very large rural population and, though it is difficult to give even vague estimates of the number of people in Roman times, it is likely that it was higher and perhaps much higher than that indicated by Domesday Book in 1086.

From their wide pattern of distribution it is clear that Roman rural settlements were not apparently controlled by simple geographical factors to any marked degree. This is even more obvious when some specific areas are looked at in detail. On the high chalklands of Wessex, for example, there were a large number of farmsteads and also many villages. The question of access to water which concerns all who see the sites today was no problem to the Romano-British farmers who lived there. They merely dug wells through the chalk until they reached the water-table. At the Roman hamlet of Woodcutts, high on the north Dorset downs, there were at least two wells, both of which have been excavated. One was 41 metres deep and the other 54 metres deep. In a very different landscape, the silt fens of eastern England, the dense pattern of settlement was achieved by remarkable feats of drainage. The courses of major rivers, including that of the Great Ouse, were changed, catch-water drains constructed to carry away water from the higher land on the edge of the Fens, large internal drains laid out and every field, road, track, garden and even individual house site was ditched around. Here, superior technology and planning overcame a hostile environment, at least temporarily, in a way that was not to be repeated until the eighteenth and nineteenth centuries.

By applying this technology the Romans were able to make potentially rich and thus valuable land economically productive. This is an important point for settlement history. In all periods where economic or demographic forces, in their widest sense, make if profitable or necessary for man to farm, and thus live, in very hostile and apparently unsuitable landscapes, he is prepared to work to either overcome the natural forces or at least modify them sufficiently to make a living.

It was these pressures which presumably produced the large Roman villages on the high mountain-sides in north-east Yorkshire, or the hundreds of farmsteads on the upland slopes of Northumberland and Cumbria. The peace which the Roman army brought to these areas and the supplies that the same army required, as well as the potential for exporting produce and animals to other areas, all combined to produce a larger population and the economic conditions to exploit the landscape. As a result, many new settlements were established in environments that were not by any means perfect for permanent habitation.

In any one of these areas it is possible to identify geographical determinants which could apparently have given rise to each particular settlement. Sheltered spots, spring lines and gravel patches can all be found. Yet at the same time the observant fieldworker can always find equally 'good' sites which have not been occupied as well as positively 'poor' sites which have certainly been settled. The location of these Roman settlements was obviously influenced more by human than by natural factors.

If the large number of Roman rural settlements and their varied locations seems surprising, it is also now clear that the settlements themselves were very diverse. Until a few years ago the traditional picture of the Roman countryside was that of a fairly well-wooded landscape with occasional palatial villas and the rare and ill-defined Roman farmstead or hamlet. As we have seen, most of the woodland had gone and settlements lay almost everywhere. But in addition these settlements were as varied in type, or perhaps even more varied, than those we can see in the countryside today.

First of all there were large villages. Some of these still survive on unploughed land and though these were probably, even in Roman times, on marginal land and thus not typical, they give us a good idea of the variety in size and arrangement.

On a spur of Meriden Down, Dorset, near the village of Winterborne Houghton, low banks, scarps and shallow ditches on the grassland mark the site of a Roman village (Fig. 29). The core of the settlement is a roughly trapezoidal area, bounded by a low bank and outer ditch with three entrances leading to the interior. Inside there is a confused pattern of at least twenty hut-sites, both rectangular and circular. This was always the main part of the village and this lay inside a much larger, roughly rectangular area bounded by a bank. Beyond the bank are the remains of the contemporary field system, consisting of small embanked and scarped paddocks of typical Roman form. Through these fields ran four separate trackways which approach the village from the north, south-east, west and north-west and lead into the large rectangular area. The only explanation for this area is that it was a 'green', though unlike our normal village greens it surrounded the village and was not enclosed by the houses. The form of this complicated pattern suggests that it was a deliberate creation, for the original 'green' must have been planned before the surrounding fields were established. The enclosed settlement was then planted inside its 'green'. The interpretation of this site, as so many others, is complicated by the fact that this village did not remain static. It clearly grew, for other house-platforms lie outside the village core and within the 'green'. It looks very much as if this growth is an example of what was to be a common phenomenon in medieval and later times, the encroachment of houses on to a village green as a result of a population increase.

A very different and even more remarkable village is that of Chisenbury Warren, Enford, on the north-east side of Salisbury Plain, Wiltshire (Figs. 30, 31). It is sited on the gently sloping, north-facing side of a shallow valley and covers some 6 hectares, as large as many deserted medieval villages. This comparison is also valid in another way for its plan is remarkably similar to many classic medieval villages. It consists of a single 'street', now a holloway, about 770 metres long. On either side of the street are some eighty rectangular platforms between 14 metres and 20 metres long, each probably the site of a house. At the east end of the street the holloway forks and within the angle are other house sites. It has been suggested that this space was perhaps once an open 'green' and that the village has expanded over it. At the west end of the village street is a clearly defined triangular 'green' unmarked by any house sites. To the north of the village are the remains of long narrow fields which are certainly Roman, not prehistoric, in date and here again it is possible that the village is the result of conscious planning.

Another variant on the Roman village is that at Overton Down, West Overton, also in Wiltshire and also partly visible on the ground (Fig. 30). Here it appears that the village consisted of a long row of conjoining enclosures, forming a 'ladder' pattern some 500 metres long and 145 metres wide, intersected in places by hollow trackways. The houses seem to have lain at the west end of the enclosures and at least seventeen possible structures have been identified on the ground. Different again, and perhaps representing an older tradition of village form, is Chysauster, in south-west Cornwall (Fig. 33). Here, the irregular group of circular stone-walled huts, set within courtyards, is Roman in date but prehistoric in appearance and arrangement and follows the pattern established by Iron Age villages in the same area, such as Carn Euny which was also occupied throughout Roman times.

All the examples of villages so far discussed still exist in some form on the ground. But there are also many villages whose plans are only revealed as soil- or crop-marks from the air. Though totally invisible, except to the aerial archaeologist, these are very impressive when examined carefully. One at Fotheringhay, Northamptonshire, is situated on a gravel terrace edging the River Nene (Figs. 30, 32). As at Chisenbury, but in a very different landscape, this settlement seems to be very close in form to a medieval one. It appears to consist of a long 'street', now edged by ditches, with plots laid off each side. If we assume each plot contained a house, then there was a minimum of thirty houses there and probably at least twice as many as that for old quarries have obscured part of the site.

Out on the silt fens of eastern England air photographs have revealed many considerable villages as well as other types of settlement. Particularly good examples are those at March in Cambridgeshire, on Hacconby Fen, Lincolnshire

OVERLEAF LEFT **29 Roman Settlements** *The detailed plans show how widely Roman settlements varied in size and form. The inset map gives a vivid impression of the density of such settlement in one small area of fenland which was newly colonized in early Roman times.*

OVERLEAF RIGHT **30 Roman Villages** *The detailed plans show three types of Roman village and the different ways in which such remains can be revealed. The inset map indicates the density of Roman settlement over a small part of Northamptonshire and Bedfordshire when compared with modern villages there. It should also be compared with the map of Iron Age settlement in the same area (see Fig. 19).*

Crosby Garrett, Cumbria (Stone Walls)
Chelmorton, Derby (Stone Walls)
Meriden Down, Dorset (Earthworks)
March, Cambs (Crop-Marks)
Holbeach St Johns
Sutton St James
. 2.5 m
. 3.0 m
Whaplode Drove
Sutton St Edmunds
. 1.8 m
Gedney Hill
. 2.8 m
. 3.4 m
. 3.6 m
Parson Drove
. 2.0 m
. 2.0 m
Roman settlement
Medieval village
Spot height
4 kilometres
Roman Settlements in South-East Lincs
Hacconby Fen, Lincs (Crop-Marks)
300 metres

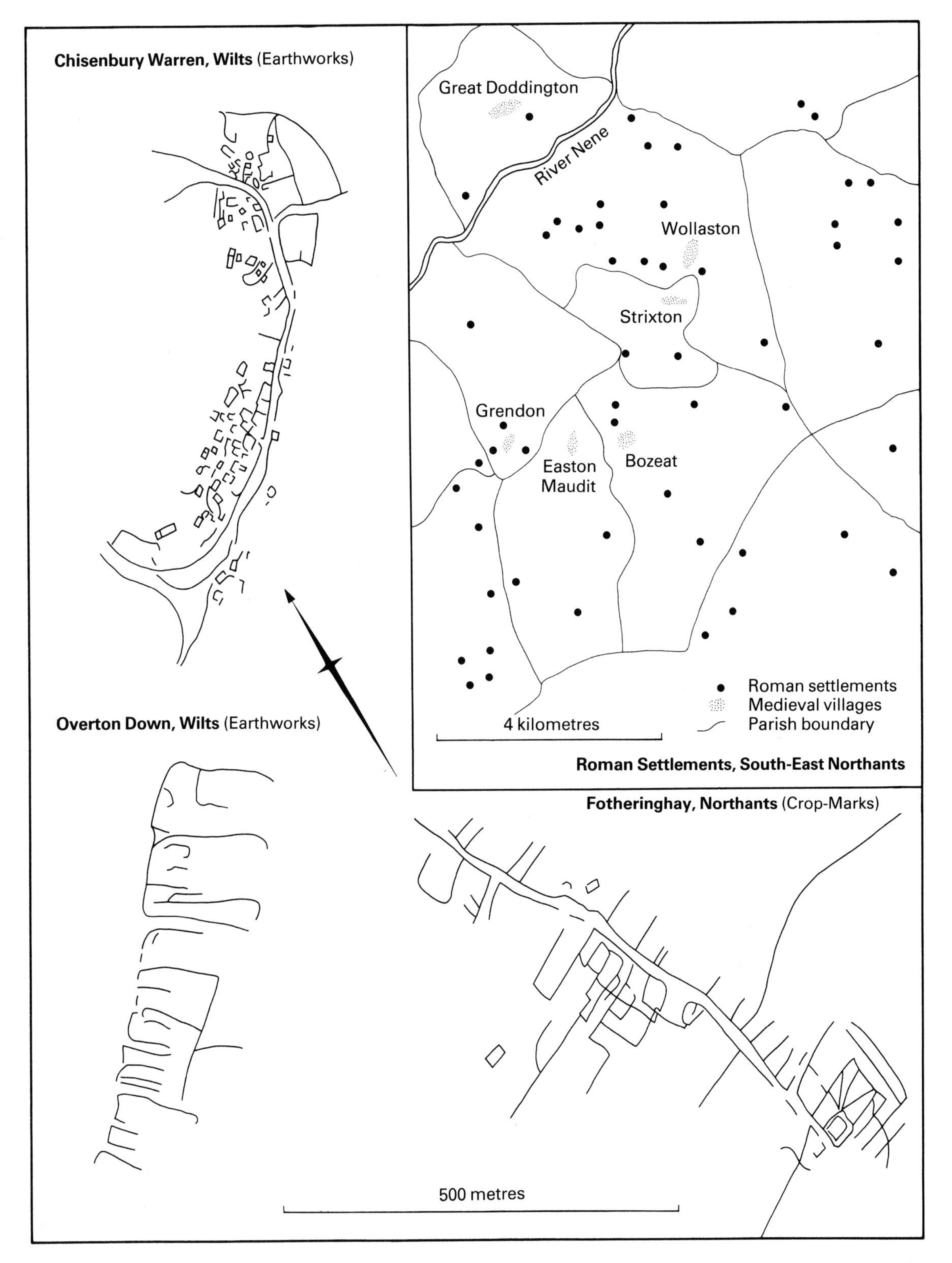
Chisenbury Warren, Wilts (Earthworks)
Great Doddington
River Nene
Wollaston
Strixton
Grendon
Easton Maudit
Bozeat
Roman settlements
Medieval villages
Parish boundary
4 kilometres
Roman Settlements, South-East Northants
Overton Down, Wilts (Earthworks)
Fotheringhay, Northants (Crop-Marks)
500 metres

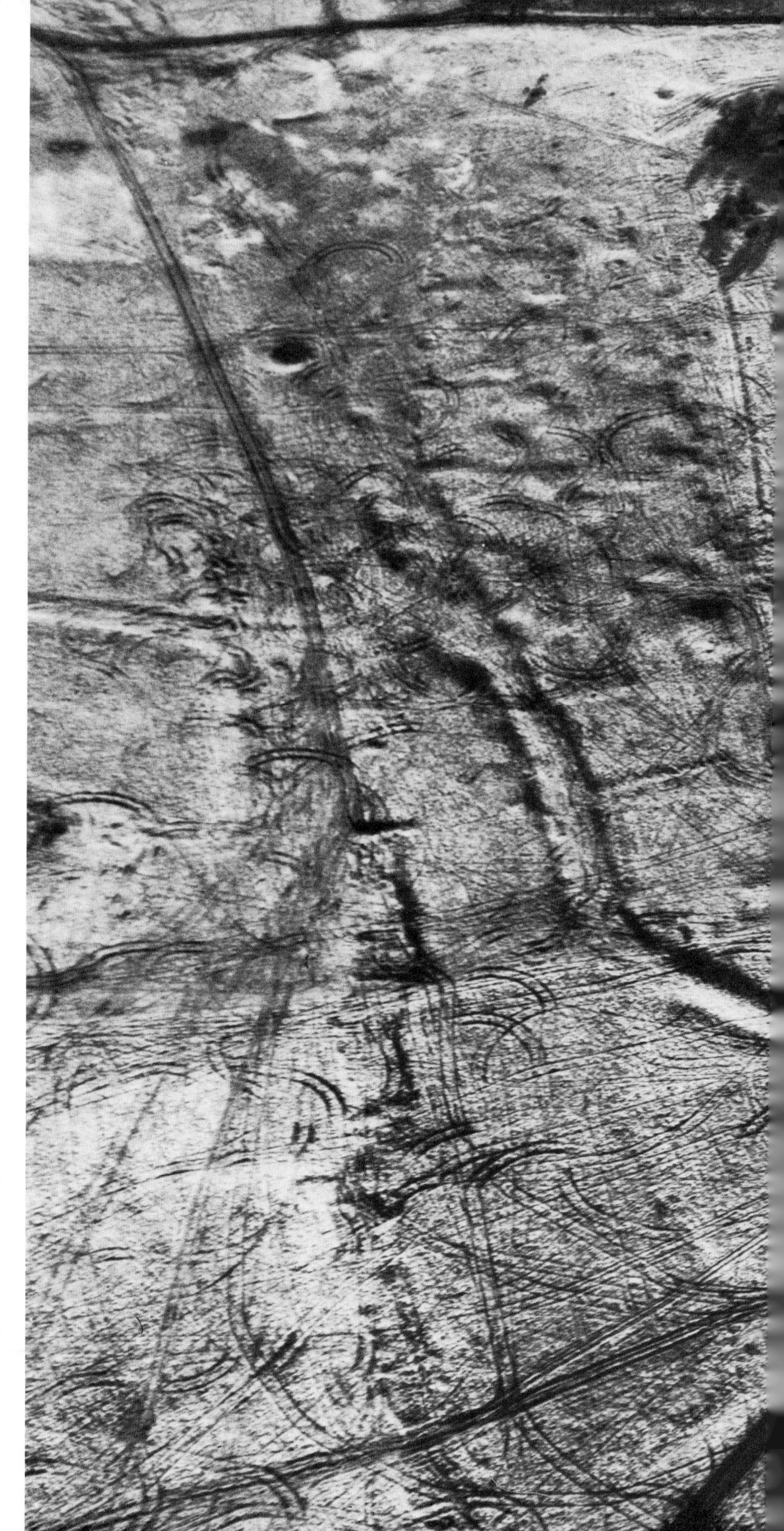

31 Chisenbury Warren, Enford, Wiltshire *Here a Roman village on the high downlands of Wessex has been preserved because it lies within an army training ground, but has been mutilated in detail by tank tracks. Its former main street is still clearly visible while the remains of some of the houses and gardens are just recognizable. This photograph can be compared with the plan of the village in Fig. 30 – north is to the right.*

32 Roman Village, Fotheringhay, Northamptonshire *Though only visible from the air, the former main street and the paddocks and gardens which once lined it are clear. The circular features are Bronze Age burial sites, perhaps indicating a much older occupation. This photograph can be compared with the plan of the village in Fig. 30 – north is to the left.*

33 Roman Village, Chysauster, Cornwall *One of the stone-walled, circular huts of a small Roman village. These structures are almost identical to the later prehistoric settlements in the same area and show the relatively small influence of Rome in these remote parts.*

and at Holbeach, also in Lincolnshire (Figs. 29, 34). At all these sites ditched tracks enter compact areas of small ditched enclosures and paddocks. On the ground vast quantities of pottery and other debris indicate large and flourishing communities. These examples are only a few of the large number of Roman villages that have been identified from the air, and are typical of many which appear as soil- or crop-marks in numerous parts of lowland England.

Moving down the scale to hamlets, these also display the same variety of form and layout. Of the Roman hamlets that have been preserved on unploughed land, a good example is that on Berwick Down, Tollard Royal, Wiltshire (Fig. 21). It actually lies only 100 metres or so north of the Iron Age farmstead described in the previous chapter and is probably an example of the usual settlement drift, this time up-slope. This hamlet consists of a roughly oval enclosure about 1 hectare in area, bounded by a scarp and ditch. A road or holloway runs across the enclosure and on either side are platforms which probably represent five or six small farmsteads clustered together. A different type of hamlet is that at Plush in Dorset. Here there is a road running into the settlement but this ends in a small open space or tiny 'green' no more than 50 metres by 40 metres. On two sides of this 'green' are contemporary fields, and the settlement itself lies to the side and below the 'green' on a steep slope. The occupied area is no more than 1.25 hectares in extent and no more than ten or twelve possible building platforms can be identified. In the north stone walls mark the sites of countless small Roman hamlets. These consist of numerous small paddocks and enclosures, often with circular or rectangular hut-sites within them. The site in Ewe Close, Crosby Ravensworth, Cumbria (Fig. 35), is perhaps the best of these, though more typical is that at Titlington in Co Durham (Fig. 28).

Turning to the Roman hamlets that have been identified from soil- and crop-marks, that at Kemerton in south Hereford and Worcester is typical. Here air photographs show a trapezoidal enclosure with one curved side, at least one internal division and a small double enclosure attached to the south-east corner. Judging from the platforms that were discovered on the ground when the land was being ploughed and the second- to fourth-century Roman pottery found there, it appears to have been an enclosed group of six or seven houses. On the fenlands of south Lincolnshire, there are hundreds of hamlets visible on air photographs, such as that at Deeping St Nicholas. This is a small enclosed area of rectangular ditched paddocks, set inside a surrounding field system. Pottery of the second century found here indicates a relatively short period of occupation.

Thousands of the smallest type of Roman rural settlement are known, but it is difficult to pick out any that might be called typical because there is such a bewildering variety of forms. Of those that still survive, many would not be recognized if they had been damaged by ploughing. One such, on Overton Down in Wiltshire, is now no more than four hut-circles, set in the sides of older, probably prehistoric fields. That at Knap Hill, also in Wiltshire, is a rectangular enclosure, presumably a farmstead, set against the bank of the ancient Neolithic causewayed camp (Fig. 9). On moorland edges in the north of England, hundreds of individual Roman farmsteads still exist, though even here local differences occur. In Northumberland, to the north of Hadrian's Wall, circular stone huts in round, walled enclosures are common. To the south of the Wall, the stone huts are set in rectangular farmyards. Elsewhere in the lowlands of England, air photographs have produced evidence of almost every conceivable type of farmstead from groups of enclosed circular huts, including one or two domestic dwellings and two or three stone sheds or byres, to farmsteads bounded by circular, oval, square, trapezoidal or rectangular enclosures.

So far we have discussed these rural settlements as relatively static places, based on the forms that are visible on the ground or from the air. The situation becomes much more complicated if we look at the results from excavations. Every type of settlement so far discussed, as well as many others, has been excavated. These excavations not only confirm the complexity of settlement form but they add a new dimension, that of change over time. In addition, they have given us details of structures and evidence as to how the buildings were used.

Of the hundreds of excavations, only a handful can be discussed here to show what can be and has been revealed. At Studland in Dorset, a Roman hamlet has been examined by Mr N. Field. It began life at the very beginning of the Roman period as a group of circular wattle and daub huts, identical to those of the later Iron Age in the same region. These huts lasted only twenty to twenty-five years and were then replaced by rectangular houses, also of wattle and daub, but with substantial stone foundations. These were altered and extended on a number of occasions, but basically were of a 'long-house' type, that is they had two rooms, one used by the inhabitants and the other for keeping animals. This hamlet was an 'open' one for no trace of a surrounding enclosure was discovered and its occupants were clearly never rich. Yet the site remained occupied until the end of the fourth century.

Quite different was the farmstead excavated by Mr B. Dix at Odell, Bedfordshire, on the banks of the River Ouse (Fig. 21). Here, a farm was established just before the Roman Conquest. This consisted of two circular wooden huts inside a small ditched enclosure. Apart from the huts being rebuilt at least twice, this farm remained unaltered in spite of the arrival of the Roman army and continued in its original form until the end of the first century AD. It was then moved 100 metres to the south-east where, after the stock pens of the first farm had been demolished, a new group of circular huts was built, this time without an enclosing ditch. These huts too were rebuilt many times, but eventually they were abandoned and a simple rectangular stone farmhouse was erected in their place. This farmhouse lasted until the middle of the fourth century when the whole site was deserted. Here we can see the influence of Roman 'civilization', in the form of a rectangular, multi-roomed house, finally appearing on the site a long time after the beginning of the Roman period.

In the Thames valley, in Oxfordshire, a different story was revealed at Barton Court, near Abingdon (Fig. 21). We have already seen that the late Iron Age farmstead there consisted of a trapezoidal enclosure or farmyard with a single round wooden hut set in one corner of its own inner enclosure. This farmstead too remained unaltered until some twenty years after the Roman Conquest when it was completely rebuilt. Then a new and larger

34 Roman Settlement, Holbeach, Lincolnshire
This is the site of one of the hundreds of Roman villages that dotted the silt fenlands of eastern England. Most have now been destroyed by modern agriculture and this is a rare survival. The tracks, paddocks and gardens, edged by ditches, still remain.

35 Roman Settlement, Crosby Ravensworth, Cumbria *One of the best-preserved Roman hamlets in the north of England. It lies in an exposed position on moorland at over 300 metres. Its stone-walled house sites, yards and paddocks remain almost completely untouched by later activity.*

rectangular enclosure was laid out with the farmyard in the northern half and a rectangular farmhouse of timber in the southern half. Here the arrival of Roman ideas and fashions was earlier than at Odell and more impressive, for though the house was only of timber, its interior walls were decorated with painted plaster in the traditional Roman manner. This farm lasted for perhaps a century and then it was abandoned and the site left empty for about a hundred and twenty years. Then yet another farmstead appeared and this time a grand farmhouse, which perhaps ought to be described as a 'villa', was built. It was set in its own garden enclosure which was inside a large farmyard of 1.7 hectares, divided into a series of paddocks or yards, one of which contained farm buildings. The farmhouse was rebuilt in the mid-fourth century and lasted probably for just under a century when it was systematically demolished and the area abandoned again.

Further north, in Northamptonshire, a Roman farmstead has been excavated just outside Northampton itself. The site was near a late Iron Age one, which it perhaps succeeded. The Roman occupation began in the late first century and lasted just over a hundred years. At this time the farm consisted of two circular wooden huts with no sign of any outer yard. Soon after AD 200 the farm was abandoned and the land on which it stood was used by a nearby farmstead which has not been excavated. Then around AD 280 a new farm appeared, this time a circular stone building 6.5 metres in diameter with a limestone-flagged floor associated with a cobbled yard. This lasted until around AD 400, or perhaps a little later, when the site was deserted. Here we have little evidence of real Roman influence, at least as far as the type of building is concerned, but of more importance this site shows the same almost ubiquitous picture of settlement movement or drift.

Not far away from this site, at Lynch Farm, near Peterborough, air photographs have revealed a huge farmstead, consisting of two conjoined yards each about 150 metres by 90 metres, both surrounded by small enclosures or paddocks. Limited excavation of the site indicated that occupation did not start until at least AD 200 and then continued without a break until perhaps AD 350 when again the area was abandoned.

In the north of England, a number of the geometrically laid out farmsteads of the Roman period have been excavated. Most appear to have been inhabited in the second and third centuries and it has been suggested that they represent a planned Roman reorganization of the landscape. The best excavated example is that at Riding Wood, in southern Northumberland. It had a trapezoidal stone-walled enclosure within which were two small stockyards and three stone-walled circular huts. The possibility that planning was an important factor in the Roman countryside has been reinforced by the results of recent excavations carried out by Messrs D. Miles and S. Palmer at Fairford, in Gloucestershire. There, soon after AD 50, a late Iron Age village was apparently removed with all its ditches deliberately back-filled. It was replaced by a neatly laid out hamlet consisting of a main street with three rectangular blocks on either side, divided by side streets and with an open space or green in the centre. Within each block and fronting the main street the excavators found the foundations of houses which had been rebuilt many times. Individual boundary fences within the blocks were shown to have been moved on a number of occasions, but the basic outline remained intact. The hamlet existed until the early fifth century when it was deserted.

This site is important for a variety of reasons, perhaps the most notable one being the fact that it may have been planned. In addition, the well-documented process of the distortion of an original layout by continued occupation is worth stressing for it is a feature which occurs widely in medieval planned settlements.

Shortage of space prevents other examples of Roman rural settlements being given. In any case they would only show what is already clear from those that have been discussed. Settlements of this period show an almost infinite variety of form and size, some were occupied all through Roman times, others only for certain periods. Elsewhere there are sometimes gaps in the occupation sequence. There is much evidence of settlement drift or movement over relatively small areas; the classical Roman influences are sometimes considerable and acquired rapidly, while elsewhere they are minimal and arrive only after many years. These characteristics – the mobility, stability, variety and even planning of rural settlement – are not of course new. They are merely a continuation of trends that had been evident in England during the previous 8000 years. But in the Roman period these features appear on a greater scale and can be seen rather more clearly.

There is one last form of rural settlement that has not yet been discussed, and that is the villa (Fig. 36). It figures largely in all books on Roman Britain and thus tends to overshadow all other types of Roman occupation sites, even the towns, in the popular imagination. But it is difficult to get agreement, even among Roman specialists, as to what a villa was. Those who go to see the splendidly preserved villas, such as those at Brading on the Isle of Wight, Fishbourne in Sussex, Whitcome in Gloucestershire, Lullingstone in Kent (Fig. 37) or North Leigh in Oxfordshire, will have no doubt as to what a villa looked like. These sites have fine stone buildings with long ranges of rooms floored by mosaic pavements and warmed by underfloor central-heating systems, often with associated complex bath suites. They seem to be the Roman equivalent of our great country houses and indicate a style of living far above the average farmstead discussed earlier. However, the villas preserved and open to the public are inevitably only a minute proportion of those which have been discovered. In fact many hundreds of villas are known and when the evidence from all of them is put together a very different picture emerges. As with all other types of rural settlement it is the variety of villas which is most striking. Certainly there are many that can be truly considered as great country mansions but there are also many others that are considerably less luxurious.

This is clear from the villas known in just one small area of England, Gloucestershire, where they are relatively common. The largest is that at Woodchester and this was a true country house, or perhaps even a palace (Fig. 36). The main part consisted of a small square courtyard some 30 metres

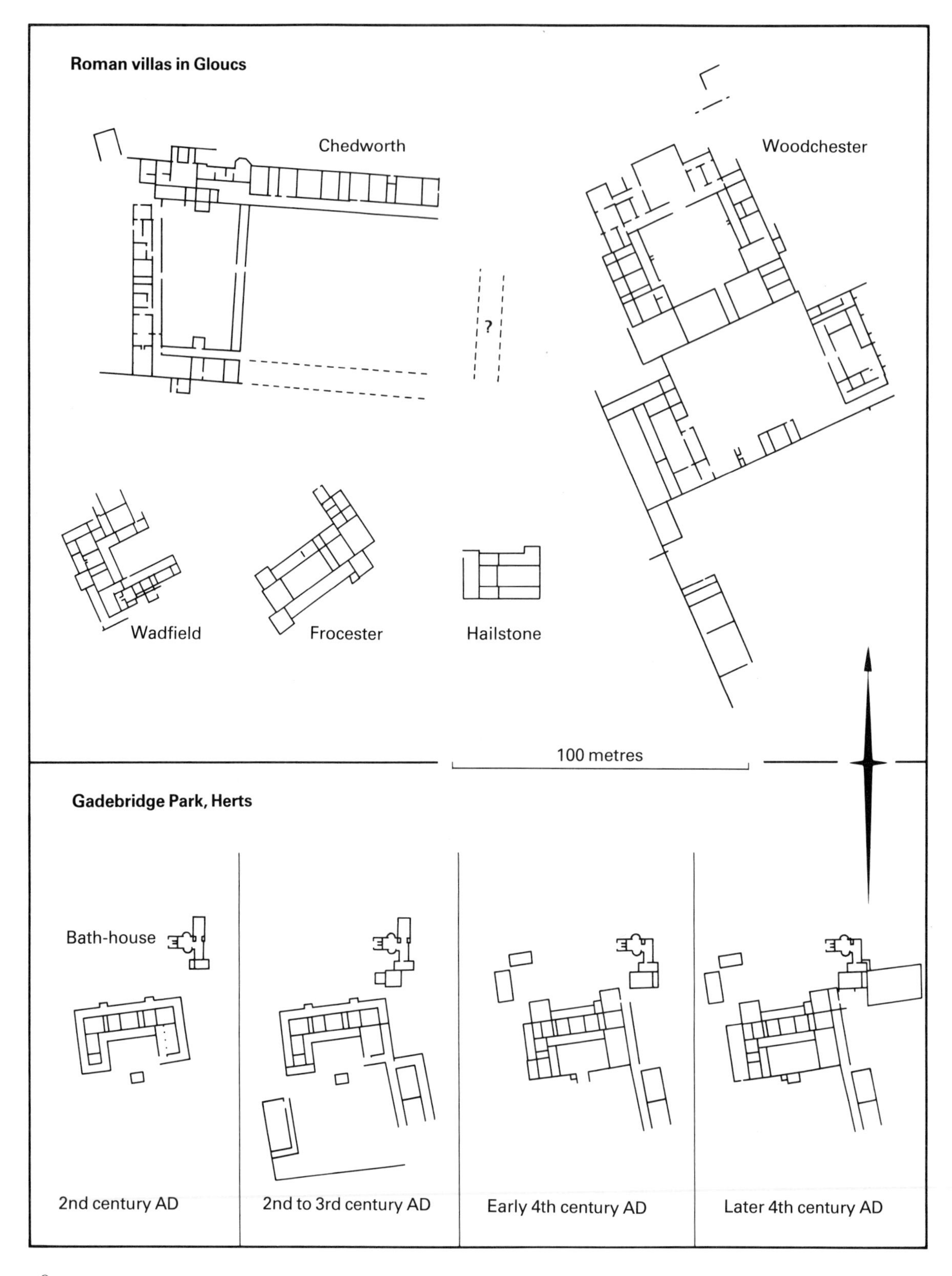
Roman villas in Gloucs
Chedworth
Woodchester
?
Wadfield
Frocester
Hailstone
100 metres
Gadebridge Park, Herts
Bath-house
2nd century AD
2nd to 3rd century AD
Early 4th century AD
Later 4th century AD

across, with the main rooms, sumptuously decorated and floored, arranged around it. Beyond lay a larger outer courtyard with buildings of much lower status around it, perhaps including a brew-house and a granary. Beyond again was another courtyard also with buildings around it. Moreover, large and impressive as this site is, it is likely that less than half of it has been excavated.

A slightly smaller but equally impressive villa is that at Chedworth (Fig. 36). It too had a fine rectangular courtyard with buildings around it, almost all with mosaic pavements in the associated rooms, and a large outer court with buildings probably around all four sides. The villa at Wadfield, near Sudeley (Fig. 36), is clearly of much lower status. Here ranges of rooms extend from the main block to edge a small courtyard. At Frocester (Fig. 36), the villa was also much smaller and was simpler too, consisting of only one range of buildings on one side of a court and garden. Even so, there were several heated rooms, mosaic floors and a plunge bath. The villa at Badgeworth was smaller still, consisting of no more than a long range of rooms with a corridor or verandah on one side, and though it probably had a plunge bath it had no mosaic floors.

OPPOSITE **36 Roman Villas** *The five villa plans, all from one county, show the wide range of size and layout which is covered by the term villa. The history of Gadebridge villa illustrates how many of these structures were massively remodelled throughout their lives.*

BELOW **37 Roman Mosaic, Lullingstone, Kent** *This magnificent pavement is one of a number discovered in the Roman villa here. It indicates the status of the villa as a great country house and as the administrative centre of a large estate.*

All these buildings may probably be defined as villas, but at the lower end of the scale they begin to resemble other stone-built structures which perhaps would not be classified as villas. The building at Hailstone, near Cherrington in Gloucestershire (Fig. 36), is a good example of a border-line case. It was a large rectangular structure 25 metres by 15 metres containing at least seven rooms, but there were no mosaics or heating system. This building does not fit the description of a typical villa, but it does show well the difficulty of defining one. For clearly the term, as archaeologists use it, includes buildings with a very large range of size, complexity, sophistication and, much more importantly, status. The term 'villa' hides all kinds of dwellings which are by no means comparable. Some can only be described as country mansions on a grand scale, others are really rather modest residences. Between them are examples of all ranges of wealth and position.

Just as significant, but less well understood, is the use of buildings associated with villas. They sometimes include servants' quarters, bath houses, stone sheds, barns and stables. When such buildings are connected with a truly huge and palatial villa it may be correct to identify the site as a wealthy man's country house. But most villas have ranges of buildings that are purely agricultural in purpose – cow houses, granaries, cart sheds, etc – which show that the majority of villas, large or small, were not elaborate private residences for the rich, but working farms. The relative grandeur or squalor of the villa itself almost certainly indicates not only the real wealth of the owner, but whether it was the home farm, whether it was sub-let to tenants or whether the farm was run by a bailiff or steward. It could equally well indicate the existence of the small, hard-working and self-made farmer who had raised himself to a reasonable position. That is, the variety of so-called villas probably covered the same range of buildings as can be found today in any rural parish of England where an eighteenth-century mansion is surrounded by a large tenanted farm, the home farm where the estate manager lives, the small tenant farmers' homes and individually owned farmsteads.

Roman villas, whatever their form, are widely scattered across the countryside, but their overall distribution is curious. North of a line across England from Flamborough Head to Morecambe Bay there are almost no villas, nor are there more than a handful in south-west England. They are few and far between in the southern Pennines and in north-west England. Elsewhere they are fairly common, though with curious gaps such as in the area of Salisbury Plain. On the other hand, considerable clusters of villas exist around what were the Roman towns of Ilchester in Somerset, Bath in Avon, Cirencester in Gloucestershire, and to the south-east of London. Other towns, and even major industrial areas, such as that near Peterborough which was perhaps the largest pottery-producing area in Roman Britain, also have an abnormally high proportion of villas around them. Why should there be this distribution? There are a number of possible explanations. First, as a reflection of the relative wealth of the people who lived in them or owned them, they may lie in what were the best agricultural areas. The lack of villas on the light upland soils, as on Salisbury Plain, and the concentration of them in, for example, southern Northamptonshire, where they are almost all on heavy clay soils, is significant in this respect. It is very possible that the same factors which led to the rich lowland areas being exploited as early as the Bronze Age were still at work in Roman times. The magnificent villa discovered by air photography at Lidgate in Suffolk in an area usually said to have been heavily wooded until medieval times is one of many examples that support this theory (Fig. 38).

Clearly though, other features also played a part in the distribution of villas. Their existence around some of the large and more favoured towns, as well as the larger industrial areas, presumably reflects the desire of the rich urban merchants and industrial entrepreneurs to establish a 'place in the country' in exactly the same way as their eighteenth- and nineteenth-century successors, and with the same variety of size, ostentation and decoration in their buildings. In addition it may well be that, around the urban areas, close to where the main impact of Roman civilization was to be seen, and also near good commercial markets for their produce, prosperous farmers could imitate their betters in the arrangement of their farmhouses. Or was it that the large estates, owned by urban dwellers but farmed by bailiffs, were more successfully exploited than elsewhere? The distribution of villas may reflect all these factors.

So far we have discussed villas as if they were a static feature in the landscape, which arrived at the beginning of the Roman period and lasted until the end. But as with every form of settlement then, before and since, villas changed over time in a very complicated way and often arose from very simple and humble beginnings. Very few villas appear early in the Roman period, or indeed arrive as fully-fledged buildings with all the trappings of villa life. The handful that are both early in date and elaborate in form from the beginning are so special that they are the exceptions that prove the rule. Thus the villa at Fishbourne, West Sussex, built on a grand scale, was almost certainly the palace of a very important Roman official, or more likely a member of the old native ruling family of Sussex. Most villas did not begin their lives until the end of the first century or early in the second, that is after some fifty years or so of Roman rule. They were then rebuilt and altered, often on a number of occasions, before they reached their greatest extent, again at different periods.

One typical villa is that at Gadebridge Park, Hemel Hempstead, Hertfordshire (Fig. 36). It was built on an empty site at the end of the first century but then it was only a wooden structure, certainly of no great pretensions, though it had painted plaster on some of its internal walls. Yet at the same time a quite elaborate detached bath-house existed, built of stone. Why there should have been this difference between the standards of the dwelling house and that of the baths is not known, but it is a relatively common feature in early villas and perhaps indicates the desire of the owners to demonstrate their status. Baths were a clear indication of Roman civilized status and thus could have been built to improve the 'image' of their owner. It is certainly not just twentieth-century people who have been concerned with status – the same preoccupation appears all through the history of settlement in England.

At Gadebridge this first wooden villa or farmhouse remained in its original form for nearly a hundred years. It was then rebuilt in stone on a much larger scale, to a plan which again is so standard to many villas that the impression is of an uncritical demand for 'Romanized' structures, in much the same way as the demand for twentieth-century inter-war suburban houses was based on the ideals they reflected. These 'standard' villas consisted of a long range of rooms with projecting wings at each end and a verandah along one or both sides, or sometimes all the way around. The Gadebridge villa in the early second century was typical of this type.

Soon afterwards, however, the probably wooden surrounding farm buildings were rebuilt in stone, on a lavish scale, with barns, stables and servants' or labourers' quarters set around a yard. The baths were also enlarged. Then for another century or so the villa remained unaltered and part of the baths fell into decay. At the beginning of the fourth century massive changes took place. The house itself was enlarged considerably, some of the farm buildings were demolished and others built on the opposite side of the house, set around a new yard. A little later the baths were again altered, this time provided with a huge swimming bath 21 metres by 12 metres. Clearly at this time the villa was much more than an average farmstead. Yet this situation lasted for only fifty years. Probably in AD 353 the whole villa and its outbuildings were systematically demolished and the site levelled except for two structures. Over the villa site cattle pens were erected and the outbuildings were apparently used by labourers engaged in looking after the animals.

What is the explanation for this sequence of change at Gadebridge? The excavator, Mr D. Neal, has given a perfectly acceptable one. He suggests that in its timber and first stone stages it was a small farmhouse which then became the centre of a large estate where a bailiff lived and to which outlying farmers brought their produce, hence the barns and the improvements to the house. The great fourth-century rebuilding with the swimming bath has been interpreted as the result of the structure being a kind of Chilterns weekend holiday hotel. The destruction of AD 353 has been said to have possibly been connected with confiscation of the estate by the Emperor Constantius because of the owner's involvement with the usurper Magnentius.

While all this is possible, indeed likely, this sequence of events will explain only the Gadebridge villa. Others have a quite different development and history. At Latimer in Buckinghamshire, only a few kilometres away from Gadebridge, the villa there was built in the mid second century when an earlier first-century timber farm was demolished. The stone villa began with the usual standard plan and was later expanded and improved, but in the third century it fell into disrepair and was abandoned for a short while. Then, just after AD 300, it was reoccupied, given a fine courtyard and substantial wings. It again declined in the middle of the fourth century but remained in use until the end of that century. The site continued to be occupied for long after this but the buildings were much poorer.

To further emphasize the variety of villa types and the contrasts in their sequences of development,

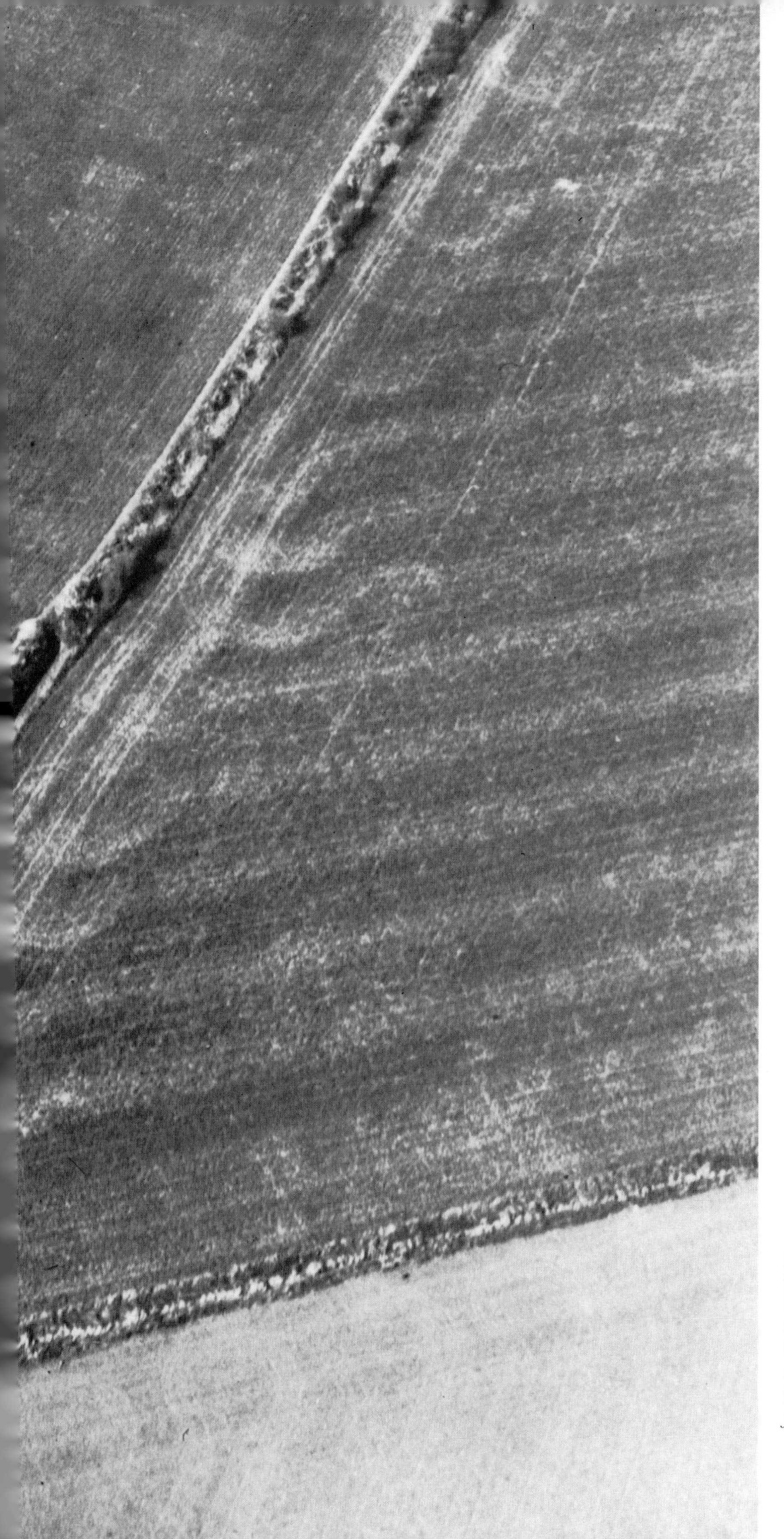

38 Roman Villa, Lidgate, Suffolk *In an area alleged to have been forested until medieval times, air photography has revealed the outlines of a great Roman villa. It was undoubtedly the centre of a prosperous farming estate.*

there is no better example than the villa at Iwerne Minster, in Dorset. It was a typical Iron Age farmstead which continued largely unaltered until the third century AD. Then a long stone building was erected with three small living rooms at one end and the rest used as a cattle shed. Around AD 300 a simple villa of five rooms with a verandah on one side was constructed, though the largest of the rooms was still used as a cattle shed. In spite of the apparently primitive nature of the occupation, the living rooms were lined with painted plaster. In this form the farm lasted until about AD 360, when it was abandoned.

There is one final aspect of Roman rural settlement which must be discussed; the estates or economic units to which the settlements belonged. We noted earlier that even prehistoric settlements were associated with territories, first for hunting and later for agriculture, with clearly defined boundaries. The same was certainly true of Roman times – the villas, farmsteads and hamlets must have been organized into tenurial and/or agricultural units and there is also documentary evidence that estates were a feature of the whole of the Roman Empire. The problem, in England at least, is to discover and define them. Archaeological evidence of estate boundaries is virtually impossible to discover and thus the only way that archaeologists can define them is by calculating possible areas of farmland or by measuring the capacities of granaries. From such work it has been estimated that, for example, the villa at Ditchley in Oxfordshire must have had at least 400 hectares of arable land and that single farmsteads in Hampshire had at least 200 hectares of land under cultivation. These figures, however, mean little for not only is the amount of meadow, pasture, woodland and waste unknown, but the boundaries or exact areas of the estates are impossible to identify. However, it has also been shown that it is possible to trace Roman estates by using archaeological and historical evidence from later periods and then working backwards in time.

The most important example of this kind of work is that that was carried out in Wiltshire by Mr D. Bonney. It is clear that most of the early Anglo-Saxon burials there, dating from the fifth and sixth centuries AD, all lie on or very close to medieval parish or estate boundaries. This suggests that the boundaries were known and were of some significance as early as the fifth century and thus by implication must have existed before then, that is in the late Roman period. Other work has made use of later Saxon charters of the eighth century and afterwards, for example in Dorset, where it is known that the Saxon settlers had arrived in significant numbers less than two centuries before the charters were written. These charters give the detailed bounds of areas of land which were to become either parishes or the basic agricultural sub-units of parishes in the early medieval period. Again the implication is that these areas of land existed at least in late Roman times. This means that, in effect, most of the parishes of medieval England and their sub-divisions were in use in the Roman period. If this is so then what were these land units? In the medieval period they were not, as is popularly imagined, just basically ecclesiastical divisions. The medieval Church tended to use old land units for its administrative, financial and parochial purposes. But even in medieval times each identifiable parish or sub-division of a parish (a township) was a basic agricultural unit. Certainly over much of the Midlands, southern England and east and north-east England, the parish or township was an area of land within which there was a single field system or unit of agriculture together with its associated meadow, pasture, woodland, wastes, fen or marsh, used solely by the inhabitants of one or more settlements situated within that territory. It may well be that the same situation existed in Roman times.

The multitude of rural settlements discussed so far were thus not set in an unorganized limbo of fields, but were each associated with a clearly defined estate or land unit, which perhaps approximated very closely to the later parish or township arrangement. If we accept this hypothesis then we see a well organized landscape in Roman times and, even more significant, the movement or 'drift' of settlement and the changes of form, all visible in the archaeological record, must have taken place within these 'estates'. There is one other important conclusion that follows from this hypothesis. As we have already seen, Roman rural settlements evolved directly from Iron Age settlements, and exhibited the same features in development. Therefore it is equally possible that some of the estates or land units which existed in Roman times were actually already in being in the late prehistoric period. Indeed there is a little archaeological evidence that certain boundaries used by medieval parochial organizations already existed in pre-Roman times, perhaps as early as the later Bronze Age. Thus it may be that the medieval parishes evolved directly from the territorial divisions that emerged as a result of population pressures and agricultural expansion in the late Bronze Age and that therefore they were already old by the Roman period.

It is not suggested that every medieval parish or township and their sub-divisions are prehistoric or even Roman in every respect. There were clearly changes over time and amalgamation and division have certainly taken place. The history of the English landscape is one of mobility and change and to assume that all these estates remained unaltered through millennia would be totally mistaken. But these basic agricultural estates, even in medieval times, were more stable than the settlements inside them. For, as we shall see, these settlements moved and were abandoned in the same way as prehistoric and Roman ones had been. Whatever happened to the settlements, the land units would *tend* to be more stable for they were the very basis of life. A settlement could move to a better site, acquire new land, be divided between two or three or a multitude of lords, but as long as people lived in the area it was in their vital interests to keep the land together as a single agricultural unit. To lose part of it could mean starvation.

It may well be that these units of land were, to some degree at least, the most stable part of the medieval, Roman and even the late prehistoric landscape. With the country divided up into these basic units of agriculture, the settlement pattern could change in a way that has been detailed in both this and the previous chapter, but only *within* the reasonably fixed boundaries of the estates. Thus the mobility of settlement which has been stressed so far in this book, and will continue to be emphasized, was probably only operative within the defined limits of the basic units of land which it was in everybody's interests to keep intact.

It must be stressed that the units of land discussed so far were the agricultural basis of society, perhaps from late prehistoric times until well into the post-medieval period. They must not, however, be mixed up with tenurial estates or units of land held together by ownership. It has already been suggested that the agricultural units could have been actually *owned* by more than one person. This is certainly true in the medieval period where 'multi-manorial' parishes are the rule rather than the exception. But it is also true that major landlords in medieval times owned many agricultural units, forming tenurial estates of very variable sizes. These were acquired, enlarged, divided and lost as a result of complex inheritance laws, social changes, invasions, civil wars, political divisions, grants to the church and much else. Thus the tenurial units were more flexible and liable to change than the agricultural units. There is no reason to doubt that the same was true in Roman or even earlier times. Thus a late Iron Age farm which developed into a great villa by the fourth century does not only show the physical development of the settlement site. It also probably reflects the gradual acquisition by one family, as a result of successful management, suitable marriages, political acumen, good economic conditions and mere luck, of other agricultural units which were welded into a tenurial whole. One Iron Age farmstead might become the administrative centre of this tenurial estate and thus end up as a palatial villa. Another Iron Age farmstead may have remained as an unsophisticated stone hut, or developed into a standard small villa, hamlet or large village, depending on whether the owner or administrator leased out the land, kept it in hand, had a semi- or actual slave-labour force or indeed, was a good, bad or indifferent landlord.

Because the tenurial units were inherently less stable than the agricultural units, it is even more difficult to establish their boundaries. Clearly the chances of such an administrative unit remaining intact into historic times, and yet still being recognizable for what it was, are extremely limited. Yet in a few places such tenurial units have been recognized. They do seem to have remained intact on occasions, simply because they eventually came into the hands of perpetual institutions such as the Crown or the Church, which had both the means and the incentive to see that the units did not fragment. For example, the land that in 1086 was held by the Bishop of Chester, a single block around Lichfield in Staffordshire and comprising some sixteen agricultural land units, was probably the remains of the land associated with the small Roman settlement of Letocetum, just south of Lichfield.

The existence of these agricultural and tenurial estates or land units in Roman and even pre-Roman times has not been generally accepted. The pure archaeologists sometimes doubt their existence for they cannot find them by archaeological means. The historians are unhappy because these estates lie beyond the limits of historical evidence. Yet everyone agrees that such estates must have existed; it is only their actual delimitations, linked through time to medieval estates, that some people find hard to accept. But these links seem far more logical than the alternative view, which is to see a total reorganization of the post-Roman landscape to suit the incoming Saxon settlers. And as we shall see in the next chapter, new evidence about these settlers and about the places they inhabited makes the idea of continuity of agricultural estates far more plausible than any kind of reorganization.

This, then, is the evidence for rural settlement in England in Roman times. It presents us with a very different picture of the country than that usually given in most popular books. Throughout most of the period England appears as a densely populated country with settlements of many sizes, forms and functions situated everywhere.

This conclusion leads to the most basic question of all with regard to settlement and one which has been avoided up to now. What was the population in Roman times, and indeed in prehistoric times, if the density of settlement was so high? There have been various estimates of the population of Roman Britain but most were worked out before it was realized just how many settlements there were in Roman times. Sir Mortimer Wheeler, in 1930, suggested that the maximum population of Roman Britain was around 1.5 million. Professor Frere, in 1967, revised it upwards to 2 million. It is now clear that such figures are far too low. It is probable that a total population of 4 million is by no means too high to accept, and a figure of 5 million is perhaps much nearer the truth. These figures must then be compared with the estimated population of England given in Domesday Book in 1086, usually said to be between 1 and 2 million. The implications of this huge Roman population are immense, particularly for our interpretation and understanding of settlement in Saxon times, the beginning of the medieval period.

Part II Medieval and Later Settlement

The end of the Roman period is usually seen as a major break in the history of England. In prehistoric and Roman times the only 'facts' are those lifted from the ground by archaeologists – the people of the time are vague, nameless and misty figures whose activities can only be seen in the results of mass movements or trends. From Saxon times onwards everything becomes much clearer. The 'truth' comes from written sources, people have names, characters and motives. Unravelling the history of settlement also seems to become much easier as the evidence from this period onwards lies all around us. Prehistoric and Roman settlements are either quite invisible or only recognizable as indeterminate bumps on the ground, or as marks seen from the air. Medieval and later settlement is still much in evidence, in some cases providing us with our homes. It would seem that, while prehistory is irrelevant to the present, medieval and later activities are the foundations on which our own landscape is based. Such views are common, but wrong. As we shall see, the reality is rather more complicated.

Certainly written evidence in all forms, from place-names through medieval taxation lists to modern newspapers, provides an increasing wealth of information through time. Yet documents themselves rarely tell us what we want to know of any aspect of history and this is especially true of the history of settlement. Documents, like the scraps of pottery from an archaeological excavation, have to be examined with care, compared and checked against others and in the end can support a multitude of interpretations. Documents are no better than archaeological material for understanding settlement history, they merely provide a different form of evidence which is equally difficult to understand.

The written record, useful though it is, is often suspect. For example, place-names can be studied and their meaning deduced. It is likely that place-name scholars are correct when they tell us that the name Farmborough, in Somerset, means the fern-clad hill, based on the fact that it is recorded in a document of 901 as Fearnberngas. But what relation this name has to the existing place called Farmborough is pure supposition. The village may have been named after a nearby hill when it was set up, it may have had an earlier and quite different name or even acquired the later name long after 901 when Fearnberngas merely referred to the surrounding land.

Likewise, how should we interpret the fact that the medieval tax collectors, when visiting the village of Edgcote in Northamptonshire in 1301, noted in their records that fifty-seven people had paid their dues. Does this mean that all the tax payers were heads of households, each with a wife and three children, thus giving a total population of around 250, or was there a high proportion of children, numerous widows and childless couples? Or indeed was everyone in the village on the day that the tax collectors called? Did some people deliberately disappear to avoid paying tax? It is known that in some places up to 20 per cent of the tax payers avoided tax in this way. All these possibilities are unknown imponderables that the historian has to take into consideration when interpreting the documentary evidence.

Nor are contemporary observers impartial and honest in their views. In the fifteenth and early sixteenth centuries there was an outcry against rapacious landlords who were clearing villages for sheep. Yet detailed studies have shown that, though this certainly occurred, in some instances tenant farmers were as much to blame as the landlords. Even objective observers do not always understand the real cause of the events they see. In the mid fourteenth century vast areas of land, reclaimed centuries before from the fens, were abandoned, together with numerous farmsteads and hamlets, as a result, it was claimed, of floods. Yet there had been dreadful disasters and floods before which did not lead to desertion. The real reason was almost certainly a general economic decline which meant it was no longer worth the effort involved in protecting and working what was marginal land.

Even more important from the point of view of settlement history is that documents do not, except on very rare occasions, record the beginning of places. Either such places came into existence before the documents that might have recorded the fact were found to be necessary or, and much more often, there was no need to write such details down. The actual existence or location of settlements had no relevance to the national and local administrative requirements of the times. From the sixteenth century onwards maps appear and are, of course, immensely valuable in charting the ebb and flow of settlement history. But even maps are not, until the appearance of the Ordnance Survey in the early nineteenth century, objective statements of the truth. They were produced for a wide variety of reasons including estate management, propaganda, prestige and even decoration. Thus they too have to be treated with circumspection. Even when maps can be shown to portray accurately the facts of settlement history we still have to understand how and why the features shown cartographically came into being. Very often this is not easy, even when dealing with the very recent past.

Over the last three decades archaeology has become increasingly important for the understanding of medieval and later settlement. Techniques of excavation, air photography and field examination, all largely developed for prehistoric and Roman sites, have been used to elucidate the settlement history of more recent centuries. Though in many respects archaeological methods have revolutionized our ideas on settlement, the basic limitations of archaeology remain and have to be appreciated. In favoured situations archaeology can often tell us when and how, but rarely why. By combining archaeological and historical methods, by no means an easy task, it is possible to some extent to make good the deficiencies of the individual disciplines. History is good at showing us how settlements worked, who lived in them, and why and when they flourished or declined. Archaeology is good at indicating beginnings and endings as well as physical movements and change. Together they give us a much clearer insight into the history of settlement than each could do alone.

In the end, however, from whatever source we receive our information, it is necessary to exercise judgement and care. A major theme of this book is that the history of settlement in England is more a reflection of man than of his environment. Yet man is, and always has been, an irrational animal and this is nowhere better seen than in the way he has treated the places in which he has lived.

-7-
The Coming of the Saxons

The evolution of settlement in Saxon times is probably the most difficult to explain in the history of settlement in England. As with prehistoric and Roman times, modern research has totally changed long-accepted ideas. But whereas the changes in the understanding of, for example, prehistoric settlements have to be accepted only by archaeologists, the changes in our view of Saxon settlement have to be accepted by a much wider and more sceptical audience. To most people prehistoric times are remote and of little interest. But almost everyone knows about the Saxon invaders and how these invaders were the people who established the English landscape as we know it.

The generally accepted story of Saxon settlement in England may be crudely, and perhaps unfairly, summarized as follows. Towards the end of the Roman period, as the Roman Empire weakened and fell apart, Saxon raiders attacked this country in large numbers. In the early fifth century the Roman army and administration were withdrawn and Saxon bands swept over the country burning, pillaging and destroying all in their path. A few remaining Romano-British people were massacred or driven west into Wales leaving an empty but potentially rich countryside for the Saxons. These early Saxons quickly found the best sites to live on. They picked out suitable places on dry gravel, at spring heads, or in sheltered valleys, and laid out the first English villages. Some villages, because of the need to protect livestock from enemies, both human and animal, took the form of the open space or green with the houses arranged around it. More often these new villages were laid out along an existing track or at the meeting point of several tracks. Elsewhere a convenient woodland clearing was chosen or made and the subsequent tracks meeting on that clearing produced a radiating pattern of streets for the new village.

Thus the basic form of our earliest villages appeared. At the same time their inhabitants gave them names that modern experts can identify as 'early'. Around each of these primary villages fields were laid out. These fields were of the open or common field type in which each villager had a number of elongated strips scattered between broad unhedged fields which were usually cropped on a two- or three-field rotation system. The fields were gradually extended by the co-operative work of the Saxon[1] settlers who cut down the primeval forest that initially surrounded these villages. Then, as the centuries rolled by, the population rose and two things happened. The first or primary villages grew bigger and the fields were extended further into the woodland. At the same time some people moved out of the villages and established daughter or secondary villages or hamlets in the wastes and forests. This second generation of villages also had greens,

[1] The term Saxon here is not used in any real ethnic sense. Strictly it denotes people who thought of themselves as the descendants of arrivals in this country in the early fifth century though, as will become clear, this was not necessarily the truth.

radiating street plans or long simple main streets as their predecessors had but, because they were established later in time, they were given names which can again be recognized today as secondary or late place-names. These new villages also developed their own field systems. The next stage is usually said to have been the arrival of Christianity and the creation of parish churches. Most villages acquired churches over the centuries and as these churches needed a well-defined unit of land, both for their financial support from tithes and to establish which people attended which church, parishes emerged with clear boundaries, usually with one village and one church within each.

As time went by further population growth led to the continuous expansion of settlement with the establishment of tertiary villages, hamlets and farmsteads in the remaining waste. So, by 1066, when William the Conqueror arrived in England, the English rural landscape was fully formed much as we see it today.

This is a splendid interpretation of Saxon England, not the least for the comfortable picture it presents of the stability and antiquity of our landscape. Particularly today, at a time of constant and often violent change in so many aspects of our lives, we can stand in the typical English village and apparently see it much as the first Saxon settlers made it in the fifth and sixth centuries. Such a view is comforting and comfortable. The sad thing is that this interpretation is quite wrong and the actual history of settlement in England in Saxon times was utterly different. Why it was so different and how Saxon settlement actually developed is a complicated story that has emerged in the last few years as a result of the work of scholars in many different disciplines.

Perhaps the most important factor relating to the history of Saxon settlement is what has already been discussed at length in the previous chapters. The old view of Saxon times depended on the fact that the first Saxon settlers came into a relatively empty landscape where only a few Romano-British people remained and thus the Saxons were able to produce an entirely new landscape of villages and fields with little or no relevance to the past. They were able to pick out the 'best' sites for their new villages and created their fields out of virgin territory.

But as we have seen this was not so. The Saxons came not to a new and relatively untouched country but to a very old one, a country where most of the 'best' places had already been occupied not once but many times, by a variety of people living in a great variety of settlements. The primeval forests had been removed, allowed to regenerate and removed on a number of occasions. More particularly, as was stressed at the end of the last chapter, by the fourth century England had a very large population, with tens of thousands of settlements ranging from single farmsteads to hamlets and villages and even to many towns. Every available area of suitable land was under cultivation. Animals were herded on the moorlands and marshes and most of the forest was cleared and its former areas cultivated or grazed. And all this activity took place within clearly marked territories or estates, often grouped together under the control of large landowners.

When the Roman Empire began to collapse, all that happened was that the protection of the Imperial army was removed and the sophisticated central government system was taken away. But the great mass of the established population stayed on, as they had to, in their homes and on their land to face up to what were to be increasingly difficult times socially and economically.

It was to this country, with this landscape, that the first Saxons came. It was therefore a land where the Saxons could only effect changes by adapting what existed, not where it was possible for new man-made landscapes to be neatly laid out. Once this is clear, it becomes evident that Saxon settlement history is by no means straightforward.

The picture is made even more complex when we look at the actual process of Saxon settlement. The first Saxons arrived not as settlers but as raiders, and in the fourth century when the Empire was still in being, not in the fifth when it was in ruins. Indeed one of the reasons for the final withdrawal of the Roman army was that it could no longer withstand the constant attacks by the Saxon raiders. Towards the end of the fourth century, the shortage of trained troops forced the inhabitants of England to hire mercenaries to protect themselves. But in the confused situation the only available mercenaries were Saxons themselves. Even more confusing, especially to those brought up on the nice, neat, simple divisions of old-fashioned history, some of the Saxon mercenaries and certainly many of the raiders themselves were time-expired Roman soldiers. The Roman Imperial army had its recruiting problems in the fourth and early fifth centuries and one solution was to bring in 'barbarians' from beyond the Empire and train them to protect the weakened frontiers. On completion of their service some of these returned to their homeland and led their followers in raids on the Empire. Others took service under the nominal control of Roman local authorities or major landowners as mercenaries to protect towns, estates or areas of local government from the depredations of their compatriots.

In this latter situation, fraternization of the most basic kind inevitably followed. This can be well seen at Cambridge where, in the later fourth century, the government of the Roman town there clearly employed Saxon mercenaries to protect them from raiders arriving via the fenland rivers. The cemeteries of these mercenaries and their families have been found just outside the Roman town and the grave goods associated with the burials indicate clearly that intermarriage between 'Romans' and 'Saxons' had already occurred before 400.

Other evidence shows the same confusing picture. The founder of the Saxon Kingdom of Wessex, whose exploits in defeating the 'Romans' were sung and told over many a Saxon hearth on winter nights for centuries before they were finally written down in the Anglo-Saxon Chronicle, was a man whose name, Cerdic, was British and not Saxon. Further, as the formal Roman government fell to pieces and economic decline and collapse accelerated, the Roman people themselves reverted to an Iron Age type of society with the development of petty kingdoms engaged in intermittent warfare with each other.

One further point, which is very relevant to the situation, concerns the actual number of Saxons who arrived in England. Professor Charles Thomas has recently estimated that during the fifth century no more than 10,000 Saxon settlers came to this country. While this may seem to be a considerable number, when this figure is compared with the estimate of a late Roman population of perhaps five million, it pales into insignificance. Even if we assume that there was a considerable fall in the population of England in the fifth century, the situation still remains much the same. The Saxon invasions and settlement appear more as the political take-over of a disintegrating society rather than as a mass replacement of population. And if, as Professor Thomas has also suggested, the political and religious institutions of Roman Britain survived in some places until around 600, we can eliminate the Saxons as a force for changing settlement type and patterns altogether. What we may have is merely a hiccup in the history of settlement caused by economic difficulties, political confusion and population decline, something that had happened before in prehistoric times and was to occur again much later.

Thus, instead of a nice clear picture of a mass of Saxon invaders arriving and wiping out or driving away the remnants of the Roman population, we have a complex scene of conflicting loyalties, mixed races, and the break up of any clearly defined political or military unity. This situation was to last for perhaps two hundred years. In addition, there is some evidence of disease, described as 'plagues' in contemporary annals. Though these are little understood, they may well have been worse in their overall effects than the much better documented Black Death of the mid fourteenth century. It is out of this confusion that the settlement historian has to determine what happened to the places where people actually lived at this time.

Again the established version of the story of Saxon settlement is that most, if not all, Roman rural sites were abandoned in the late fourth century or early fifth century as the Saxons moved into their new villages. That a very large proportion of these sites was abandoned cannot be denied. However, two points are worth noting. Firstly, by the very nature of the process of settlement movement which has been documented in the previous chapters, a certain number of settlements would have been abandoned in these times even if the Saxons had never arrived. Secondly, in the past, archaeologists examining late Roman sites assumed abandonment when they found that there was no evidence of coins or pottery or well-built structures dating from beyond the late fourth century. More careful modern excavations, using new techniques of recovery, have shown that in many cases the apparent abandonment did not take place but a different and very much poorer occupation continued. Given the chronic political, economic and social situation of the period, this is only to be expected. A splendid example of this sequence was discovered by Professor K. Branigan at the Roman villa at Latimer, Buckinghamshire. As we have already seen, the villa was rebuilt on a lavish scale in the early fourth century, as were many similar places. By the mid fourth century the building was in disrepair and decay and at the end of the fourth century the villa buildings were finally abandoned. Yet occupation did not cease. Timber buildings were erected almost immediately just outside the ruined villa and for another century people continued to live there, though the timber buildings were abandoned and replaced in entirely new positions no less than three times before the site was finally deserted.

Even more significant is the villa at Rivenhall in Essex, examined by Dr and Mrs W. Rodwell. There, in the fourth century, a large aisled building was added to the existing structure and, though the rest of the villa was abandoned in the later fourth century, the addition continued to be used until well into the fifth century. Its aisled construction would perhaps have been acceptable for communal living and may well have formed an ideal building for the traditional Saxon 'hall'. When another villa, at Totternhoe, Bedfordshire, was abandoned in the late Roman period, two cottages were erected nearby made from material from the villa's gatehouse. These cottages remained occupied until perhaps the mid fifth century.

Less pretentious Roman farmsteads often have evidence of continued occupation long after the end of the Roman period. One example is that at Barton Court, near Abingdon, Oxfordshire (Fig. 21). We have already noted the long sequence of occupation there from late Iron Age to late Roman times. The large late Roman farmhouse was certainly occupied until the end of the fourth century and probably well into the fifth. Then it was systematically demolished and replaced by a group of small huts in a slightly different position, These lasted until the sixth century. A similar late-Roman farmstead excavated at Orton Longueville, Cambridgeshire, was shown to have had a farmstead of fifth- and sixth-century date built alongside it, whose inhabitants used at least one of the earlier Roman paddocks.

However, not all Roman sites with early 'Saxon' occupation on them were settled continuously. Even with careful excavation, many still show the inevitable gap in the sequence. At Willington, on the River Trent in Derbyshire, a Roman farmstead, abandoned in the fourth century, was not reoccupied until the sixth century.

The nature of the post-Roman houses, as revealed by excavation, is of two forms. On some sites the remains of well-built and obviously substantial timber buildings have been discovered which may be interpreted as 'halls' or communal dwelling houses for extended families. These may be 10 metres by 5 metres or even longer. However, the traces of such halls are not easy to find and indeed have often been totally destroyed by later activities so that nothing of them remains. Far more common in excavations of this period are what have been called sunken floored huts. These are basically rectangular or oval pits which were clearly surrounded by timber walls and covered by roofs. Much ink has been spilt by archaeologists as to whether there were suspended timber floors over the pits, or even whether they were strictly dwellings at all. On the best preserved sites these sunken huts are often associated with timber 'halls' and the former have been interpreted as store sheds and working places. However, in terms of general early Saxon or post-Roman settlement patterns, these arguments need not concern us. The sunken huts are an indication of settlement of some kind in this period and, assuming that the slight traces of the associated 'halls' have gone for good, we can use the distribution of these huts to reconstruct the pattern, location and form of Saxon settlement. For while even a few years ago only a handful of these sunken huts had been discovered, now we have evidence of many hundreds. What they tell us about early Saxon settlement is of great interest as they show clearly that this settlement was very different from the old established ideas.

First, the overall distribution of these huts is very widespread. They have been found in large numbers in southern and eastern England, especially in Essex, Bedfordshire, Kent, Oxfordshire, Dorset, Cambridgeshire and Norfolk, but they have also been found in the midland counties, such as Staffordshire and Leicestershire, as well as in the north of England in Yorkshire. They occur on a wide variety of soils and in very varied situations: on limestones, sands, gravels and clays; in river valleys, on heathland, on chalk downland and in clay vales. They have been discovered as individual huts, scattered across the river terraces of the River Thames near Oxford, or along the chalk escarpment near Dunstable in Bedfordshire, in small groups just outside Aylesbury in Buckinghamshire, as a single hut in the centre of later villages as at Grantchester in Cambridgeshire, or within major Iron Age and Roman settlement complexes as at Keston in Kent.

39 Prehistoric, Roman and Later Settlement Movement *These three simple parish maps encapsulate much of the settlement history of England. In Iron Age, Roman and Saxon times, settlement was dispersed, constantly changing and subject to regular abandonment. In the medieval period nucleated settlements were established but they too have disappeared in several cases.*

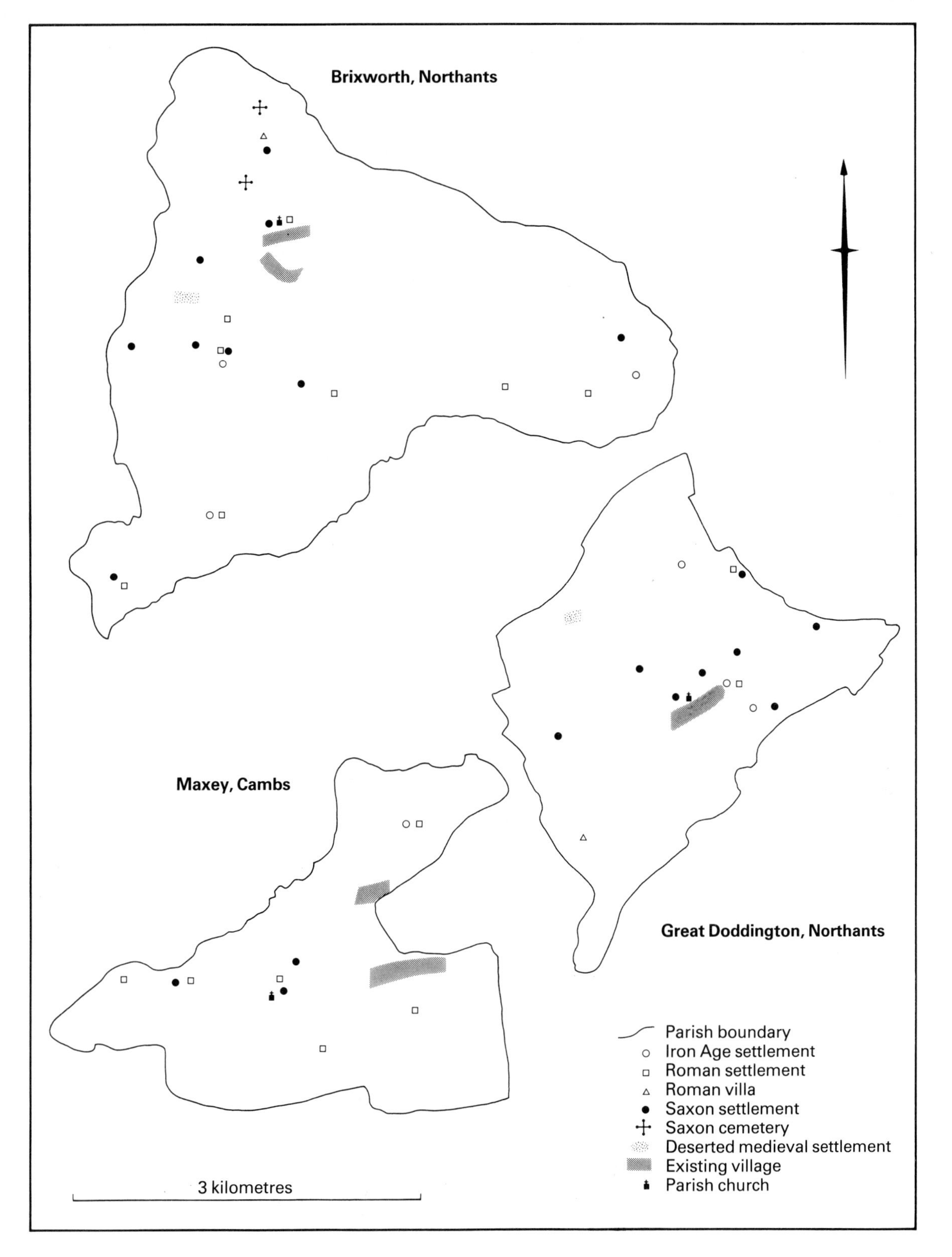
Brixworth, Northants
Great Doddington, Northants
Maxey, Cambs
Parish boundary
Iron Age settlement
Roman settlement
Roman villa
Saxon settlement
Saxon cemetery
Deserted medieval settlement
Existing village
Parish church
3 kilometres

40 Maxey, Cambridgeshire *The medieval parish church is now quite isolated from its village. Yet from the air it can be seen to be surrounded by settlement remains of earlier periods. While many of the ditched enclosures are probably of prehistoric or Roman date, the small dark 'blobs' are actually early Saxon huts. These show that Saxon Maxey was not only short-lived but had an arrangement unlike any later village.*

More important, whatever the exact purpose of these huts may have been, they are far from the traditional idea of a 'Saxon' village and must represent the remains of isolated farmsteads and small hamlets with no clear form or shape which can be related to anything that follows them. While the close dating of these huts is not easy, the evidence suggests that many were of the fifth or sixth century and that most were short-lived, few being occupied for more than a century at the most before being abandoned and their inhabitants moving on elsewhere.

The evidence from excavation, important though it is, has a limited value in assessing the real pattern of settlement in the first two or three centuries after the end of Roman times. By its nature, excavation tends to be limited and is often the result of chance discovery. More important from our point of view are the results of detailed field examination of specific areas which have produced a picture of the total pattern of settlement at this period. This work involves the most careful and systematic walking of large areas of ground and the recording of every piece of pottery of whatever date. This type of work has been going on for a number of years in Northamptonshire and two specific parishes may be taken as an example of the kind of results that are obtained.

At Great Doddington, a little to the east of Northampton, the evidence for eight small 'Saxon' settlements has been noted (Fig. 39). These are scattered all over the parish with no obvious preference for 'good' sites and only two are near the existing village. Another site lies on top of a very large Roman occupation area and appears to be its direct successor.

Even more spectacular are the results from the work at Brixworth, north of Northampton. There, no less than nine small settlements of the fifth and sixth centuries have been found, all but one some distance from the present village. Of these, one was certainly a building erected inside the walls of a ruined Roman villa and another was associated with a late Roman settlement area (Fig. 39).

Impressive as these results are, it has to be realized that even they almost certainly do not give us the complete picture. For at these and at other places only a small proportion of the land of the parish is available for close examination. Obviously much is covered by woods, roads, permanent grassland and built-up areas which prevent any finds being made, and at Brixworth, for example, one-fifth of the parish has been quarried away for ironstone which has totally destroyed all the evidence. In fact, it is possible to calculate that, on the average, no more than thirty per cent of any parish in Northamptonshire can be examined in this way. The implication is that seventy per cent of the possible archaeological evidence is lost or irrecoverable. It is important to realize this when the settlement pattern of any period is being studied, but in the case of the early Saxon period it means that, at Brixworth for example, there may have been as many as thirty or forty small 'Saxon' settlements scattered over the parish. Again this is a far cry from the older ideas of a single 'Saxon' village.

Similar detailed work, on an even larger scale, has been carried out in the Soke of Peterborough, Cambridgeshire, in the last few years. There sixteen 'Saxon' settlements, one covering as much as 13 hectares, have been found in eight parishes. One of these parishes is Maxey, where three settlements, all quite remote from the later medieval village (the existing village), have been found (Fig. 39). In view of the problems connected with establishing the origins of medieval villages to be discussed later it is of more than passing interest that one of these Saxon settlements lies adjacent to the now isolated parish church (Fig. 40).

Not all parts of England have produced such a density of early 'Saxon' occupation. This is partly the result of a lack of detailed work in other areas. But it is also probably because there was a considerable fall in the total population of England in the fifth and sixth centuries, compared with the very high levels in late Roman times which the dense pattern of settlement then suggests.

Other areas which have been subjected to the same intensive examination as Brixworth and Great Doddington have not produced the same results. Again in Northamptonshire, the parish of Marston St Lawrence, near Brackley, has been examined in great detail for over twenty years. There, though vast quantities of prehistoric and Roman material have come to light, including eleven Roman settlements, not a single early 'Saxon' settlement has been found. The existence of a large late sixth-century cemetery and a perhaps contemporary settlement indicates later occupation, but at the moment there appears to be an almost complete gap of some two centuries duration in the settlement of this parish.

Even more striking is the evidence from West Yorkshire. In spite of very careful examination of large areas of land no Saxon occupation has been found. This may be because the remains of settlements of this period are particularly difficult to identify. Mr T. Williamson, working in north Essex, has been able to locate, very easily, a large number of Roman sites, all situated on heavy clayland. But it was only after the most careful examination of some of these, literally on his knees, that fragments of the very friable Saxon pottery came to light, indicating that occupation had continued into the fifth, sixth and seventh centuries.

It may seem that the inference to be drawn from all this evidence is that early 'Saxon villages' as such did not exist. However, if we return to the results of excavation we find that this is not true as over the last fifteen years or so a number of 'villages' have been discovered and excavated.

But the results of these excavations do not square with the traditional ideas of a Saxon village. First of all, some of these villages are very small. Indeed the term village is perhaps misleading as by later medieval standards most might more strictly be called hamlets. Moreover, the majority have no definable plan as is characteristic of later villages. There is rarely any clear street system, and certainly no trace of neat greens, back lanes, or continuous building lines. All that usually exists is a cluster of ill-defined houses. The closest analogy in the modern landscape to a plan of these settlements may be the dispersed hamlets of south-west England and the northern hills. Indeed it may be that the remains of 'Saxon villages' can still be seen in these places.

Another important feature of these settlements is that most of them lie on land which can hardly be described as good, and on specific sites may be termed 'poor'. That is, they are marginal settlements and certainly not on the 'good' sites which the Saxons were usually said to have chosen with so much care. It is true, of course, that the 'good' sites are occupied by existing villages, whose origins are more difficult to ascertain, but the existence of these marginal settlements in Saxon times is a new factor which must be taken into account. A further feature of those settlements which have been excavated is that, like their prehistoric and Roman predecessors, they were relatively short-lived; none appears to have been occupied for more than a century or so.

Finally, and perhaps most disconcerting of all to those people who like their history precise and easy to understand, none of these villages is associated with 'early' Saxon place-names, which thus calls into question the whole basis of place-name evidence in explaining the origins and growth of Saxon settlement.

There are several specific examples which illustrate the truth of these generalizations. The existing village of Chalton in Hampshire is a typical chalkland one, tucked away in a valley between the high downlands (Fig. 41). There is some evidence of fifth-century occupation here as well as at some of the late Roman sites in the area. However, the excavated village lay away from the existing settlement on top of a wind-swept hillside in, to our eyes, a very uncomfortable situation. The excavation probably recovered the total plan of the settlement and nearly fifty buildings were found, only four of which were sunken-floored huts. The rest included large rectangular timber structures, 9 metres by 5 metres or more in area, which must have been dwelling houses or 'halls'. There were also a number of smaller huts in the 7 metre by 4 metre range as well as a few very small buildings.

The overall plan of these buildings showed no coherent arrangement. Most were aligned north to south or east to west, but no streets were discovered nor any obvious central space or green. The dating of the site proved to be difficult but it was probably seventh-century and certainly the settlement appears to have had a very short life, perhaps no more than a century or so.

In a very different position was the settlement of Catholme (Fig. 41). It lay in the valley of the River Trent on a slight gravel terrace overlooking the river, just south-west of Burton-on-Trent in Staffordshire. Here, only part of the site was excavated but even so some sixty-six timber buildings were recovered. This seems to have been a substantial settlement, but the structures were by no means all contemporary and the excavator thought they represented no more than five or six farmsteads, continually rebuilt over a period of four hundred years. Each farmstead consisted of a group of timber 'halls' or sheds, surrounded by fences or ditches and connected to each other by trackways. Again no coherent plan was visible and the comparison with many of the existing farmsteads in, for example, south-west England is a very close one. Yet, unlike them, the settlement had a relatively short life, probably beginning just before 500 and being abandoned soon after 900. It has been suggested by Mr S. Losco-Bradley, the excavator, that the final desertion was perhaps due to the disruption caused by the Danish colonization of the area at this time, and indeed the name of the settlement, *Cat-holme*, is

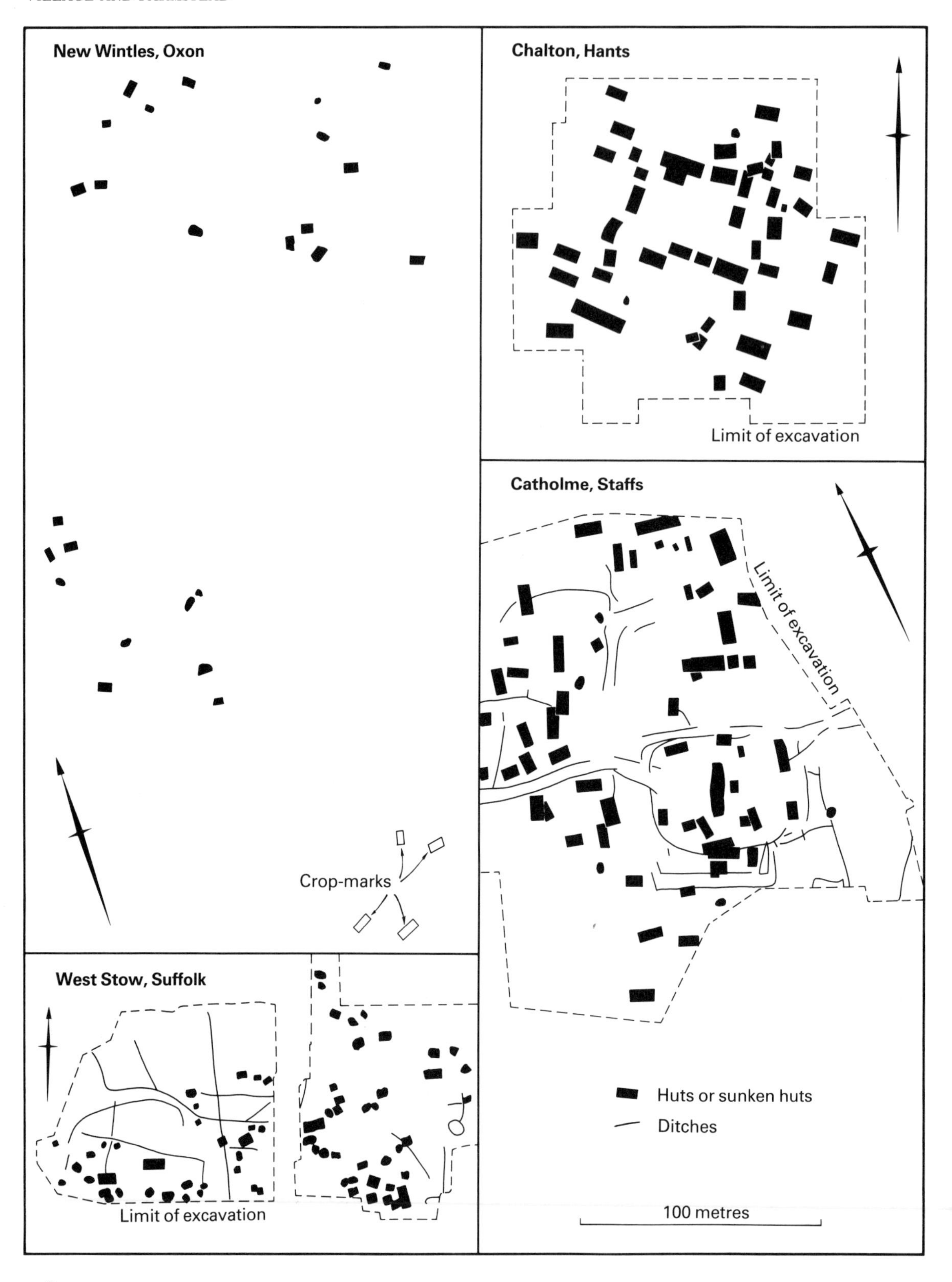
New Wintles, Oxon
Crop-marks
Chalton, Hants
Limit of excavation
Catholme, Staffs
Limit of excavation
West Stow, Suffolk
Limit of excavation
Huts or sunken huts
Ditches
100 metres

Danish in origin, Here, almost for the first time in this book, a clear historical event has been suggested for the abandonment of a settlement. From now on others will be put forward. All may well be acceptable, though we can rarely be sure whether they were the true and only cause of abandonment or only a contributory factor in a much more complex set of interrelated events and conditions.

Different again was West Stow which lay on the heathlands of north-west Suffolk, on the edge of the valley of the River Lark (Fig. 41). The site was occupied in prehistoric times, though not continuously, and again in the early Roman period. But the main late Roman settlement in the area, a large villa, lay some distance away. This villa was certainly occupied well into the fifth century, but the 'Saxon' settlement was first established around 400. It may be that West Stow represents a place where incoming Saxon settlers or indeed mercenaries found an unused corner of heathland on an otherwise flourishing estate and built their houses there and perhaps protected the estate from later arrivals.

LEFT **41 Saxon Settlements** *Four examples of excavated Saxon settlements. All have different plans, but none bear any relationship to the traditional idea of a Saxon village.*

BELOW **42 West Stow, Suffolk** *This modern reconstruction of the Saxon settlement excavated nearby gives a vivid picture of the nature of villages of this period.*

The actual structures found by Dr S. West included a large number of the usual sunken-floored huts, and, more importantly, at least six large 'halls'. These and the huts were scattered about with no understandable form and no streets or tracks were discovered. The settlement appears to have been a group of perhaps half a dozen farmsteads which seem to have existed for about two hundred and fifty years until the mid seventh century (Fig. 42).

Yet another early 'Saxon' settlement is that at Mucking, in south Essex, on a plateau overlooking the Thames estuary. Again the site is an unattractive one, yet with a long history of intermittent occupation stretching back into the early prehistoric period. Yet while the Neolithic, Bronze Age and Roman settlements were fairly compact, the 'Saxon' structures, almost all sunken-floored huts, were scattered over a wide area set within abandoned prehistoric and Roman fields, and with no coherent pattern whatsoever. The settlement had a relatively short life lasting perhaps only a century or so after its establishment soon after 400.

The settlement at Bishopstone, East Sussex, was sited close to the sea on a ridge between the River

Ouse and a small tidal inlet. Twenty-three buildings, mainly rectangular timber huts or 'halls', but including three sunken-floored huts, were recovered, again showing no overall plan. The lifespan of the settlement was probably a little over a hundred years.

The final settlement worth noting is that at New Wintles, near Eynsham, Oxfordshire (Fig. 41). Here, scattered over an area of almost 3 hectares, were timber and sunken-floored huts, arranged in two groups, all probably of sixth- or seventh-century date and perhaps representing only a single farmstead which had been continually moved. On the other hand the huts excavated formed only a tiny part of the whole site. Air photographs show crop-marks of many more sunken hut sites stretching to the south for over a kilometre, almost to the existing village of Eynsham.

One last feature of this early to mid Saxon period that is probably connected with settlement is the number of large Saxon cemeteries which are known from many parts of England, especially in the east and south east. In the past, the interpretation of the siting of these cemeteries has always posed problems as most of them are situated some distance from the existing villages which, it was assumed, they were related to. Now it is clear that these cemeteries belonged to settlements on quite different sites. Thus, at Bishopstone, a large cemetery with 117 burials lies next to the excavated village, while at West Stow there are two cemeteries close at hand. It is probable that the location of many early Saxon cemeteries may be an indication of their so far undiscovered associated settlements.

The existence of these 'villages', hamlets and isolated farmsteads in the early Saxon period has implications for the interpretation of the wider landscape. If the neat nucleated village did not exist at this time then it is unlikely that the common or strip field systems which ultimately lay around them could have existed either. Though not our direct concern in this book, it is worth noting that recent research on field systems has also indicated this and has suggested that in fact many of the occupiers of the early 'Saxon' settlements continued to use the late Roman fields and only modified these gradually over a long period.

Much more important from the point of view of settlement is the problem of the origin of the medieval parish or estate, for if the Saxon nucleated villages did not exist in early or even mid-Saxon times, where did the familiar parish come from? One possible explanation is that they appeared with the establishment of the Christian churches with which they were of course inextricably associated. However, we know from early Saxon land charters that many estates, later to be known as parishes or townships, were in existence long before the churches were built. As we saw in the last chapter, many scholars now see parishes as originating at least in the Roman period and as having been derived, with certain inevitable modifications, from the tenurial grouping that existed in Roman times or even earlier. Thus the early Saxon rural settlements discussed above were not scattered randomly across the landscape, but lay within established units of land from which their inhabitants gained their food and livelihood.

As with Roman and even prehistoric rural settlements, these occupation sites certainly moved about through time, but this movement was within the existing confines of the estate boundaries. The closely packed nature of settlement, at least in some areas, would have precluded the taking over of other people's land, and the boundaries would therefore have tended to have been relatively stable. Thus, what we seem to have in early Saxon times, as in the preceding periods, is a fixed network of estates within which the pattern of settlement constantly changed in response to political, social and economic events or conditions.

This then is the evidence, largely archaeological, of rural settlement in the three centuries or so after the end of the Roman period. What does it mean and can we draw a new picture of 'Saxon' settlement to replace the traditional one? It appears that parts of early 'Saxon' England were characterized by widespread settlements, of varying size and form, ranging from isolated farmsteads to village-like conglomerations, and with the same characteristics of movement, drift, and short lives that we have seen in the preceding 3000 years or more. The only limitations were the already fixed boundaries of agricultural units or economic estates. This is important for it means that the Saxon period is not marked by any break in settlement pattern and type but is a direct continuation of the long-established situation. Thus the real changes in the pattern of settlement must have occurred after mid Saxon times.

The important conclusion that follows is that the coming of the Saxons as such did not have a profound effect on the settlement pattern. The changes that did take place were not as a direct result of this racial influx while the similarity of settlement over wide areas of England in these centuries, both within and beyond those zones traditionally said to be settled early by the Saxons, could only have resulted from a non-cultural explanation of the settlement pattern.

This pattern of varied, small and mobile settlements, does, however, partially bridge the gap between the prehistoric and Roman settlement pattern and the later medieval one. Clearly many of the earliest 'Saxon' settlements are the direct successors of late Roman ones while, on the other hand, a large number of 'Saxon' settlements were to be transmuted into nucleated medieval villages, in ways to be discussed in the next chapter.

Yet, in another sense, the early Saxon period does mark a break with the past. As we have seen in the previous chapters, the history of rural settlement in England, at least in late prehistoric and Roman times, is one of increasing density associated with a growing population and an increased exploitation of the land. In the early Saxon period, perhaps for the first time in 2000 years, there was a retreat of settlement, abandonment of land and presumably a marked drop in the total population of the country. In some areas, such as West Yorkshire, no early or mid Saxon settlement has been found at all. More significant, perhaps, are those areas which, in later medieval times, are known to have been forested and yet which were certainly densely occupied in late Roman times.

The abandonment of settlement may not always have been a feature of the immediate post-Roman years. Evidence from the parish of Stanion near Corby in Northamptonshire shows that woodland regenerated here after the early Saxon period. Medieval and post-medieval documents show that the whole of the south of the parish was completely forested, certainly from the thirteenth century onwards. The parish had extensive woodland within its boundaries in the late eleventh century and perhaps long before. Now this woodland has almost all disappeared, probably cleared for agriculture in the seventeenth or early eighteenth centuries. Yet within the area of the woodland not only are there no less than ten Roman settlements, but at least four small early 'Saxon' settlements have been discovered scattered across the landscape. These indicate that the woodland, later to become part of the great Royal Forest of Rockingham, could not have started to regenerate until at least the sixth century, and perhaps even later.

The smaller number of 'Saxon' compared with Roman sites in Stanion may suggest that there was already a decrease in the number of settlements in the area, but as the discoveries at Stanion were not made as a result of systematic fieldwork these results may be open to question. A stronger case comes from the Soke of Peterborough, Cambridgeshire, where the fieldwork was meticulous and carried out by experts and where the same features occurred. Though sixteen Saxon sites were found, twenty-five Roman settlements were noted and these, together with the six or seven already known, do indicate a fall in the number of settlements in the early Saxon period. Further, while the Roman settlements, and indeed the earlier Iron Age sites (of which twelve were found), all lie on a great variety of soils, including gravels, sands and heavy clays, the 'Saxon' settlements lay only on light soils and no Saxon sites were found on the boulder clay areas which are known to have been forested by the early medieval period.

Thus it appears that, at some time in the early to mid Saxon period, there was a considerable abandonment of settlement. This probably varied in scale from place to place but may be explained only by a large decrease in the population of England. This conclusion again is in sharp contrast to the usually accepted picture of the Saxon period as one with a steeply rising population associated with the continuous expansion of settlement.

Why there should have been this fall in population in these centuries is, as yet, unknown, though the fact that it took place cannot now be denied. It may well be that disease, largely unrecorded except as ill-defined 'plagues', especially in the fifth century, took a massive toll of the existing population. But equally the disturbed times, politically, socially and economically, may have played a part. We still do not fully understand the social mechanisms that control birth rates and which have been shown to affect population rise and decline, even in more recent times, as much as or more than disease, warfare, or even lack of food. Climatic changes, too, as yet equally ill-defined, may have been important. In conclusion it can be said that we are now beginning to understand the development of early 'Saxon' settlement in England and to see that it is very different from the traditional picture, but the processes involved in that development remain obscure.

One final problem of early 'Saxon' settlement, already touched on in passing, is that of place-names. The explanation of the distribution of early English place-names depends on the traditional idea of the establishment of nucleated villages by the first Saxon settlers which, as we have seen, is no longer acceptable. This means that, if the place-name scholars are now correct in identifying certain place-names, notably the topographical ones, as being the earliest, they cannot originally have been related to the settlements that they are now associated with. Indeed the same is true of many later place-names. These names must have once referred to settlements abandoned by at least the seventh or eighth century and must have been subsequently transferred to the ones that now exist. In essence then we seem to have not only mobility of settlement but also of place-names. This may not be strictly true for, if the topographical place-names are indeed the earliest, it may well be that these names actually once referred not to specific places but to the whole area in which a group of settlements lay, or at least to a major topographical feature within it by which it could be identified. Such an area would most likely be the agricultural unit or estate, and in time the parish or township to which we referred earlier and which we can be reasonably sure existed well before the beginning of the Saxon period.

This then is our view of early Saxon times; it is a view of an English landscape without the villages with which we are so familiar. Where then did our villages comes from? If we move forward in time and look at the details of rural settlements towards the end of the Saxon period in the eighth, ninth and tenth centuries there is, apparently, very little difference from the previous pattern. Although there is, at the moment, considerably less evidence for this period than for the previous one, yet many of the earlier features of rural settlement are still apparent. The settlements themselves remain small, many continued to be relatively short-lived, but, and perhaps most important, they still bear no relationship to the later villages even when they are beneath them.

Perhaps the best example of the latter point is the settlement of Goltho just east of Lincoln. The site was a deserted village, finally abandoned in the late fourteenth and early fifteenth centuries, where the arrangement of the streets and the traces of individual houses and gardens were clearly visible as banks, ditches, scarps and holloways. From these it was possible to see that Goltho, in late medieval times, was a fairly typical village, comprising a long main street with houses on each side and with a side street, also lined with houses, approaching from the north-east. In one of the angles formed by the two streets lay the manor house, chapel and other houses and gardens. Because the site was about to be destroyed for agricultural purposes, part of the village and the manor house site were excavated by Mr G. Beresford, with remarkable results. These indicated that the medieval village, with its street system and regular arrangement of crofts or gardens, was not laid out until the tenth or eleventh century. Before that the 'village', such as it was, lay south-east of the later one, partly beneath the medieval manor house site. Yet it was not an early Saxon village. There had been Roman occupation on the site but this ended in the fourth century and the area was left unoccupied until the eighth century. Then rectangular timber houses were erected, probably alongside a street, though this was quite unrelated to the later street pattern. These houses lay inside ditched and fenced paddocks or gardens. In the late ninth or early tenth century, these houses were removed and the first of a series of timber halls and outbuildings was erected which, after many alterations, eventually became the medieval manor house.

Goltho perhaps indicates a stabilization of settlement, in that from the eighth century until the fifteenth century occupation of some form existed on the site. But it also shows that the mid to late Saxon settlement was not only different in form but also in specific positioning from the medieval village. Finally, it gives us the first date we have had so far for the establishment of a 'real English village', a point we shall return to in Chapter 8.

The existence of mid to late Saxon settlements very close to later villages but apparently of a formless nature and unrelated in morphology to the subsequent layout has been noted in a number of other places. In Hampshire, at Bishop's Waltham, excavation immediately west of the present village revealed a group of timber houses dating from the late tenth to the early eleventh centuries. These presumably represent part of an earlier Waltham founded and abandoned long before the later village was laid out. The area was certainly occupied for only a short time before the inhabitants moved elsewhere as in the eleventh century cultivation began on the site and continued for three hundred years.

Yet alongside these mid to late Saxon settlements, associated in some way with later villages, there were also occupation sites of the same period which were quite unrelated to subsequent habitation. One was near Gosport, Hampshire, where, in an area with no immediately preceding or subsequent occupation, a group of timber structures that were occupied in the ninth and tenth centuries has been discovered. A similar group of timber buildings on an isolated site has been found near Brandon, in Suffolk. The present village is neatly aligned along a main street running down to the River Little Ouse. The mid-Saxon settlement was found a little to the west close to the river. This example suggests settlement movement of the type which is by now familiar. The parish church at Brandon also stands apart from the village to the south-west. Though no direct evidence of early settlement has been found there, it has been postulated that perhaps the earliest Saxon Brandon was around the church and that the village first moved north-east and then east to its present position.

That movement or settlement 'drift' was occurring throughout the Saxon period as a whole is well illustrated at the site excavated at Odell on the River Great Ouse, in Bedfordshire. Its earlier development has been noted in a previous chapter (Fig. 21). The late Iron Age farm was replaced in the first century by a new farmstead a little to the south-east. This lasted until the fourth century when the settlement seems to have moved well to the east where it continued until the eighth century. Towards the end of this latter period, there was some reoccupation of the area of Roman habitation.

This continuing feature of settlement 'drift' and even large-scale abandonment now being identified as still occurring in the late Saxon period means that, once again, the long accepted version of settlement development at this time needs to be revised. The old concept of continuous expansion of population from the existing nucleated villages, which resulted in the establishment of secondary settlements in outlying or marginal areas, now seems to be suspect. Certainly it is increasingly hard to prove, although, with a rising population towards the end of the Saxon period, it must have occurred to some extent. The only apparently clear evidence for it is found in the 'secondary' place-names given to outlying hamlets and farmsteads situated near the limits of parishes or townships which appear to have been cut out of pre-existing larger units. As we have seen, however, the interpretation of place-names is not as straightforward as it once seemed. It may well be that many of the apparently 'secondary' settlements are either just as old, or older than the allegedly early ones, or they may be merely remnants of the earlier mobile Saxon pattern. That secondary settlements could develop can be proved, but even then archaeology has shown that the process is much more complicated than we have hitherto imagined.

At Ribblehead, high on the Yorkshire Pennines the remains of a small farmstead, consisting of three rectangular stone buildings set round a courtyard, were discovered. In such a position a possible interpretation was that it was a medieval farmstead, or a monastic sheep grange, abandoned in late medieval times. Yet excavation revealed that in fact it was of ninth-century date, was occupied for only a very short time and was probably an arable rather than a purely pastoral farmstead. The reasons for its desertion seem to be clear; the cultivation of the surrounding land seems to have led to rapid soil erosion and the production of a barren limestone pavement. The establishment of a farm here may well have resulted from expansion of population in the lower valleys which forced farmers into more unsuitable and hostile territories. Nevertheless its early foundation and short-lived existence show how little we understand of the development of apparently secondary settlements at this time.

A very different aspect of secondary settlement or 'colonization' is allegedly visible in northern and eastern England. Such settlements here are said to be the result of the Scandinavian invasions and settlement of the ninth and tenth centuries. Not only is there good historical evidence for the widespread occupation of land by people from Scandinavia, but there are also the ubiquitous Scandinavian place-names attached to villages. Indeed, perfectly reasonable hypotheses of settlement development have been worked out in many places in eastern England. There we find large villages with true 'Saxon' place-names or with hybrid Saxon/Scandinavian names. These have been assumed to be the 'early' Saxon villages, some of which were taken over by the Scandinavian newcomers. Beyond these villages in the more isolated places there are others, often smaller, with pure Scandinavian names. Such villages are usually said to have been later settlements of the ninth and tenth centuries founded by Scandinavian people occupying the gaps left in the landscape by the Saxons.

Unfortunately such a splendidly obvious and neat theory receives a severe blow when the archaeological evidence from the later deserted villages with impeccable Scandinavian names is considered. Calceby on the Lincolnshire Wolds, for example, which has been described as 'an archetypal Scandinavian colonizing settlement', has produced, unusually for most deserted villages, a sequence of pottery and occupation debris of early Saxon to late Saxon and medieval date. At other places villages with Scandinavian names do not appear to have existed until the twelfth or thirteenth centuries. Archaeological evidence for occupation of 'Scandinavian' villages before the Scandinavian arrival is now accumulating and once again the use of place-names as an indicator of settlement origins is becoming suspect.

However, while it is now clear that the pattern of Saxon settlement was not at all what it is traditionally supposed to have been, we can be sure that most of what were later to be medieval parishes, townships or estates were in existence, as there is a wealth of documentation from all over England for these, mainly in the form of Saxon land grants, charters or wills. Thus change in settlement at this time can be proved to be taking place within these estates, just as it had done probably for the previous two millennia. The arrival of formal Christianity in the late sixth century was followed by the gradual establishment of parish churches. The Church with its accompanying administrative needs inevitably required a financial as well as a religious basis on which to operate. In purely monetary terms this was achieved by imposing a tax, tithes, on the people who came under its jurisdiction. As tithes were paid, often in kind, from the produce of the land, it was inevitable that the Church came to regard the basic unit of agriculture as the area from which tithes were drawn. The estate and parish therefore tended to become synonymous. The fact that it was then very much in the interests of the Church to ensure that the boundaries of the Church became sacrosanct meant that established divisions became more permanent than ever before. The places where people actually lived were almost irrelevant. These could move or be moved at will for any reason at all, but the boundaries of the land from which the Church derived its income could not be altered. The whole weight of the power of the medieval Church ensured that they were not. Thus the old estates became even more rigidly controlled, while settlement continued to move about as necessary.

This factor also partially explains the varied positions of churches. When the very first churches were built there were probably three major factors behind the choice of their location. The first, laid down in the original instructions to St Augustine when he came to convert the 'heathen', was that they were to be positioned on already sacred or pagan sites in order to ensure continuity of worship. Some of these sites, such as that at Knowlton in Dorset where the church lies within a great prehistoric temple or henge, were already isolated. Others, as at Maxey in Cambridgeshire, where the church stands on an apparently prehistoric burial place, were then within or near an existing settlement which subsequently moved.

Another factor which controlled the siting of the church was the fact that the land on which it stood was given by the local lord or community. This land may have lain within, or near, or quite remote from the existing settlement depending on what was available. Thirdly, with the predominantly dispersed pattern of settlement of the Saxon period, individual churches were often positioned in or close to what was, at that time, the largest settlement. In subsequent centuries, as we shall see, continued movement, drift or abandonment may have meant that churches that were once within settlements found themselves either standing alone or positioned near their limits and that once isolated churches came to be at the centres of flourishing communities or remained forever on their own. Thus the interpretation of the positions of churches in relation to earlier or existing settlement patterns has to be treated with considerable care.

By the eleventh century then, the pattern of settlement in the English landscape was probably far from what has been traditionally imagined. England was not then, as has often been assumed, a country of nucleated villages, some 'old', some relatively 'new', each surrounded by its strip fields. Almost the only recognizable features from the present landscape, apart from some churches, were the parish or estate boundaries. Within these boundaries lay a curious pattern of hamlets and farmsteads, many on the sites of today's villages though very different in form. The rest lay scattered across the landscape in, to our eyes, very unlikely positions. Many of these settlements may have been in existence for centuries, others were brand new. It was a landscape which any Bronze Age, Iron Age or Roman farmer would have instantly recognized, for it had been thus for millennia. We, however, would have found it entirely unfamiliar. It was not until post-Saxon times that the rural landscape came to resemble our own.

-8-
The Making of Villages

The nucleated village is usually said to be typical of England but in fact it is not very common over England as a whole. Village England is really a broad zone stretching from the south coast through the Midlands to the north-east. Nucleated villages are extremely rare in the south-west, over large parts of East Anglia and in the south-east. Elsewhere, in parts of central southern England, along the Welsh Marches and over large sections of the north-west, they are only part of a much more complex pattern including many hamlets and isolated farmsteads. Indeed it might be said that nucleated villages, far from being a normal form of settlement, are an aberration, especially in view of their late development and limited distribution.

The basic problem connected with the history of these villages, as Chapter 7 made clear, is that few if any existed by 1000. Where nucleated villages now stand there was either no occupation at all or occupation of a very different type or form from that which came later. At the same time, however, we are faced with a well-known and remarkable document which tells us, apparently without a shadow of doubt, that almost all the villages that now exist in the English landscape were there in the eleventh century, together with many others which have since disappeared. This document is Domesday Book, compiled in 1086 on the orders of William the Conqueror, so that he might know exactly what his new kingdom consisted of and what it was worth for taxation purposes. This magnificent record has been the Bible for all scholars interested in the history of settlement in England for it gives us the first complete picture of the English landscape, apparently listing the villages that existed at that time and recording the area of land belonging to each village and the use to which the land was put, i.e. whether it was arable or pastureland, or woodland.

How, then, can we reconcile the evidence from Domesday Book, which gives us a view of late eleventh-century rural England that is not very different in outline from what we can see today, with the evidence from archaeology which seems to indicate a very different pattern. It is obvious that either the archaeological record or Domesday Book must be wrong, or that we are misinterpreting the evidence from one or both. Although archaeological methods and archaeologists are by no means infallible, as has often been proved, the sheer bulk of evidence now available from the archaeological record seems to indicate that there is something wrong, not with Domesday Book itself, but with the way in which we have interpreted it.

First of all it is important to note that Domesday Book does not actually list *villages* which existed at that time. It describes the *land* held by various lords and sub-tenants and lists what was of value on that land, whether it was woodland, meadow or people. These land holdings may be akin to later medieval manors, though much scholastic ink has been spilt over the question as to whether they were indeed true manors at that time. For our purposes it will help if we call the land holdings described in

Domesday Book manors, for they certainly consisted of areas of land over which lords had certain rights and within which people lived. These lands or 'manors' are identified in Domesday Book by name, most of which are now the names of existing villages. But nowhere in Domesday Book does it say that these names *are* those of villages, only that they are the names of land holdings or manors. Modern scholars have equated land holdings with villages and this assumption, and assumption it is, has become the accepted truth.

Many years ago W. G. Hoskins, in what is arguably his most important work, 'The Highland Zone in Domesday Book', pointed out the fallacy of equating villages with the manors of Domesday Book. He showed that, in south-west England at least, though Domesday Book records land holdings in exactly the same way as elsewhere, in fact villages did not exist there in the eleventh century and nor do they today. Professor Hoskins proved that Domesday Book is actually describing a landscape not of villages but of isolated farmsteads and small groups of cottages in this part of the country. Subsequent workers have found that the same applies to other areas of England, notably parts of the heathland of central southern England and along the Welsh Marches. In these places, as in the south-west, it can be seen that Domesday Book is not describing villages, which did not and never have existed there, but is listing in bureaucratic jargon the valuable assets in a landscape with a dispersed pattern of settlement. If this is so, could it be that elsewhere in England Domesday Book is often describing a similar picture and that the archaeological record is perhaps giving us a more accurate view.

So, if these nucleated villages did not exist at the time of Domesday, where did they come from? From the archaeological point of view, the fact that many of these villages are still lived in creates difficulties, for few people want their homes and gardens torn apart by excavators looking for evidence of their origins. However, it is possible to carry out excavations on the sites of the many thousands of villages which were abandoned in later medieval and post-medieval times, for a variety of reasons which will be discussed later. These excavations can tell us much about the arrangements of such villages, their history and the reasons for their final depopulation. And they can also give us many clues as to their origins. The most important feature of these excavations is that they show that most villages do not exhibit the arrangement that they retained to the end of their lives until what seem to be extraordinarily late dates, and dates that often conflict not only with the evidence of Domesday Book but also with that of place-names.

The difficulties involved in reconciling Domesday Book, place-name interpretation and the archaeological record are exemplified by the case of Faxton in Northamptonshire (Fig. 43), a village with a long and complex history whose life did not finally come to a close until the 1950s. The name Faxton has been interpreted as a possible combination of the English word *tun* or farm and *Fákr*, a rare Scandinavian personal name. If this is so then the name of the village was originally Fákr's tun or the farm of Fákr. This would suggest that Faxton must have come into existence by the ninth century at the latest. The evidence from Domesday Book is more convincing and here Faxton seems to be described as the 'manor' of Fextone, which was then held by the King. In it were the usual valuables which are always listed in Domesday Book, including enough arable land for twelve ploughs, sixteen acres of meadow and twenty-one people, described as six serfs, six villeins and nine bordars. On the traditional interpretation of Domesday Book Faxton would seem to have been a flourishing village with a relatively large population. On the assumption that the bordars and villeins were the heads of households, a widely accepted interpretation, it would mean that the village of Faxton in 1086 was a community of between sixty and eighty souls, relatively large by the standards of that part of Northamptonshire in which it lies. Faxton village, on a high dry sandstone spur surrounded on three sides by deep clay valleys, may thus be seen as a well-situated settlement of undoubtedly ancient origins.

Unfortunately the archaeological evidence shows that this was not so. The now deserted site of the village was subjected to large-scale excavation by Dr L. Butler before all the remains of the abandoned houses, streets, gardens and even the church were totally destroyed for modern agriculture. This destruction, though regrettable in some ways, was also useful in that the site could be fully examined afterwards for fragments of pottery and other material which might shed light on its origins. This work thus supplemented the more restricted but detailed scientific excavations.

The results of both are a shattering blow to those who believe in the accepted interpretation of

Domesday Book. The excavations uncovered the remains of rows of medieval peasant cottages, each set in a rectangular garden plot, lining the main streets in various parts of the village. But nowhere was anything earlier than 1150 discovered and it was quite clear that the pattern of houses, gardens and streets did not come into being before the late twelfth century. Indeed part of the village was not laid out until about 1200. The results obtained by examining the site after it had been ploughed supported the excavations, for again no pottery or objects earlier than 1150 to 1200 were discovered, except for some evidence of a much earlier Roman site.

It appears therefore that the medieval village of Faxton did not exist in 1086 and that the place called Faxton, apparently described in Domesday

43 Faxton, Northamptonshire *This photograph, taken in the 1950s, shows the village at the end of its life. Only four houses remained, though the outlines of former streets, gardens, paddocks and house sites were still clear. A few years later three of the houses were pulled down and the earthworks destroyed by ploughing. Pottery uncovered by this ploughing, combined with the evidence from excavations, showed that the village originated not in Saxon times but in the twelfth century.*

Book, must have lain elsewhere or was not a village at all. Where this putative Faxton was has not yet been discovered. It presumably lay within the area of land later known as the parish of Faxton but it was certainly not on the site of the medieval village.

Faxton is not an isolated and unusual case and many similar examples can be quoted from all over England. In the same county, for example, the deserted villages of Wythmail and Lyveden have both been excavated and then examined again after they were destroyed and neither has produced any evidence of occupation before the later twelfth century.

The deserted village of Wawne in north Humberside tells a similar story. Again examination before and during the complete destruction of the site showed that the earliest occupation was not until the twelfth century. At Gomeldon, in Wiltshire, the earliest occupation discovered was of twelfth-century date and the same results have been obtained at the deserted village of Holworth in Dorset.

There are, of course, many villages where pre-eleventh-century occupation has been discovered and which therefore support the record of Domesday Book. But, as the discussion of Goltho in the last chapter made clear, this occupation is often quite unrelated to the later layout of the village concerned. Elsewhere, even when the village can be shown to have already acquired its medieval plan before the eleventh century, it is often clear that this plan was a very recent feature at that date.

At the deserted village of Clopton in Cambridgeshire the site was certainly occupied in Roman times and probably in the fifth century as well. There was also some habitation there in the seventh century but widespread settlement did not begin until the tenth century and the arrangement of the village as it was towards the end of its life did not appear until the late thirteenth century. At Upton in Gloucestershire some remarkable stone peasant's houses have been excavated but these were found to be of thirteenth-century date. Beneath them was evidence of earlier occupation, but this began only in the ninth century.

At other places it is clear that the present village is the result of a marked change in position, perhaps beginning in the late Saxon period but continuing well into the medieval period. This movement of settlement has been particularly well recorded in Norfolk. There the most characteristic feature of the modern landscape is its isolated medieval churches, which have puzzled scholars and laymen alike for many generations. As a result of the careful work by Dr P. Wade-Martins it is now becoming clear that these churches have been isolated following long-term settlement drift. The parish church of Longham today stands alone, except for a single farm, and the rather sprawling village lies over one kilometre to the east and south-east (Fig. 44). Meticulous fieldwork has shown that the earliest village, dating from mid Saxon times, lay around the church. This was quite a small settlement, perhaps consisting of only a handful of farmsteads. In the succeeding centuries it expanded and by the tenth century there was a considerable area of occupation around the church. Then, in the eleventh century, the village moved to the south and was laid out around a large L-shaped green. Soon afterwards the village began to move again and by the fifteenth century was arranged around an even larger green to the east. Similar movement or drift has been identified at a number of other places in the same area.

All the examples so far, except the last, have been of villages which were later deserted. As was noted earlier, it is because they have been abandoned that archaeologists have been able to investigate their true development. Of course, the fact that such villages were later deserted might mean that they were unusual although, once the process of continuous change is recognized, this argument is difficult to accept. Moreover, although there are considerable problems in establishing the origins of villages that still exist, the work that has been carried out on these villages confirms the results obtained from those which have been deserted. There is rarely any evidence of continuous occupation from early Saxon times through to the medieval period and in many cases no evidence at all of occupation until the ninth century or later.

At Fladbury in Hereford and Worcester the chance discovery of some burials led to an excavation in which ninth-century occupation, including a large timber building, was discovered. However, there was nothing earlier, except for some material dating from the Bronze Age. This writer, always aware of these problems, has spent much of his life in two villages, one in Wiltshire and the other

44 Movement in Medieval Villages *Three villages in Norfolk where detailed work has shown to what extent movement can and did take place in the medieval period.*

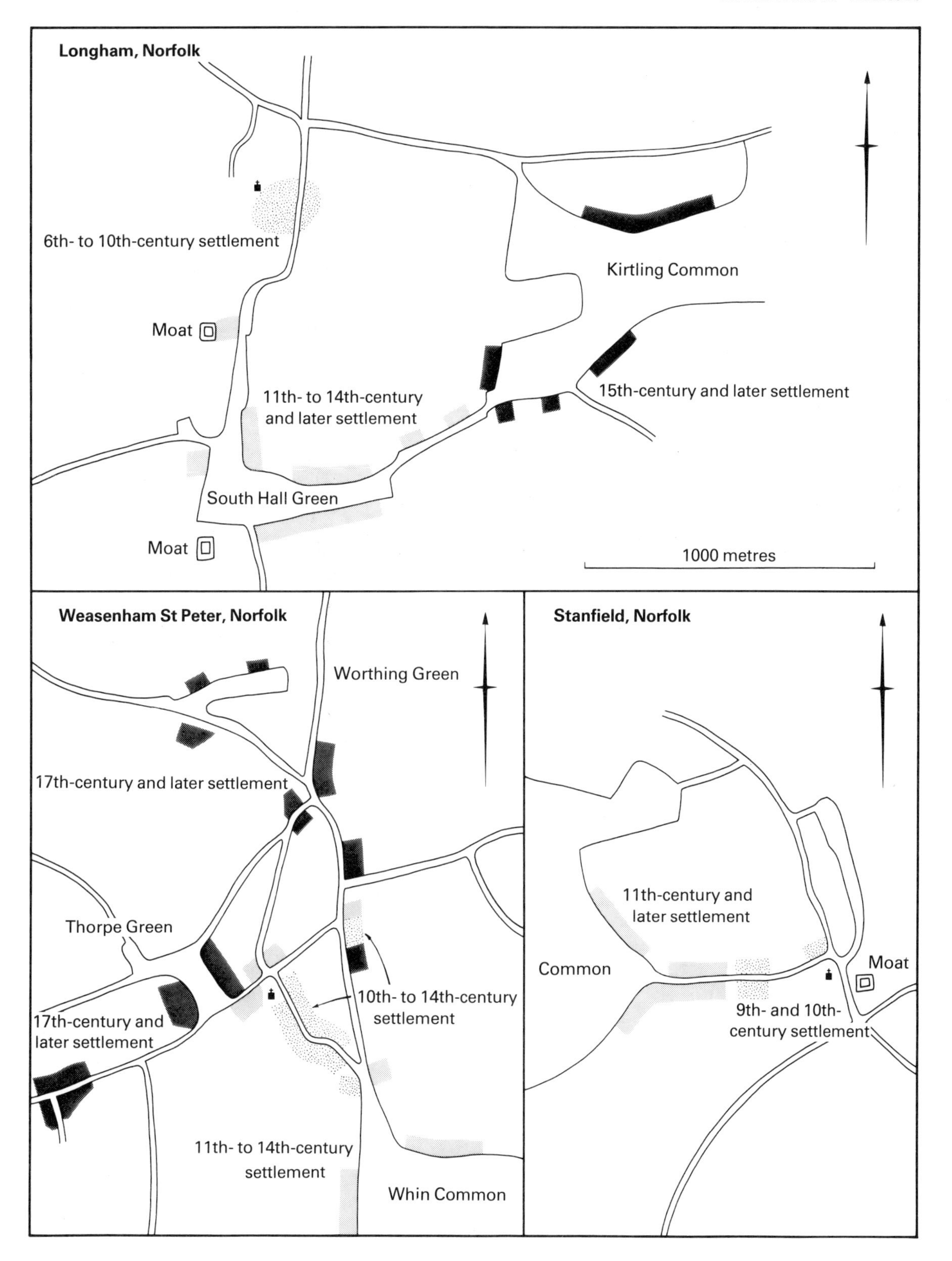
Longham, Norfolk
6th- to 10th-century settlement
Kirtling Common
Moat
11th- to 14th-century
and later settlement
15th-century and later settlement
South Hall Green
Moat
1000 metres
Weasenham St Peter, Norfolk
Worthing Green
17th-century and later settlement
Thorpe Green
17th-century and
later settlement
10th- to 14th-century
settlement
11th- to 14th-century
settlement
Whin Common
Stanfield, Norfolk
11th-century and
later settlement
Common
Moat
9th- and 10th-
century settlement

in Cambridgeshire. Yet in spite of the most careful examination of every modern disturbance, foundation trench, garden and roadwork, he has never found any indication that either village existed before the tenth century. Very careful work, spread over twenty years, at Marston St Lawrence in Northamptonshire, has produced massive evidence of intermittent prehistoric and Roman occupation but no Saxon material of any date within the village.

At the beginning of this chapter we pointed to the fact that in many parts of England there is good evidence that Domesday Book is covering up the existence of a dispersed pattern of settlement, consisting mainly of farmsteads and hamlets. The implication of what has been discussed here is that the same pattern existed over much of the rest of England and that it has since been destroyed by later changes. The reasons why this pattern has remained in some areas, for example south-west England, Essex and along the Welsh Marches, will be discussed later but its very existence has led scholars to see it as very old (Fig. 69). If we journey to Devon today the pattern of scattered farmsteads seems to be very similar to that of prehistoric, Roman and Saxon settlement elsewhere (Fig. 70). As a result it has been suggested that in such places we do indeed have the remnants of a truly prehistoric and Roman settlement pattern that has remained unchanged by the events of medieval times. To some extent this is so but we must not fall into the trap of being convinced that it is absolutely so just because it seems obvious. For though the overall pattern of dispersal is similar to that of earlier times and so very different from the nucleated villages of Leicestershire or Warwickshire, two important points are worth noting. Firstly, as we have seen, it is possible that the pattern in these latter counties and elsewhere was not a nucleated one until a relatively late date and secondly, even the apparently ageless and stable pattern in south-western England, the west Midlands and parts of East Anglia also altered in detail through time, even though it retained its generally dispersed form. We shall return to this problem in the next chapter.

In summary, the archaeological evidence for rural settlement in the late Saxon and early medieval period reveals a continuously changing pattern, very similar to that of the preceding 5000 to 6000 years. Domesday Book, far from giving us a picture of an old and stable landscape which we can still recognize, allows us a partial view of a complex process of change which is difficult to interpret. Despite this denigration of England's most famous historical document and the indication that it may be describing an English landscape which was still primarily one of dispersed settlement, it is also true that Domesday Book was written at a time when the pattern of rural settlement in England was to some extent beginning to become more stable.

Within a century or so on either side of the Norman Conquest many English villages did come into existence in a form which, at least in morphological terms, we can still recognize today. The major questions therefore are how and why this should have occurred on such a scale for the first time in the history of settlement in England and why the changes should have been limited to a relatively small part of the country. The short answer is that we do not know. Many hypotheses can be put forward though none is entirely satisfactory. Certainly no racial invasion or political event could have been involved for the spread of some four centuries during which the process operated is too long. Nor can climatic changes be invoked for there is nothing in the historical record or in palaeoclimatological evidence to indicate any major alterations in our weather. It is also difficult to explain what happened in general economic or social terms.

One favoured explanation is to invoke demographic evidence. Slim though this is, it would appear that the population of England was rising rapidly at this time after the disastrous fall from the high levels of the late Roman period. Yet sharp population rises had occurred before, especially in the Bronze Age and Roman times, and these increases had not resulted in the nucleation of settlement to the extent that happened in late Saxon and early medieval times. Nor does the distribution of nucleated settlements equate exactly with the areas that Domesday Book records as being most densely populated in the eleventh century. Indeed, in 1086 dispersed patterns of settlement were often recorded in the areas of densest population, as is the case over much of Essex and Suffolk.

Another point which is perhaps significant is that at the very time when village nucleation was taking place in fairly restricted parts of England, some historians have seen indications that the typical common or open field system that is known to have eventually surrounded these villages was also coming into being. Is there a link between the development of a true open field system with its accompanying rights of common grazing and complex organizational structure and the nucleated villages that usually go with these systems? It seems that in many cases this is possible though why these changes should have occurred, is not clear. Even if we invoke an increasing population resulting in a growing demand for food and a shortage of land, this does not explain why settlement should become nucleated. The open field system could, and in some places certainly did, operate successfully without a nucleated village at its centre.

The best way to go about trying to understand the process of nucleation and thus the origins of the typical English village is to look carefully at those villages that still exist. The village that we can see today is the result of considerable modern and indeed earlier change, so we need to go back in time to look at how these villages were in the sixteenth or seventeenth centuries, if possible by using old maps or documents although maps are rarely available before the later sixteenth century. Apart from this historical and cartographic evidence, which enables us to remove most recent alterations, there are also some other techniques available which can help us to understand the origins of a village. The most useful of these is metrological analysis, the accurate measurement of the size of house and garden plots.

There are four principal ways in which a nucleated village might have come into existence; by steady growth from a single place, by the agglomeration or the growing together of a number of initially dispersed places, by the collapse of a dispersed settlement pattern into one of nucleated villages, or by being deliberately planned.

Steady growth from an initial farmstead is perhaps the most obvious and widely accepted reason invoked for the appearance of a nucleated village. A farmer living in a single farmstead might have two sons. On the father's death, one son takes over his father's house and the other builds a new one nearby, though the original land is still worked as a single unit. Continued growth of this family would produce first a hamlet and later a fully-fledged village. Such a sequence of events certainly did occur and in the post-medieval period the first three stages are documented in upland areas. However it is very difficult to prove that any specific medieval village came into existence in this way. The known examples of the process from relatively recent times would suggest that the hamlet stage is usually characterized by an amorphous form with no clearly defined plan and with individual farmsteads and cottages arranged in a seemingly arbitrary way in what might be termed a loose cluster. This may possibly indicate that the many villages with totally amorphous plans could have originated in this way. While this might be true, two points are relevant. Firstly, it is not necessary for such growth to be formless. If there was a pre-existing road across the area then the subsequent village may well have taken on a much more regular form with houses arranged along a single street. Likewise, if the original hamlet grew up at the junction of a number of roads, this junction might well have become an open space or green with a remarkably regular appearance. A good example of what might be described as the retarded first stage of this process may be seen at Lydlynch in Dorset, where a triangular green lies at the junction of three roads. Today there are only three farmsteads around this green and the same number existed in the fourteenth century. This settlement may have come into being in the twelfth or thirteenth centuries as a result of the colonization of former woodland and it has never grown any larger. Yet if circumstances had led to growth, today there would be a 'green village'.

The second point worth making is that even villages with amorphous plans may not have had that form originally. Because of the considerable changes to villages at a later date it is impossible to be sure that those which seem so obviously to have grown gradually from one farmstead did not have entirely different origins. Thus, while continuous growth from a single farmstead is theoretically likely, given the undoubted rise in population in late Saxon and early medieval times, it remains very difficult to pinpoint specific examples with any confidence.

The second possible cause of village formation, agglomeration, is related to the first. This involves a group of dispersed but closely set farmsteads growing into discrete hamlets which finally coalesce to form a single nucleated settlement. The resulting village plan is usually termed either composite or polyfocal. As with steady growth, the early stages of this development are difficult to prove but the identification of possible original foci is often much easier and a large number of villages have been suggested as having this origin. A good example, and one of the first to be so recognized, is Great Shelford near Cambridge. It illustrates well both how this type of village can originate and the problem of identifying agglomeration from existing village plans.

Great Shelford is now almost a suburb of Cambridge and shows no obviously explainable

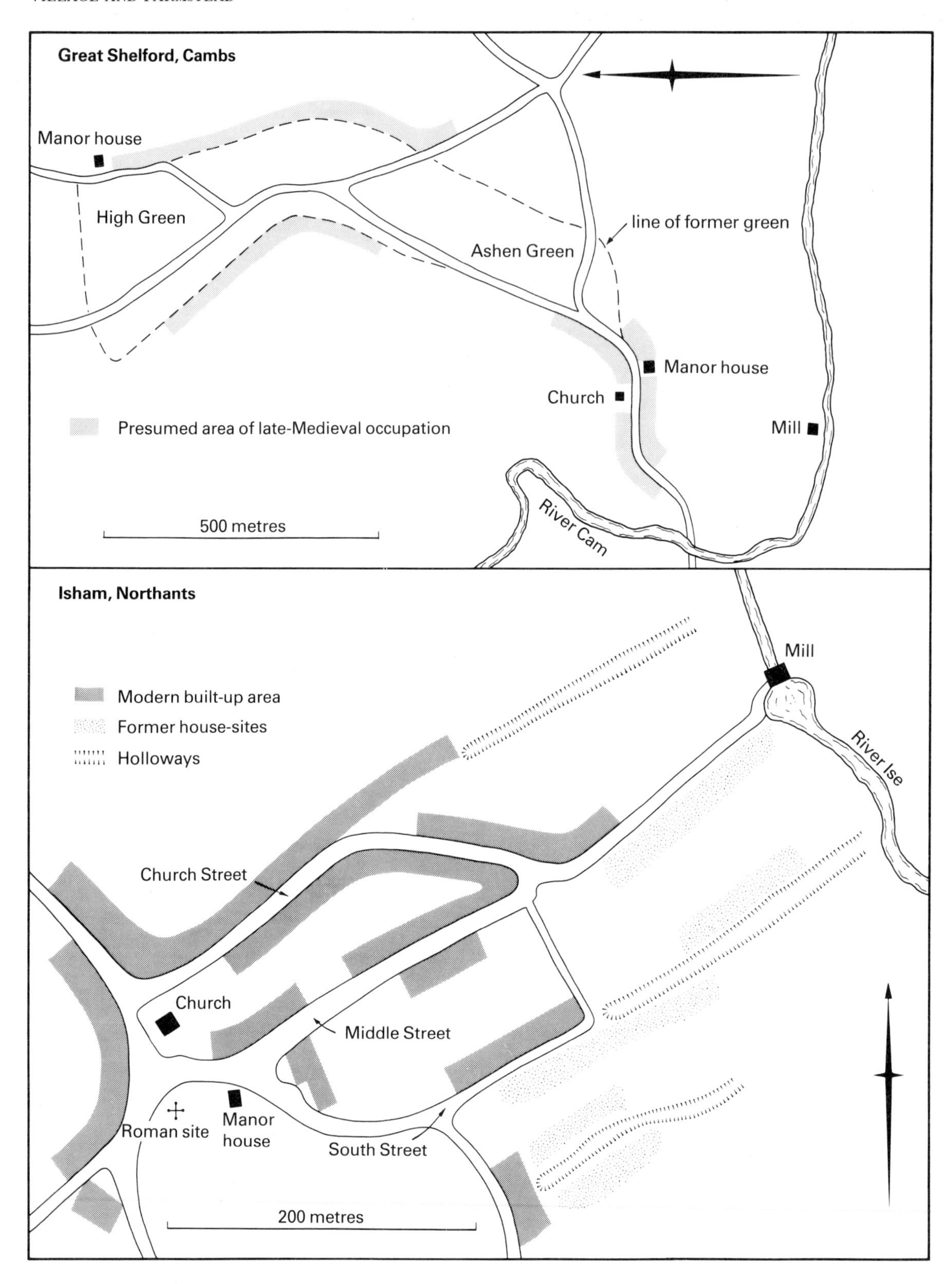
Great Shelford, Cambs
Manor house
High Green
Ashen Green
line of former green
Manor house
Church
Mill
Presumed area of late-Medieval occupation
River Cam
500 metres
Isham, Northants
Mill
Modern built-up area
Former house-sites
Holloways
River Ise
Church Street
Church
Middle Street
Roman site
Manor house
South Street
200 metres

45 Origins of Medieval Villages *Two ways in which a village could come into existence. At Shelford, two small hamlets, each centred round a manor house, gradually expanded to form one large village. The resulting green survived until the mid-nineteenth century when it was enclosed and Shelford took on a completely new shape. The remains of former streets and house sites at Isham indicate that its arrangement was once very regular and was probably planned.*

form (Fig. 45). If we go back to late nineteenth-century maps, which were made before the massive modern expansion, the village plan is still inexplicable. The Enclosure Map of 1834 reveals much more, including the existence of a huge green with houses along two sides and with extensions along a street at either end. Earlier documentary records indicate that the green was once even larger. However, late medieval records and other sources suggest that the 'green' itself was probably a late foundation occupying an area of former meadowland between two small and quite discrete settlements. Both these settlements were centred on separate manors whose existence can be traced back to the late eleventh century. Here we seem to have clear evidence of an original polyfocal village which has become an amorphous nucleated one. That this process is likely to have been extremely common is proved by the work on similar villages all over England and many scholars now claim to have recognized polyfocal villages. Indeed, in south Cambridgeshire, around Great Shelford, it has been estimated that at least a quarter of all the villages may be polyfocal in origin.

The conscious decision by a group of people to abandon their dispersed farmsteads and hamlets in order to occupy a single site is yet another way in which a village could have come into existence. As with villages which have appeared as a result of steady growth, this process is one which is close to the traditional idea of village development. The first 'Saxon villages' that were said to have appeared in the fifth century have often been interpreted as the result of groups of Saxon settlers picking 'good' sites and establishing fully-fledged villages. Though, as we have seen, such villages did not appear in early Saxon times, it is possible that the process could have occurred in late Saxon times with the abandonment of the dispersed settlement pattern that seems to have existed until then. Again, the mechanism which would trigger such a change in the pattern of settlement is difficult to imagine, especially at the scale on which it has occurred. It is possible that in some cases the trigger was a need for defence in time of war, or during a period of intermittent raids by outsiders, while the effects of major changes in agricultural techniques, social behaviour or economic pressures might be responsible in others, though none are documented on a national scale. However, while it is possible that such events and changes could have produced nucleation in individual places or regions, they are hardly likely to have been a primary cause of the nucleation of settlement over much of England.

So far we have examined three possible processes which could have produced nucleated villages; steady growth, which is likely but cannot be proved, agglomeration, which seems to have occurred on a large scale, and the collapse of a dispersed settlement pattern or settlement 'balling', which is also likely to have occurred on a small scale. The last process, conceivably the most important of all, though perhaps conceptually the most difficult to accept, is that of deliberate planning.

Consciously planned villages are, of course, a well recognized feature of the English landscape. However, the well-known examples date mainly from the eighteenth or nineteenth centuries and are associated with emparking or industrial schemes (see p. 211 below). The possibility that medieval villages might equally well have been planned by local lords is perhaps more difficult to accept. Yet even the traditional picture, now discredited, of early Saxon villages being founded by fifth-century invaders had within it, implicitly, the idea of planning. The scholars who first examined village plans over fifty years ago were often struck by the extremely regular nature of village greens in some areas, or by the extraordinarily regular pattern of houses and garden plots on either side of neatly aligned streets. Such regularity was explained as the result of the control of individual Saxon leaders or war-lords who arrived in the fifth century, picked out suitable sites, and then laid out villages in which their followers could settle. Now that there is evidence disproving the existence of early Saxon nucleated villages, it is possible to transfer this idea of planning forward in time to the late Saxon and early medieval periods and to replace early Saxon war-lords by medieval lords of the manor.

Can we, however, either prove that planning did take place or that it occurred at this period? Recent research by Roberts, Sheppard and Allerston, notably in the north-east of England, has shown without doubt that the process could and did occur. Especially in Northumberland, Durham and North Yorkshire, many villages are so regular in their layout that a planned origin seems to be the only explanation. These villages usually consist of rows of almost exactly regular house plots facing a straight street or geometrically shaped green. Complex analysis of late eleventh-century tax assessments and other records, together with detailed examination of the surviving arrangements of house plots, greens and streets, has proved that many of these villages actually came into existence soon after 1070. The main questions therefore are why this planning should have occurred and whether all the regular villages in northern England are of this period. The answer to the first question is relatively easy as it was in the late eleventh century that northern England was devastated, first by the Scandinavian raids along the coast in 1066 and then by William the Conqueror's 'Harrying of the North' in 1069–70, which was far more savage and widespread. As has been said, 'the scale of the resulting devastation was enormous, judged by its impact on chroniclers familiar with the normal activities of medieval armies and with the ravages associated with Scottish raids'. Indeed Domesday Book itself, written sixteen years after the events of 1069-70, is an eloquent testimony of the state of northern England then, with manor after manor all described as 'waste'. Yet the actual places known to have been devastated do not equate exactly with the distribution of regular villages so that the situation is not quite as simple as it first appears. Most of these regular villages lie on estates held by major landlords. They seem to have been established, sometimes on new and sometimes on previously-inhabited sites, by these lords who attracted to them free tenants from other areas. In other words, these villages were established, at least in part, for purely commercial reasons. Not all lords were commercially motivated and sometimes it seems that local survivors from the devastation were also grouped into new villages as well. These people were not free tenants but had strict manorial services imposed upon them. Occasionally villages of this kind are places with regular layouts, but more often they have rather amorphous forms and may be only the re-establishment of an earlier settlement.

There are very many examples of these regular villages in northern England and illustrations of them are common, especially in popular literature where they are usually described as typical villages.

46 Cold Kirby, North Yorkshire *At first sight this neat village, set high on the moors, looks like a modern planned estate. It is indeed a planned village but probably of the eleventh or early twelfth century. The stone-walled gardens fronting the houses are relatively modern and date from the enclosure of the parish in the early nineteenth century. Originally this space was a large open green.*

Amongst the best known are Cold Kirby in North Yorkshire and Milburn in Cumbria (Figs. 46, 47), but there are others of equally striking appearance both in the same area and elsewhere. However, the major problem, as with most topographical studies, is to identify those villages which were planned at this time. In the case of Milburn there can be little argument and many other northern English villages

OVERLEAF **47 Milburn, Cumbria** *Another planned village set around its original green. Walworth would have looked almost identical if it had not been deserted (see Fig. 59).*

can also be identified as planned settlements if modern alterations and accretions are ignored by returning to the pattern depicted on older maps. Other planned villages are not so easy to identify because of alterations which took place in the period before maps were made. The plan of Carlton, in Co Durham, for example, shows that it still had a very regular form in the nineteenth century (Fig. 50). Today the regularity has been largely destroyed by subsequent expansion. A study by P. Allerston of planned eleventh-century villages in the Pickering district of North Yorkshire, using such cartographic evidence, revealed that eighteen out of twenty-nine villages examined were certainly planned. Yet this writer has recently re-examined most of these twenty-nine villages on the ground and has found that almost all of them have minor banks, scarps, ditches and holloways within and around them indicating the sites of former houses, gardens and streets. The original form of some of the villages had been partly obscured by later development.

One of the villages, Pockley, was described in the original survey as an 'unplanned village of elongated form' (Fig. 48). So it appears on both modern and ancient maps but when it is examined on the ground, and all the abandoned garden boundaries and former house sites noted, a different picture emerges. It then becomes clear that the northern part of the village is a planned settlement of typical form. An addition, which was probably also planned, consisted of houses set around a green which was later built over. The south-western part of the village, which accentuates its elongated form, is a small agglomeration of cottages and farmsteads which might either be a further addition or the remains of an earlier village which pre-dated the planned one.

The result of this work was to suggest that of the eleven alleged unplanned villages in the area, no less than five had good evidence of planning while two others were possibly planned. Thus twenty-three, or perhaps twenty-five, out of twenty-nine adjacent villages in a small area of North Yorkshire seem to have been planned from the outset. Elsewhere in northern England the proportion of such villages is by no means as high although much more careful field examination would no doubt increase their number considerably.

There can be little doubt, therefore, that a very large proportion of the existing villages in the northern part of England were planned as new settlements in the late eleventh or early twelfth

48 A Planned Village and its Development: Pockley *A close examination of the layout of the existing village of Pockley, on the left, together with the traces of former house sites and abandoned hedge lines, enables the landscape historian to reconstruct its arrangement in medieval times. The diagram on the right suggests at least two stages of planning as well as what is either an original nucleus or a later extension on the south-west of the village.*

centuries. But what of the other parts of England where nucleated villages are also the normal form of rural settlement? There we have no clear event, such as the Harrying of the North or late Danish raids, which might have led to the establishment of planned villages. Neither have modern scholars applied themselves to the analysis of midland and southern English villages to the same extent that they have to those in the north. Yet the archaeological evidence, summarized earlier, does suggest that the first appearance of many nucleated villages in southern and midland England, whether planned or not, was also in the eleventh or twelfth centuries. Is there, therefore, evidence of planned villages in other parts of England despite the lack of a disaster to provide the impulse which created them? Indeed there is, though their establishment cannot be dated as closely as has been possible for villages further north. The evidence lies, as usual, in the villages themselves and in their documented history though neither has been examined with a critical eye. The difficulty is that interpretation of village shapes is conditioned by our preconceived notions of how a village should have originated, that is in the early Saxon period, and of how, once established, a village never changed beyond slowly increasing in size. Thus, the often neat and regular plans of many midland villages have been explained as early Saxon co-operation. Similarly, the apparently amorphous plans of many others have been interpreted as the result of slow expansion from some original focal point. However, if we accept that villages can be planned at a relatively late date, and that subsequently massive alterations did take place, then an examination of many villages leads to the discovery of much that is new and important in terms of explaining their possible origins. One example will show both such results and, perhaps more importantly, the methods involved in this sort of work.

The modern village of Isham, south of Kettering in Northamptonshire (Fig. 45), is now a seemingly

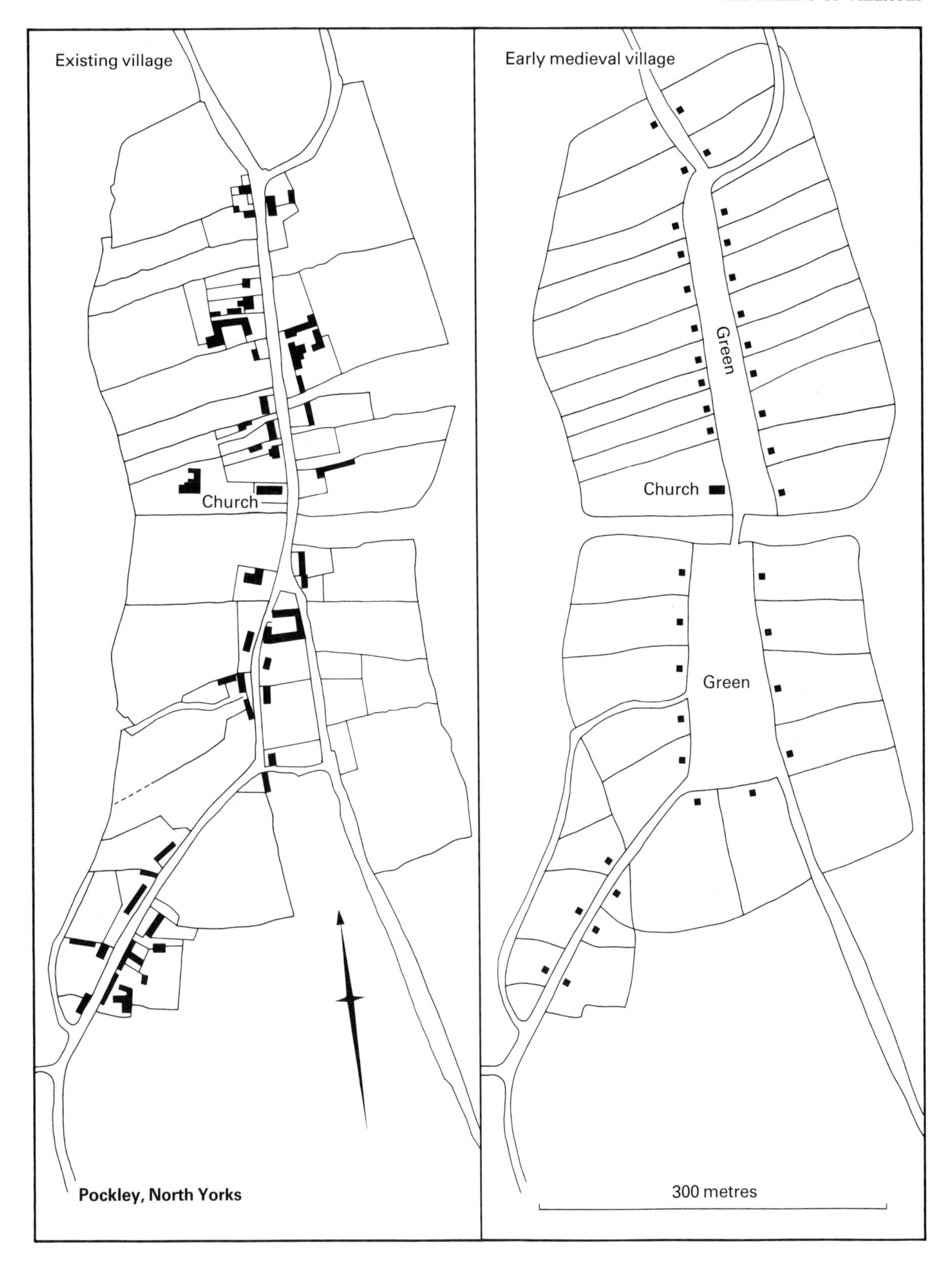
Existing village
Church
Pockley, North Yorks
Early medieval village
Green
Church
Green
300 metres

formless village lying on either side of the Wellingborough-Kettering road with its medieval church in the centre. A map of 1800, the earliest that exists, shows that at that time the village lay only to the east of the main road. It was arranged along a single street, Middle Street, with the church at the western end and with back lanes on either side named Church Street and South Street, which were also partly built up. At the east end Middle Street ran on beyond the village down to the River Ise and the mill. The back lanes turned inwards to meet the main street at the eastern edge of the village. Ground examination of the area, however, shows that the lines of both South Street and Church Street continue as deeply worn holloways running parallel with Middle Street as far as the river. In addition the sides of both holloways and the eastern extension of Middle Street are lined by the remains of former houses and gardens. Even more interesting was the evidence from air photographs, taken in 1947, which showed traces of yet another holloway, parallel to the rest and a little further south, with evidence of house sites alongside it. These remains have now been destroyed, but local archaeologists who watched the destruction were able to prove that medieval houses once stood here for they discovered their foundations and large quantities of twelfth- to fifteenth-century pottery.

Thus the original plan of Isham now becomes clear. It was not amorphous as it is today, nor a street village with back lanes as it was in 1800, but probably had four parallel streets, all lined with houses. Clearly it is difficult to explain such a plan as the result of steady growth, agglomeration or balling. Only conscious planning could have produced it and thus we may call it a planned village. But what is the date of this planning? The village is recorded in Domesday Book in 1086, though as we have seen this may not necessarily mean very much. However, an excavation carried out in 1966 at the west end of the village found evidence of extensive occupation which commenced in the ninth or tenth centuries and continued until at least the fourteenth century. The earliest material lay directly on top of the remains of an early Roman settlement which may have begun life in the late Iron Age. There was no late Roman or early or mid Saxon material. It seems likely then that Isham came into being in the ninth or tenth centuries as a planned village, though its regular plan has been distorted by later changes.

Isham is only one example of a planned grid village in Northamptonshire, a county where village forms have been intensively studied. There are fourteen other places which can be shown to have begun their lives with a plan based on a simple grid. Considering the changes which have taken place in many villages there, it is remarkable that so many original plans of this type can still be recognized. In addition there are many other villages, for example Newton Bromswold, which though of simpler form, can be identified as having planned origins (Fig. 49). In fact no less than 23 per cent of all the existing villages in Northamptonshire may well have come into being in this way, perhaps in late Saxon or early medieval times.

A similar picture is emerging from other places in the Midlands and the south. Work in Somerset by Dr A. Ellison has certainly shown that regular villages are not uncommon and Isle Abbots (Fig. 50), Long Load and Wearne, all near Yeovil, Somerset, have been recorded as especially good examples. Okeford Fitzpaine, in Dorset (Fig. 51), is

49 Newton Bromswold, Northamptonshire *This village not only illustrates the effects of massive shrinkage, but also its planned origins. The former neat and regular arrangement of crofts or gardens occupied only one side of its main street. Beyond lay arable land, still marked by medieval ridge-and-furrow ploughing.*

OVERLEAF LEFT **50 Medieval Planned Villages** *These four villages, of very varied form and from very different parts of England, all exhibit evidence of planning. Carlton, with its regular layout, is obviously planned, as is Isle Abbots. Castle Camps is known to have been established after the construction of the great castle even though its site has been largely destroyed. Braunstonbury is also now deserted, but the arrangement of the surviving traces of roads and house sites, as well as its relation to other settlements in the parish, indicates that it, too, was a planned village.*

ABOVE RIGHT **51 Okeford Fitzpaine, Dorset** *The original late Saxon village lay around the church. Probably in the twelfth or thirteenth centuries a planned extension, including a large green, was added. Subsequently this green, which lay on the right of the picture, was built over.*

BELOW RIGHT **52 Eltisley, Cambridgeshire** *Here the great triangular green as well as the name, 'the clearing of Elti', suggest an original Saxon woodland settlement. The reality is very different. The green appears to be the result of a medieval re-planning of an older village.*

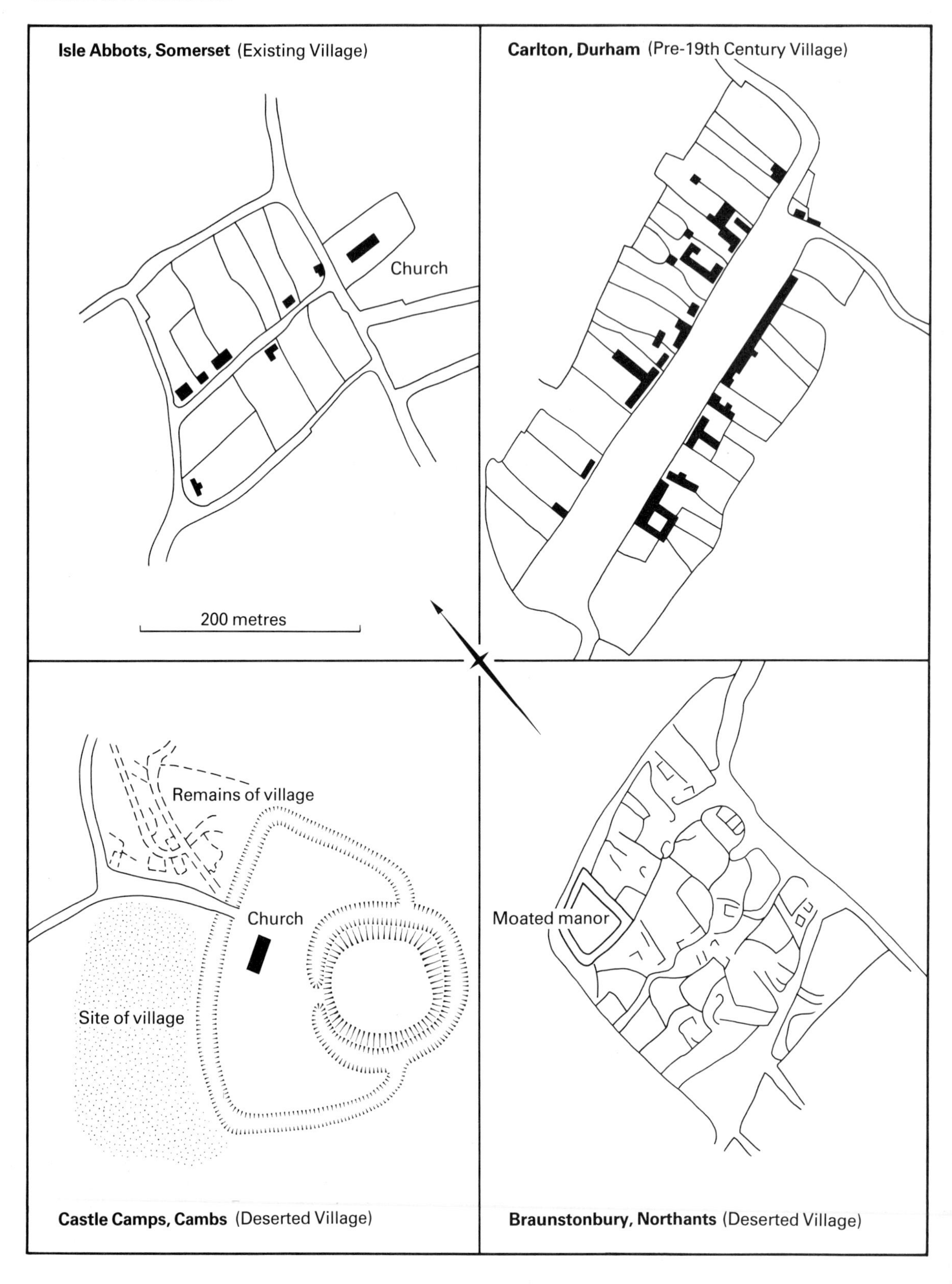
Isle Abbots, Somerset (Existing Village)
Church
200 metres
Carlton, Durham (Pre-19th Century Village)
Remains of village
Church
Site of village
Castle Camps, Cambs (Deserted Village)
Moated manor
Braunstonbury, Northants (Deserted Village)

53 Castle Camps, Cambridgeshire *The medieval church now stands alone within the ramparts of the long-deserted eleventh-century castle. It was built to serve the inhabitants of the castle and of the village which grew up around. Both village and castle were abandoned in the fifteenth century (see also Fig. 50).*

another planned village, though the green which was part of the original layout has long since been built over. Trevor Rowley, writing of the villages of Shropshire, has noted that 'there are a number of linear villages ... many of them appearing to incorporate an element of planning', and he goes on to list at least five of them. Other villages which could have had planned beginnings include Wigston Magna in Leicestershire, Old Weston in Cambridgeshire and Wickham in Hampshire. In some cases the story is complex. Eltisley, in Cambridgeshire, is a polyfocal village, made up of two quite separate parts (Fig. 52). Yet the magnificent village green is almost certainly the result of a remodelling of one half of the original village in medieval times.

Finally, there are a few places which can definitely be explained as planned villages or which can be dated to the eleventh century or soon after because they grew up around or were added to early Norman castles. The majority of Norman castles were either placed close to existing towns or villages for strategic or tactical reasons, or stood alone in isolated places and were soon abandoned, but a handful can be shown to have acquired villages after they were constructed. These villages were planned or grew up in response to the domestic needs of the castle.

An example of a village of this type is Castle Camps in Cambridgeshire, where the great motte and bailey castle of the de Vere family was planted soon after 1086 on an empty site (Figs. 50, 53). Shortly afterwards a village appeared just outside the bailey and remained there until the castle was abandoned in the fifteenth century when the village also vanished. Part of the site of the village of Castle Camps can still be recognized by its isolated church, by the remains of its old streets, now holloways, and by the slight traces of former house sites which line them. Spreads of medieval pottery from the modern arable land indicate where the rest of it once stood. As we saw at Isham, such holloways and house sites reflect the former arrangement of a village long since deserted. In contrast, some existing villages were replanned when a castle was added to them. Folkingham, in Lincolnshire, has a plan which includes a spacious green or square (Fig. 54). This may have originated in the twelfth century and was possibly laid out by Henry de Beaumont, its lord and builder of the adjacent castle.

The remains of deserted villages, which will be discussed in more detail later, can also help to prove the existence of planned villages. As many of these villages were abandoned in the fourteenth and fifteenth centuries, the form of the old streets, paddocks and gardens is likely to be much closer to the original plan than the street systems and arrangements of houses in existing villages which have been subject to changes in the more recent past. Thus surveys of the remains of deserted villages can be particularly valuable.

The survey of the deserted village of Braunstonbury, near Daventry in Northamptonshire, is a particularly good example of work of this type (Fig. 50). When the large area of apparently meaningless scarps, banks, ditches and hollows was mapped out it became clear that the village had a remarkably rectilinear plan when it was finally abandoned, probably in the fifteenth century. The whole site is contained within an almost square enclosure, with the moated manor house site in the north-west corner and two small 'greens' in the north-east and south-east. The area occupied by the houses appears to have had continuous banks dividing it into rectangular blocks. Some distortion has obviously occurred as a result of later changes, but the overall appearance is such that a deliberately planned beginning is by far the most likely explanation. Other deserted villages in the same part of Northamptonshire which also show evidence of planned layouts include Braunston Cleves in the same parish, Muscott in Norton, Glasthorpe in Flore and Newbold in Catesby. In other counties obviously planned arrangements of deserted villages have been noted. Riseholme, Croxby, Orford and West Firsby, all in north Lincolnshire, and Walworth in County Durham (Fig. 59) are exceptionally good examples.

So far we have based our argument for planned villages on their physical shape and arrangement and have only accepted the likelihood of planning where regular layouts occur. However, a more confusing picture emerges from work on the villages of Holderness, in Humberside, by Dr M. Harvey. Many of the planned villages of northern England which we have already discussed had new field systems laid out around them when they were founded. In Holderness there is similar evidence of total reorganization of field systems in the late eleventh or early twelfth centuries. Yet none of the villages there have any features which would suggest that they are planned. Harvey has examined the parish of Preston in some detail and has shown that its fields were laid out anew, probably in the late eleventh century. But the village of Preston is an extremely elongated one, consisting of a string of houses set in irregular closes and extending for nearly four kilometres. In addition there are minor nuclei in the centre and at the ends. This suggests that the present village expanded from small hamlets, that is that it is a polyfocal village rather than the result of planning. On the other hand, as Harvey has pointed out, the actual linkage between the hamlets may have coincided with the planned redevelopment of the fields. It is not beyond the realms of possibility that these links may be the result of a conscious policy to produce a linear settlement whose arrangement would then fit the new field layout that consisted of one large open field on either side of the village. Such a situation, if it is true, might mean that many thousands of villages whose layouts do not show any elements of planning could nevertheless be the result of deliberate development. This conclusion has considerable implications for the understanding of nucleated villages.

Even without this possibility there still seems to be overwhelming evidence for the fact that a large number of medieval villages were deliberately created, sometimes on new sites, but often on older ones. The period in which this happened seems to lie between the ninth and the thirteenth centuries and, if the evidence from northern England is accepted, the new villages were often created for financial or commercial reasons. At first sight this may seem curious, but the ninth century also saw the beginning of planned towns and this process of deliberate urban foundation continued until well into the fourteenth century. Thus we seem to have a period when both towns and villages were being planned, perhaps for the same reasons. It seems likely that the creation of planned settlements of whatever size or function was all part of a single process.

Where planned villages are concerned there is no need to look for basic geographical determinants in their siting. Clearly the lords responsible for the new

54 **Folkingham, Lincolnshire** *The church stands away from the present village, probably marking the site of the original settlement. The village today, with its spacious rectangular green or square, is certainly the result of planning, perhaps by Henry de Beaumont in the early twelfth century.*

villages would not have planted them in totally unsuitable situations but the 'ideal' position need not have been necessarily that which was eventually chosen. Indeed, some of the sites of planned villages look positively hostile and better positions in the surrounding area can often be found. Cold Kirby on the North York Moors, for example, is perched on the edge of a deep valley with its rectangular green neatly aligned to receive the full blast of easterly gales and with no easily accessible water (Fig. 46). Not far away is Newton-on-Rawcliffe, situated on the highest point in the area and again with no obvious water supply (Fig. 55). Here, as with many of the planned villages of North Yorkshire, there is a small pond at one end of the regular green. These ponds are probably original and very necessary features of such villages. However, despite these examples, geographical considerations were not completely ignored in every case. The regular situation of villages in south Leicestershire on the summits of dry hills, well away from the wet clay valleys, or the lines of villages at the foot of the Lincolnshire Wolds, are clearly the result of physical determinants. But the fact that not all villages in these areas conform to the general rule, and also that even within a generally favoured position there can be a variety of actual sites, shows that other factors besides geography were at work.

The only restrictions on the siting of villages were the boundaries of the territories within which their inhabitants obtained food and other basic necessities. Some of these territories, as we have already seen, were certainly already in existence in late Roman times and perhaps for long before then. By the twelfth century many had taken on a new role as parishes, for by that time numerous churches had appeared and these demanded fixed boundaries to the land which provided them with tithes, their financial support. The power of the medieval Church, once established, tended to make the boundaries of these new parishes even more permanent.

BELOW **55 Newton-on-Rawcliffe, North Yorkshire** *This pond, set at one end of the neatly planned village green, probably dates from the founding of the village in the twelfth century. It was a very necessary feature for a place set on the high moors.*

RIGHT **56 Medieval Settlements and Estates** *These three parish maps show the complexity of the settlement pattern in medieval times, as well as the internal sub-divisions or economic units into which these parishes were once divided.*

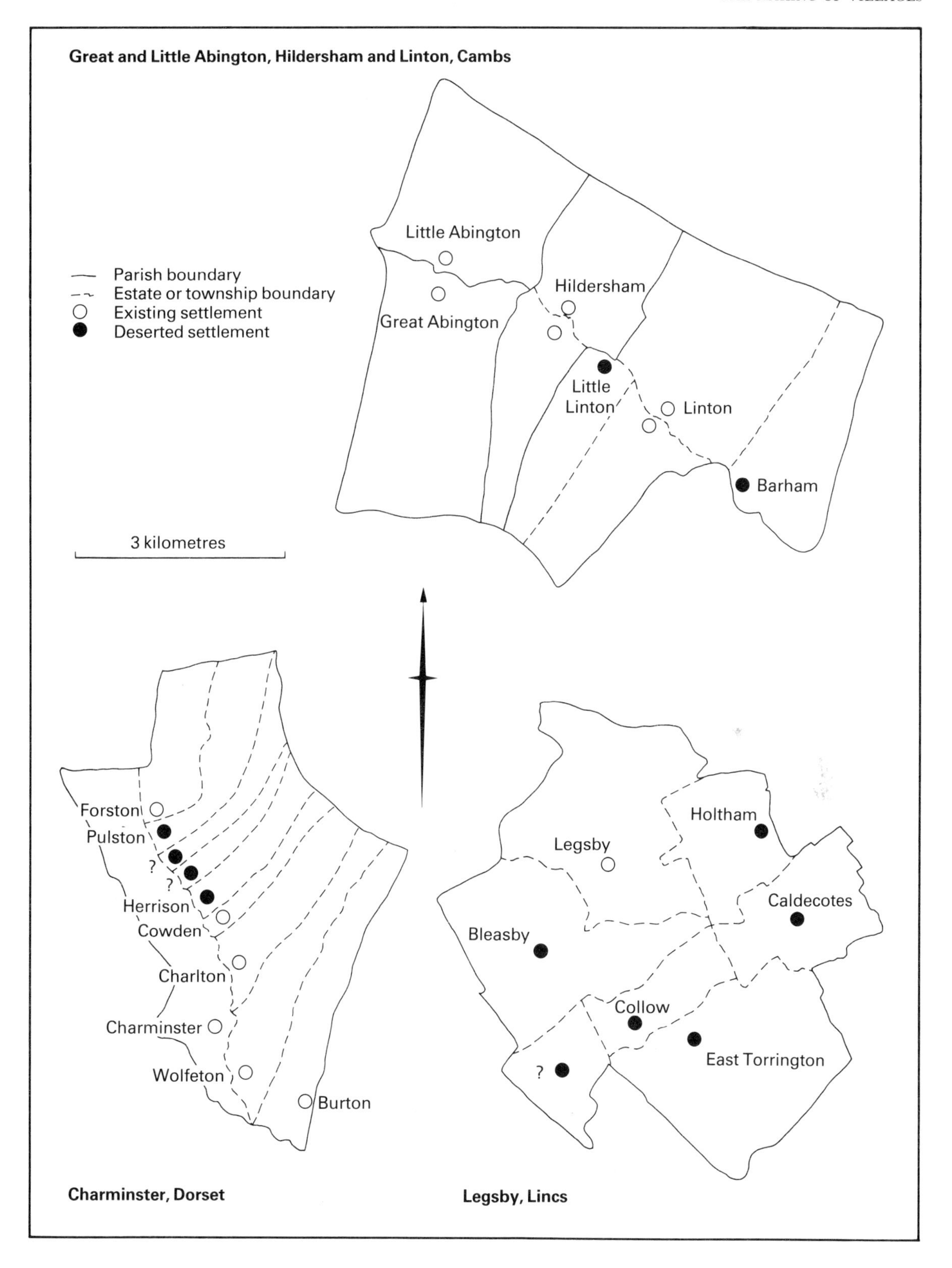
Great and Little Abington, Hildersham and Linton, Cambs
Parish boundary
Estate or township boundary
Existing settlement
Deserted settlement
Little Abington
Great Abington
Hildersham
Little Linton
Linton
Barham
3 kilometres
Forston
Pulston
?
?
Herrison
Cowden
Charlton
Charminster
Wolfeton
Burton
Charminster, Dorset
Holtham
Legsby
Caldecotes
Bleasby
Collow
East Torrington
?
Legsby, Lincs

Not all territories, however, became parishes. In many places, especially in the north of England, a single church often sufficed for very large areas of land which were made up of a number of separate territories. The parish boundaries were therefore established around groups of territories or estates which elsewhere would have been individual parishes. These territories, ultimately centred on a village or even a number of separate settlements, continued as agricultural and sometimes tenurial units and were known as townships. Even outside northern England many medieval parishes were made up of more than one estate or territory. In Northamptonshire, the parish of King's Sutton was composed of the village of King's Sutton and its land, the two separate hamlets of Upper and Lower Astrop and their land, the village of Walton and its land and the hamlets of Great and Little Purston, each with their own land units. Indeed, work in Northamptonshire has shown that almost half the medieval parishes in the county had two or more agricultural units within their boundaries.

In the chalklands of southern England the situation was just as complex. There medieval parishes were often made up of as many as six or eight land units, known as tithings, each comprising a narrow strip of land extending across the downland and into the valleys to the very small villages associated with them. At Charminster, in Dorset, there were no less than ten units of agriculture each centred on a separate village or hamlet (Fig. 56). Subsequent desertion of some of these settlements has blurred our view and only meticulous fieldwork and documentary research can indicate the original situation. Indeed, at Charminster we have evidence on the ground for settlements which are unrecorded in documents and thus we do not even know their names.

In Lincolnshire, similar work has shown that almost the whole county was once divided up into numerous agricultural units, each with its own settlement. Thus the present parish of Legsby can be shown to have been composed once of seven separate estates, again each with its own settlement, of which only Legsby has survived as a village (Fig. 56). Even in a county such as Cambridgeshire, where large single settlement parishes seem to be ubiquitous, research has revealed a similar pattern (Fig. 56). The boundaries of all these land units, which by the medieval period we can define with confidence, were probably from late prehistoric times onwards the only real determinants which controlled the siting of settlements other than the whims of their occupants.

-9-
The Changing Village

By the thirteenth century nucleated villages had appeared over approximately half of the English countryside. Although the rural landscape was now similar to that we can see today the settlement pattern that had emerged was not a stable one – the processes of movement and change that took place in earlier periods continued. In contrast to earlier changes, however, those that occurred in the thirteenth century and later took place in a period of recorded history so for the first time it is possible to produce plausible reasons for them. This is useful and interesting, not only for what it tells us about medieval settlement but also because the same factors probably caused similar changes in settlement over the previous eight or nine thousand years.

Perhaps the most important cause of settlement change is alteration in population. Though the pre-eleventh-century population of England is not known, Domesday Book of 1086 does give a rough idea of the number of people living in this country at that time and the most widely accepted figure is around 1½ to 2 million. By the early fourteenth century this had risen to around 4 to 4½ million but, with the arrival of the Black Death in 1349 and with the recurring though lesser outbreaks of the Plague later, the population of England fell catastrophically to about 2½ to 3 million before beginning to rise again in the fifteenth century. Such variations in the total number of people inevitably caused expansion and contraction of settlement on both a national and a local scale. Other factors causing settlement change which were almost as important but perhaps less obvious include climatic variation, war, border raids, changes in communication patterns, administrative decisions, commercial enterprise, as well as the effects of a continuously varying economic climate.

There are a number of aspects of physical change resulting from these influences recognizable in English medieval villages though, as will be clear, in many cases more than one may be visible. The first of these is the simplest, that of continuous uncoordinated expansion following a rise in population. As the national figures given above indicate, this was a marked feature of the twelfth and thirteenth centuries and the surviving records of many thousands of individual villages also show this. Thus, the village of Stanford on Avon, Northamptonshire, if indeed it existed then on its later site, can be estimated to have had a population of perhaps 80 to 90 in 1086. By 1377 there were probably about 170 people living there. Such an increase is by no means exceptional and thus the need for existing villages to expand physically is obvious. This growth certainly must have taken place although it is difficult to prove either archaeologically or by the examination of the physical appearance of villages. The process might have involved continuous ribbon development along existing roads or tracks leading from the village, thus accentuating the basic shape of an already linear village or one set around a road junction.

One example of this type of growth may be seen at the village of Walgrave in Northamptonshire, though there the evidence of it is only available because the expansion was quickly reversed and the newly occupied area abandoned. At Walgrave an old holloway, once a street, runs south-west from the main part of the village. Along it are the sites of former houses, each standing within an embanked plot which was once a garden. Within these gardens the faint traces of medieval plough ridges can be seen which continue undamaged beyond the rear boundaries of the plots thus showing that this part of the village was established on former arable land. This seems to indicate a sudden expansion and, shortly afterwards, an equally sudden contraction.

At Canon's Ashby, in south-west Northamptonshire, the evidence is even better and the size of the village is reasonably well documented. In 1086 it contained perhaps between 50 and 65 people. By 1301 the population had risen slightly to around 75 to 90 people, but by 1343 there were perhaps just under 200 people there. Thereafter the population fell, probably as a result of the Black Death, and in 1377 there were around 100 inhabitants. Between 1489 and 1492 the village was swept away and only the abandoned streets and house sites remain. These enable us to see how the increased population of the fourteenth century was accommodated. The presumed early part of the village lay near the parish church but at its northern end is a regular extension of house sites and former garden plots. At the rear of these plots, and between them and an old hollowed trackway through the medieval fields, is a block of very battered medieval plough ridges which have been truncated by the plot boundaries. Here again, as at Walgrave, we can see how a medieval village expanded over its own fields in response to its population explosion. Though the site has not been excavated, the existence of late thirteenth- and early fourteenth-century pottery in the area accords with the records of population and suggests that the expansion took place around 1300 or soon after.

A variant on this type of unplanned growth may be seen at Burwell in Cambridgeshire (Fig. 57). There the existing nucleated village is of complex form, but at some time in the medieval period a detached settlement appeared to the north separated from the older part by a distance of only 100 metres. This settlement, of linear form and called North Street, still exists. Its origins are indicated by the fact that it has a sinuous curve and lies parallel to and exactly matches a similar curving ridge to the east of it. This ridge was a headland between strips in the common or open fields where the plough was turned as it reached the end of each strip. It is probable that North Street was itself originally a headland with strip fields on either side. Thus, here again a village has expanded across its own fields. The date of this expansion is not known but it had certainly occurred before 1351 when North Street was recorded for the first time. At Cottenham, also in Cambridgeshire, the same type of extension over earlier fields has been identified by J. Ravensdale (Fig. 60). Both at Cottenham and at Burwell there are other complex developments which will be dealt with later.

Encroachments on former village greens, which were a way of accommodating an expanding population, often took place. In medieval times, and indeed later, village greens were not necessarily as sacrosanct as they are today. There is evidence from all over England of encroachments, though dating them is almost impossible. Barrington in Cambridgeshire has one of the largest greens in the country, yet within it there is an oval area, now occupied by houses, which has clearly been taken from the original green. No date can be assigned to this encroachment though it had certainly taken place by the early seventeenth century for some of the existing houses are of that date. At Lower Slaughter in Gloucestershire (Fig. 58), the seemingly ageless stone-built cottages that edge the stream are actually built on an earlier green, though again when the encroachment took place is not known.

The second way in which villages were changed in the medieval period was by adding planned extensions, as opposed to gradual and unorganized expansion. There is much evidence for these both from existing villages and from the layout of deserted villages. Although a rise in population is the most obvious reason for a change of this kind, there are sometimes other and more complex motives. At Sawston in Cambridgeshire a straight street, with plots measuring 80 metres by 10 metres, was laid out on the north side of the existing village

RIGHT **57 The Complications of a Village Plan**
Burwell is a typical example of a complex village whose present appearance is the result of movement, planning and expansion (see also Fig. 66).

OVERLEAF **58 Lower Slaughter, Gloucestershire**
Set on the banks of a tiny Cotswold stream, this village seems to have changed but little over the centuries. In fact these houses, or their predecessors, have been built over an earlier green which once occupied the river frontage of the village.

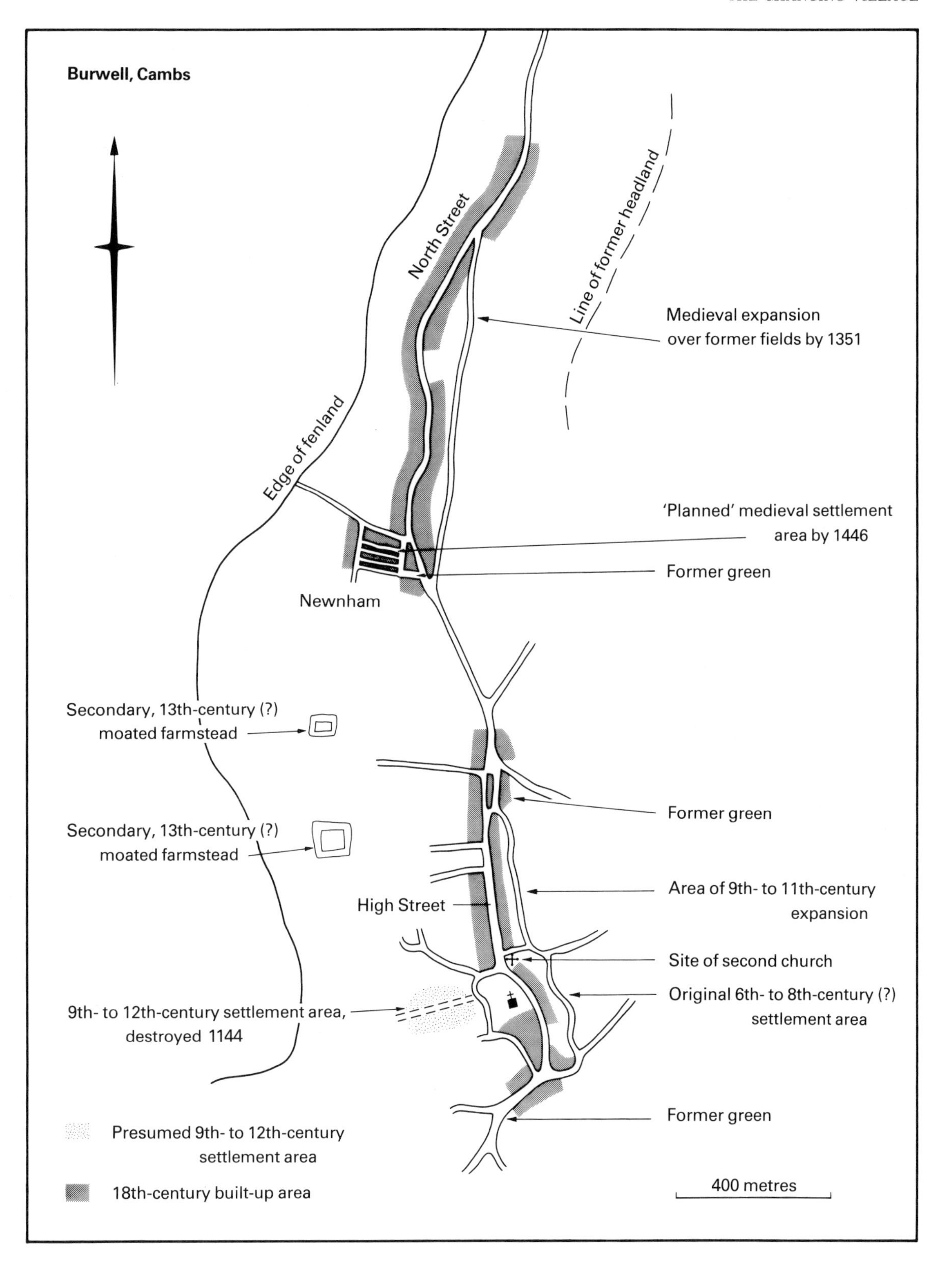
Burwell, Cambs
North Street
Line of former headland
Medieval expansion over former fields by 1351
Edge of fenland
'Planned' medieval settlement area by 1446
Former green
Newnham
Secondary, 13th-century (?) moated farmstead
Secondary, 13th-century (?) moated farmstead
Former green
Area of 9th- to 11th-century expansion
High Street
Site of second church
Original 6th- to 8th-century (?) settlement area
9th- to 12th-century settlement area, destroyed 1144
Former green
Presumed 9th- to 12th-century settlement area
18th-century built-up area
400 metres

and remains there today. At Kirk Merrington in County Durham the addition to the original village, itself planned, seems to date from about 1200. At Elkington in Lincolnshire the superbly preserved deserted medieval village has evidence of a deliberately created long extension to the east of it. In Somerset, the village of Shepton Beauchamp appears to have two planned extensions; at Sibbertoft, Northamptonshire, while there is only one extension there is also an external green around which houses have never been built. This may be an unfinished addition. At Walworth in County Durham the now deserted village also shows what is probably a planned extension (Fig. 59).

Though planned extensions are common, only in a few places has enough work been carried out to date them and to indicate their true origins. One such place is Cottenham, Cambridgeshire (Fig. 60). The village plan is highly complicated but has been worked out in detail by J. Ravensdale. The original part of the village comprises a large rectangle divided by narrow sinuous lanes. To the north lies a roughly triangular area which was in medieval times the site of the main manor house and its demesne land. It is likely that this arrangement dimly reflects a late-Saxon planned origin but more certain is that the two parts of the village which extend north and south from the old centre are later additions. The northern part, which stretches for

RIGHT **60 The Complications of a Village Plan** *Cottenham is another village which exhibits a complex story of expansion, planning and destruction throughout its life.*

BELOW **59 Walworth, Co Durham** *The modern farmstead, left of centre, stands in the middle of the almost square original village green. The traces of the houses and their gardens which once surrounded it are picked out by the light snow cover. Such a plan cannot have developed by accident and Walworth must have been a deliberate creation, perhaps of the early twelfth century. The long, narrow field in the right foreground, though ploughed over in both medieval and recent times, shows slight traces of yet more house sites aligned along a former straight street. This may represent a later planned extension to the village, probably in the thirteenth century.*

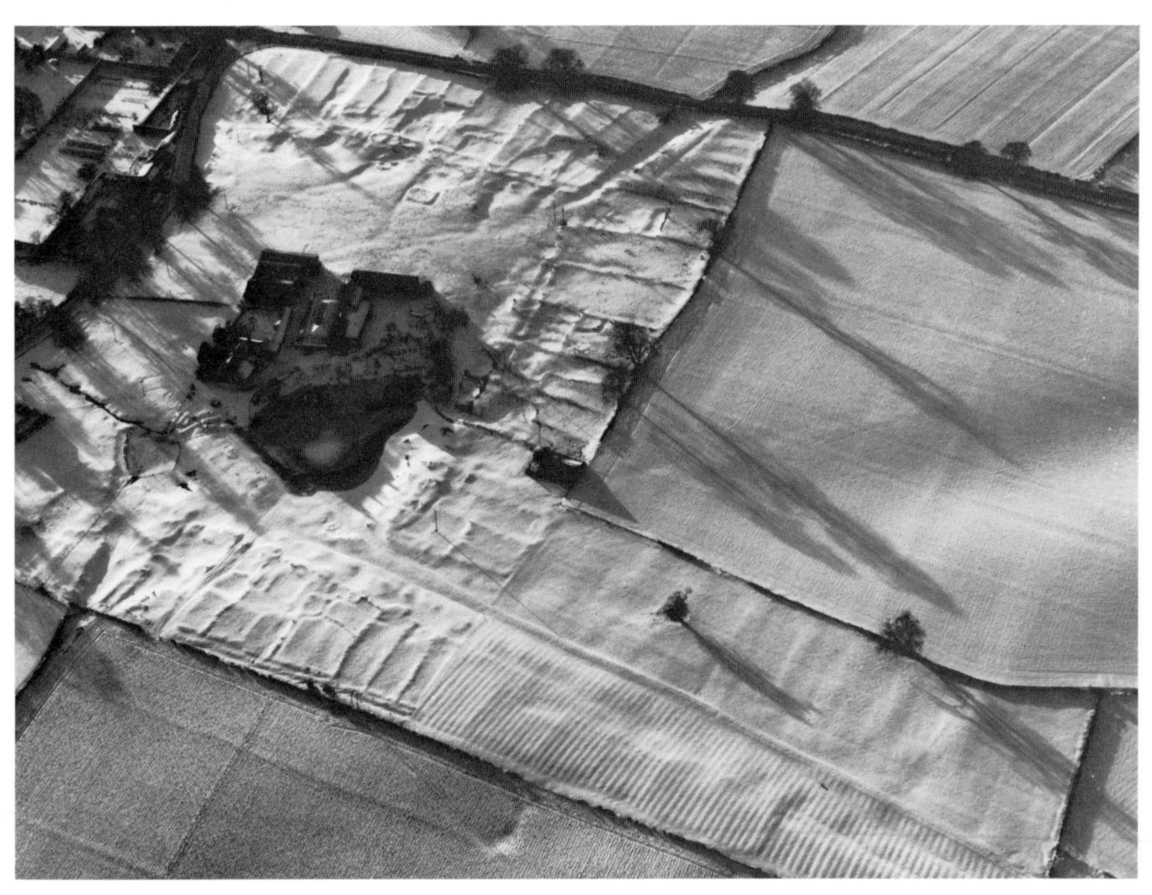

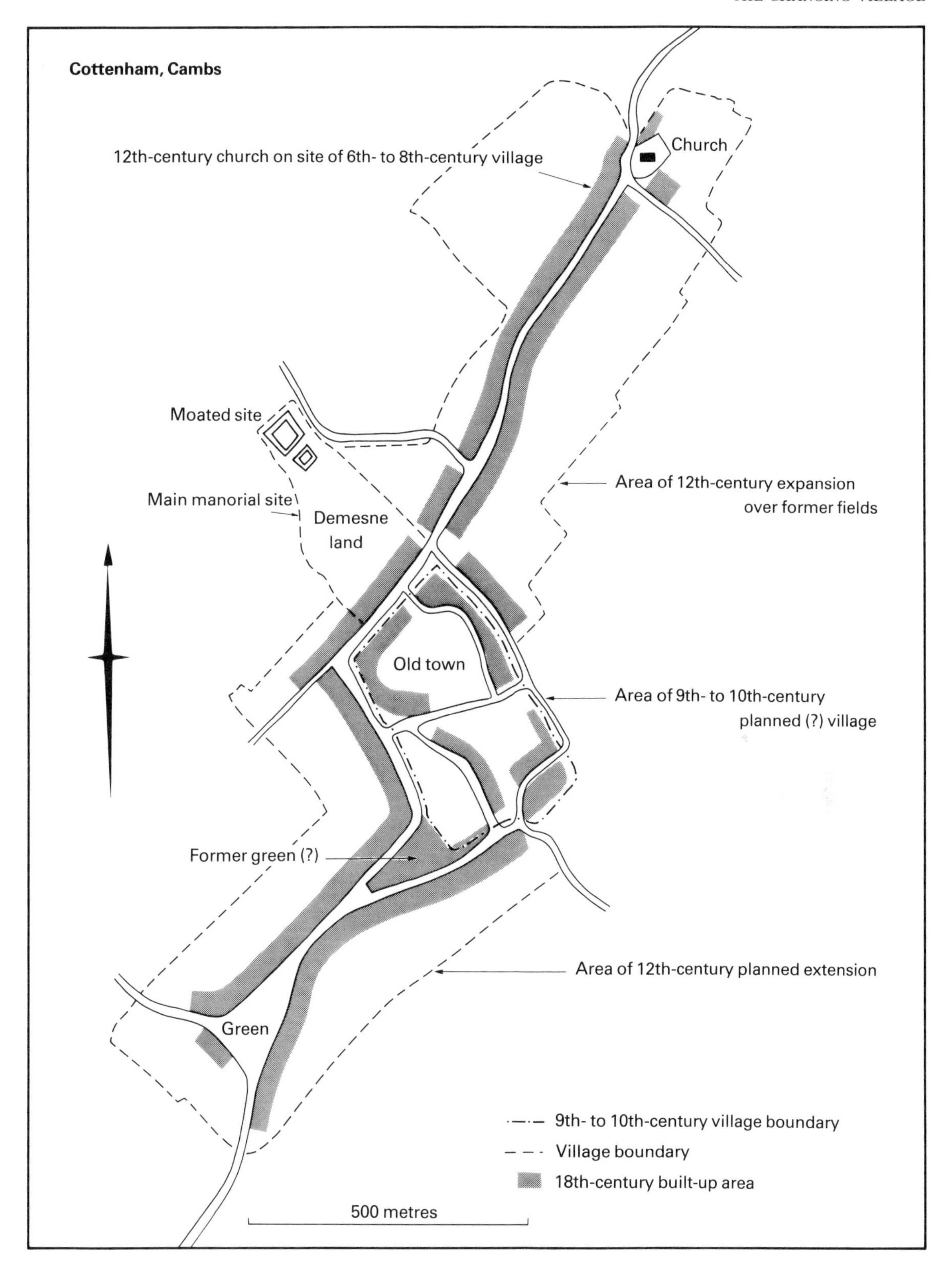
Cottenham, Cambs
Church
12th-century church on site of 6th- to 8th-century village
Moated site
Main manorial site
Demesne
land
Area of 12th-century expansion
over former fields
Old town
Area of 9th- to 10th-century
planned (?) village
Former green (?)
Area of 12th-century planned extension
Green
9th- to 10th-century village boundary
Village boundary
18th-century built-up area
500 metres

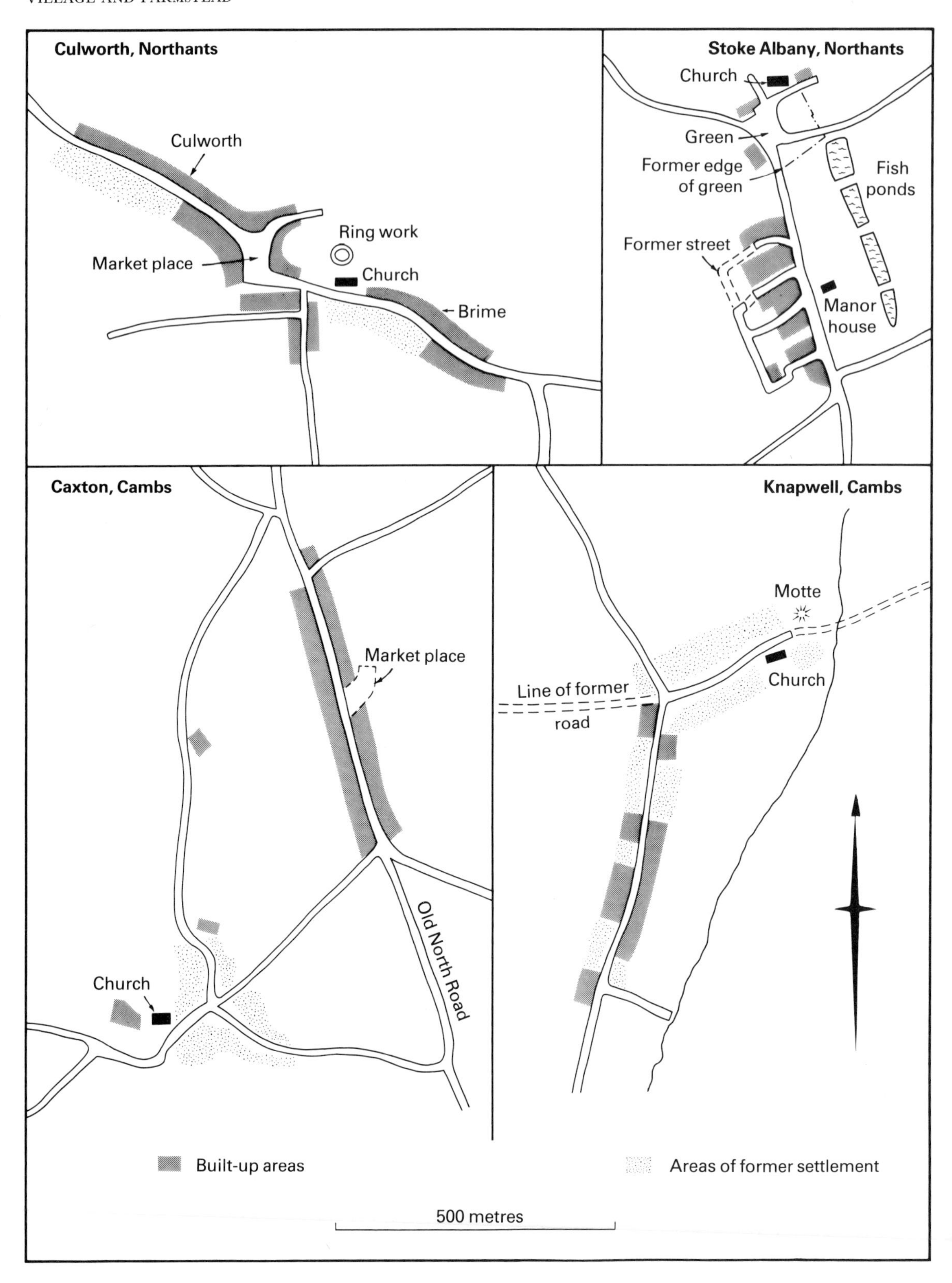
Culworth, Northants
Culworth
Ring work
Market place
Church
Brime
Stoke Albany, Northants
Church
Green
Former edge
of green
Fish
ponds
Former street
Manor
house
Caxton, Cambs
Market place
Old North Road
Church
Knapwell, Cambs
Motte
Church
Line of former
road
Built-up areas
Areas of former settlement
500 metres

almost 800 metres to the parish church, appears to have been developed over earlier strip fields whose former divisions are still preserved in the existing property boundaries. Dr Ravensdale has suggested that the church was moved to its present site in the twelfth century and that the village subsequently expanded towards it. He thought that the reason for this may have been the need to erect a new church near a fenland water course so that the necessary stone could be brought more easily to the site. While this is possible it may be that the church was positioned on the fen edge because it was an ancient sacred site, and it is more likely that the mid-Saxon village was located there before it moved south. Whatever the reason, it seems that the part of the village between the late Saxon centre and the church does represent expansion over former fields.

The southern extension is more relevant to our argument. While it too certainly lies over former strip fields, it also has a neat rectangular form, a large triangular green at its southern end and traces of what seems to be a matching green, now built over, at its northern end. This part of the village belonged to a manor which was one of a number of new fees or sub-manors created in the twelfth century by the Bishops of Ely as they strove to maximize their resources. There seems little doubt that the whole extension is a result of conscious planning.

Though less well documented, Burwell in Cambridgeshire (Fig. 57) shows the same process of expansion and planned additions – Newnham, in particular, with its neat arrangement of parallel streets, is a fine example of this process. Another village with a planned extension is Stoke Albany in Northamptonshire (Fig. 61). The original village lies on relatively flat ground near a small stream and is set around a now triangular green though the traces of an earlier and much larger green are detectable. A later part of the village lies 250 metres away on the hillside above. This consists of four roughly parallel streets laid at right-angles to the road leading south from the old part of the village and so forms a simple grid-like plan. Opposite this grid stands a superb late medieval manor house. Below the latter in a subsidiary valley lie the manorial fishponds and watermill. Though the date of the new part of the village is not known, it may be connected with William de Albini who held the manor of Stoke Albany in the thirteenth century and who certainly constructed the fishponds and also created a deer park there which still survives.

61 Change in Medieval Villages *All these villages illustrate changes long after their original establishment. At Culworth a new market place has been inserted between two separate earlier villages. Stoke Albany has had a new planned section added to it. At Caxton the village has been replanned on a new site, probably for commercial purposes, while Knapwell has turned itself through 90 degrees following an alteration to the local communication pattern.*

A very different form of addition to a village is that at Landbeach in Cambridgeshire, where the village's highly complex development has again been worked out by Dr J. Ravensdale. It was probably a planned village based on a grid that was perhaps laid out in the eleventh or twelfth century. Later ribbon development took place along the road to the south. In the fourteenth century, perhaps as a result of the Black Death, much of the old part of the village was abandoned and most of its population lived in the southern part. In the early fifteenth century the extreme northern part of the old village, then empty of buildings, was turned into a village green, apparently by the landlord, Corpus Christi College, Cambridge. This green survived until the nineteenth century when it was enclosed and built over.

This example is perhaps unusual, for although there are many other cases of village 'greens' appearing as planned additions, these were generally produced by a different method and for purely commercial reasons. The period from 1100 to 1300 was a time of considerable economic activity. This resulted in the establishment of hundreds of new towns by kings, ecclesiastics and lay lords, both great and small, who wanted to take advantage of the increasing commercial prosperity of the time. At the level of the village, this drive to increase lordly finances is evident in the number of market grants that were issued at that time, now one of the commonest documents to survive in the national archives. Such grants were issued by the Crown, often for a substantial consideration, to lords of the manor allowing them to hold weekly markets in their villages. People would then pay a suitable fee to the lord in order to conduct their business at these markets. Hundreds of villages, all over England, acquired these market grants which date mainly from the thirteenth century when trade was at its most buoyant. Few of the markets succeeded and hardly any survived the economic decline of the fourteenth century. Yet many left their mark on the villages. Numerous lords created market places in their villages and these often altered the shape of the village entirely.

In the Cambridgeshire village of Whittlesford the narrow street which runs away from the main High Street at a curious angle suddenly widens to form a small triangular 'green', with a pond on its northern side. Today it is known as 'The Green', but in earlier times was known as 'The Market Green'. It was created in 1206 alongside what was then an empty lane by the lord of the manor, Baldwin de Tony, when he received a market grant. The market had failed by 1460 but the existence of the market place led to the expansion of the village along the lane towards it instead of further along the main street as would have been expected. Thus the whole development of the village was altered and all because of a commercial venture which was not successful.

The consequences of obtaining a market grant may be seen even more vividly at the village of Caxton, also in Cambridgeshire (Fig. 61). The eleventh-century village lay about 400 metres to the west of the old Roman road, Ermine Street. Its site is now marked by the isolated parish church, abandoned holloways and considerable quantities of eleventh- to early thirteenth-century pottery in the surrounding fields. By the thirteenth century Ermine Street had regained its importance as the main road from London to the north. With the commercial potential of this road in mind the lord of the manor, Baldwin de Freville, obtained permission in 1247 to hold a market at Caxton. However he actually built the market place along the Roman road and then moved the village to it. The sharply curving boundaries of the gardens of the new Caxton, which remain to this day, show that it was laid out within the strip fields of the old village. Large monastic houses also often replanned the villages that lay near them. At Cerne Abbas in Dorset (Fig. 62) the main centre of the village, including its market place and the street leading to the gates of the great Benedictine monastery there, seems to have been entirely replanned, perhaps in the thirteenth century. Culworth in Northamptonshire is yet another example of a change in village shape resulting from a market grant (Fig. 61). In the late eleventh century there were two settlements close together, one known as Culworth and the other as Brime. In 1264 the lord of the manor was granted permission to hold a market and he laid out a square market place between Brime and Culworth. Houses and shops were built around it and the two villages became one.

Some of these examples involve the actual movement of all or part of the village. This mobility of apparently fixed nucleated villages is now known to be extremely common and took place for reasons quite unassociated with market grants. The results of movement, which enable us to recognize the process, are abandoned streets, house sites, paddocks and gardens, or occupation debris alongside existing villages. As we shall see, these are also the characteristic features of shrinkage and thus such remains must be interpreted with considerable care. Nevertheless, it is now clear that, in medieval times, movement was at least as common as shrinkage. Much of the detailed work on village movement has been carried out in Northamptonshire and many of the best-known instances are therefore in that county.

A very good example of movement has been recognized at Lilbourne in Northamptonshire (Fig. 80). The great Norman motte and bailey castle there must be a familiar sight to any observant traveller on the M1 just south of its junction with the M6. In the early twelfth century this castle and the parish church which still stands next to it were surrounded by the village of Lilbourne, then perched on the edge of the River Avon. By the thirteenth century the village had moved some 200 metres to the south on to land which had been arable up to then. The new houses were set along an old track and their gardens or yards were placed within earlier open field strips and thus curved back from the road. Later, perhaps in the fourteenth century, the village moved again, this time further to the south on to the top of a hill where it still remains. This final position was perhaps the result of deliberate planning, for the existing village is arranged around a now much reduced green whose original form was an almost exact rectangle. Not far away is the village of Yelvertoft. Here the original village lay in a narrow valley alongside its manor house. At some unknown date in the medieval period the village moved up the valley side, across its own fields and repositioned itself along an old trackway. Traces of the positions of the old houses were left behind as well as the abandoned manor

62 Abbey Street, Cerne Abbas, Dorset *This straight street once linked the village market place to the great Benedictine Abbey which stood at the far end (not the building in the photograph). The street and the market area are almost certainly the result of replanning the village, perhaps in the thirteenth century.*

The Old
Market
House

house site and, as at Lilbourne, new garden plots were created out of the curving strips of the existing fields. All these features remain on the ground today.

Such movement is also well recorded in other areas. In Cambridgeshire the village of Knapwell (Fig. 61), with its church in the centre, was originally positioned along an east-to-west trackway which led down to a small stream. We can be sure that the village was in this position in 1143 for in that year the Abbot of Ramsey, lord of the manor, built a small motte to protect the village. This motte still stands close to the stream crossing. As time went by this east-to-west trackway became less important and was replaced as a through route by the present main road 2 kilometres to the north. The most important road in Knapwell parish then became the lane leading south into the fields of the village. Gradually the village moved from the east-west road to the north-south trackway. This did not take place suddenly but over many centuries and even in the eighteenth century the old manor house still stood opposite the church. In the end, however, the village had turned through ninety degrees and expanded in an entirely new direction. But even then change continued for after the village had reached its new position another process, shrinkage, occurred producing the present scattered arrangement of houses separated by abandoned plots. The importance of changes in communication patterns, as illustrated at Knapwell, was perhaps the major factor in causing movement in medieval villages. Certainly in Northamptonshire the majority of instances of village mobility can be related to changes in the relative importance of roads. At Harringworth, for example, the original linear village, lying along a north-to-south road which ran down into the Welland Valley, eventually became an equally linear village extending east to west along the valley.

Yet not all movement was the result of changes in communications. The now isolated and ruinous church at Segenhoe in Bedfordshire is the visual reminder of a different story (Fig. 63). It appears that, by late Saxon times, there was a small village around this church. In the late eleventh or twelfth

63 Segenhoe Church, Bedfordshire *This is all that survives of the late Saxon village which moved away to a new site, probably in the twelfth or thirteenth centuries. It remained a parish church until the nineteenth century, hence the Georgian alterations.*

century a castle was erected some distance away on a prominent hill, then called (in Norman-French) Rougemont, or red hill. The result was that the village of Segenhoe gradually moved to this castle and acquired its Anglicized name Ridgmont. Here, unlike Castle Camps in Cambridgeshire, the new village survived the abandonment of the castle and remained a flourishing community. Indeed it took on a new life in the nineteenth century when it was rebuilt by the Dukes of Bedford as an estate village for Woburn Park. The inconvenient old church was then finally replaced by a new church in Ridgmont.

All the processes of alteration to medieval villages so far examined have been directly or indirectly connected with a rising population. The last process involves the reverse situation, that of a population in decline. At first sight it may seem odd that this should occur when population was, at least until the mid fourteenth century, increasing. Yet decline and abandonment did take place locally even at times of rising population and in the fifteenth and early sixteenth centuries occurred on a national scale due to economic events which had relatively little to do with population change.

Evidence of shrinkage is very widespread in English villages. It is probably safe to say that there is hardly a village in England which does not have at least one or two empty plots where houses once stood. Evidence of shrinkage varies from isolated abandoned house sites in a large, flourishing village, to very extensive areas of abandoned streets and former house sites associated with a handful of dwellings as at Ludborough in Lincolnshire (Fig. 64). At the end of the scale, of course, extreme shrinkage merges into desertion and the dividing line between the two is very difficult to define. Moreover, the reasons for shrinkage in the medieval period were often those that also caused complete desertion – desertion was rarely sudden and was usually the ultimate end of a long process of slow shrinkage. Although evidence of shrinkage is common, the problems connected with dating and explaining it are considerable. This is partly because

64 Ludborough, Lincolnshire *A fine example of a massively shrunken village with former house sites, gardens, paddocks, streets and even fish ponds now all preserved in grassland. The core of the surviving village still retains part of its original green, though this was once much larger and very rectangular. This suggests that the village had a planned origin and then expanded piecemeal before it shrank to its present size.*

the process continued all through the medieval period and indeed up to the present day but there is a lack of detailed documentation from medieval times that usually prevents the accurate identification of many presumed examples of shrinkage of that period. Furthermore, the process of shrinkage often appears to have been very complex and was not just a steady decline.

Many of the examples of medieval and later villages described and illustrated in this book have evidence of shrinkage alongside their other features. Yet in almost every case the reasons for the decline are quite unknown and very often even the time of its occurrence is not recoverable. Thus at Knapwell, Croxton and Lilbourne we know only that shrinkage had occurred before the eighteenth century, while at Culworth and Isham pottery found on the sites of the early villages suggests that the decline took place in the fourteenth or fifteenth centuries (Figs. 45, 61, 80, 84).

Though evidence of shrinkage is usually visible today in the form of abandoned settlement remains, there is other evidence which is sometimes associated with it. The village of Arrington, in Cambridgeshire, is now very small but it was clearly once much larger as the earthworks of former houses and garden plots near the church show well (Fig. 65). When did its decline take place? Surviving records show that in 1086 Arrington had between 65 and 80 people and by 1279 the population had risen to between 160 and 200. The complete rebuilding of the parish church in the late thirteenth century on a sumptuous scale was perhaps related to this large increase. By 1325 the population had fallen to around 100 to 125. The reason for this is not known, but it might plausibly be suggested that the abandonment of part of the village occurred at this

65 Arrington Church, Cambridgeshire *The seventeenth-century blocking of the arcades shows that the medieval church was greatly reduced in size at that time. This perhaps followed the considerable fall in the population of the village in the previous centuries.*

time. Yet by 1377 the population had risen again to perhaps around 150. Later it fell once more and certainly by 1676 there were only about 70 people. It was in the late seventeenth century that the parish church had its aisles demolished and their windows reset in the blocked-up nave arcades, probably because of the reduced population. Soon after the population rose again to around 100 by 1728 and to 190 by 1801. It is thus impossible, without excavation, to say whether the settlement remains relate to the early fourteenth-century decline or to the later one. The situation is complicated by the fact that the village also moved sideways at some time to reach the nearby Ermine Street and this had certainly taken place by the early seventeenth century. Arrington illustrates well the problems of identifying, dating and explaining shrinkage in medieval villages.

Though we have rightly stressed that shrinkage, and indeed desertion, are the result of a fall in population, there are examples of shrinkage, or rather abandonment, of parts of villages for very special reasons unconnected with population decline. At Burwell in Cambridgeshire (Figs. 57, 66), the land just west of the parish church is occupied by the remains of an unfinished castle built by King Stephen in 1144 as one of a series of defence works against the rebel Geoffrey de Mandeville. From field examination as well as from excavation it has been shown that this castle was built on land occupied by a street lined with houses which were deliberately destroyed to make way for the castle. The same is true at another of these twelfth-century castles, Rampton, also in Cambridgeshire. Such deliberate destruction not only altered the shape of the contemporary village but also ensured that later growth took place in new directions.

Desertion, the last of the factors that led to major changes in medieval villages, is perhaps the best known of them all though it is often misunderstood. The existence of medieval deserted villages is certainly familiar to many people but their number is perhaps not generally realized. At the present time, about three thousand have been identified with certainty and many more remain to be discovered. Desertion is thus clearly an important aspect of medieval settlement history, although the reasons why it took place are not often appreciated. In the popular mind the deserted medieval village is seen as the result of the Black Death of 1349, while more widely-read laymen will also suggest that many were wiped out by rapacious sheep farmers in the fifteenth or sixteenth centuries. Yet as always the real situation was much more complicated.

Firstly, abandonment of settlement is not just a phenomenon of medieval times. As we have already seen, desertion was common throughout prehistoric, Roman and Saxon times as merely one aspect of settlement change and movement. This same abandonment of habitation has continued to the present day. Thus there is nothing surprising in the occurrence of medieval desertion. Unless medieval times were very different from all other periods, desertion should have taken place and this is precisely what did happen. Moreover, there was no one reason why desertion took place – at any one time or in any one area it may have been linked to climatic, social or economic changes at both a local or a national level. Although it may be of considerable interest to understand why and when a particular village was abandoned, it is necessary to see the overall process of desertion merely as one aspect of settlement development.

One other point needs to be stressed. We can establish the time of and the reason for the final desertion of many villages, yet in almost every case we find that abandonment is the final act in a long drama of weakness, decline and shrinkage. Except for a few rare examples, all villages that were abandoned, for whatever reason, had certain defects which marked them out from their fellows, sometimes centuries before. They may have always been small or badly sited in relation to communications or soils. They may already have been reduced in size following climatic change, or by natural disasters, pestilence or economic forces. For whatever reason, they were already weak.

The earliest depopulations after the Norman Conquest were probably those enforced by William the Conqueror during the Harrying of the North and later in his creation of the New Forest in Hampshire. The results of the Harrying have already been discussed but in the case of the New Forest the area involved was generally poor land and the existing settlements were both small and weak. Thus they could be easily removed to provide a hunting ground for the Norman kings. It is also important to note that at least some of the villages cleared away to make the forest were later resettled, another very common but often forgotten aspect of medieval desertion which has been a feature of settlement abandonment at all periods.

It has sometimes been claimed that the Civil War of 1135–54 led to desertion, though few examples

66 Burwell Castle, Cambridgeshire *Early in 1144 King Stephen ordered the construction of this castle as part of a plan to contain a baronial rebellion led by Geoffrey de Mandeville. It was built on part of the village of Burwell which was destroyed to make way for it. Traces of the original village gardens can be seen projecting from beneath the spoil heaps outside the castle ditch near the top of the photograph. In August the same year, while still incomplete – hence the spoil heaps – the castle was attacked by de Mandeville who was killed in the assault. The whole area was then abandoned. (See also Fig. 57.)*

have been identified. Ulceby in Lincolnshire has been suggested as a victim of the war as it was clearly abandoned after 1118 and in the late twelfth century sheep were grazing on its site. Yet it, too, was repopulated and indeed it is still there today.

The twelfth century was also the period when many of the great Cistercian abbeys were founded. The rules of the order laid down that Houses should be sited in remote places away from the attractions and temptations of the world. These rules were also useful to the founders and original supporters of these abbeys as they were able to give large areas of poor land to the new Houses and at the same time gain the admiration of their friends and salvation for their souls. As a result many Cistercian Houses were founded in marginal areas and often near settlements which inevitably were small and weak and which could be cleared away without major difficulties. The Cistercian Abbey of Pipewell in Northamptonshire, founded in 1163, was established on the site of the village of Pipewell which then lay on the edge of the great medieval Rockingham Forest. Pipewell was a small settlement with perhaps only thirty or forty people living there in 1086 and so was easily swept away to make room for the new abbey. Yet when the abbey was dissolved in 1538 and its magnificent buildings demolished, the village of Pipewell was re-established. By 1720 at least twenty people lived there and today its population is about the same as it was in 1086.

Surprisingly, perhaps, there was considerable depopulation in some areas during the prosperous times of the thirteenth century. This is especially true of Norfolk where a number of villages which were abandoned during this period have been identified. Here Dr P. Wade Martins has suggested that over-exploitation of relatively poor soils in the face of a continuously rising population finally took its toll and forcibly ended the lives of some villages. One such is Grenstein in central Norfolk which seems to have disappeared some time after 1266. Its last inhabitants apparently drifted away to nearby Tittleshall. In many other places, too, the inhabitants of villages on marginal land over-exploited the soils, and though these places often survived they were seriously weakened, shrank to small hamlets, and were thus more susceptible to pressures on them in the succeeding centuries. In the same general period there was another factor which, in the extreme north of England, both weakened and killed many smaller settlements. This was the incessant Anglo-Scottish warfare and, more especially, the almost continuous small-scale raids across the border.

Later, in the early fourteenth century, general economic decline set in all over the country. From late Saxon times until the thirteenth century, climatic conditions for arable agriculture were exceptionally good, indeed far better than today. It has been estimated that even in upland areas the chances of crop failure were as little as one year in twenty. But from the late thirteenth century the climate became colder and wetter and the chances of crop failures increased dramatically to a maximum in the late fourteenth century, when the crop in one year out of three failed on marginal land. Documented examples of desertion as a result of climate deterioration are rare but archaeological excavation can show this process quite well. At the deserted villages of Barton Blount in Derbyshire and Goltho in Lincolnshire, the excavator was able to show that by the late fourteenth century the heavy clay lands surrounding these villages were becoming too difficult to cultivate, apparently because of increased rainfall. The result was an abandonment of arable land and a change to pastoralism, in these cases to cattle ranching. This in turn meant that the villages were almost completely abandoned and the inhabitants moved away, often to other villages on drier land which, in any case, had had their own populations devastated by plague and where there was thus room for the new immigrants.

This brings us to perhaps the best known of the factors which caused desertion, the Black Death of 1348–9. This plague was certainly devastating in its immediate effects as it has been estimated that it cut the population of England by up to a half. Yet, the appalling suffering apart, it seems that the Black Death did not actually cause permanent desertion of many villages. Detailed research has consistently failed to identify more than a handful of English

villages which can be proved definitely to have disappeared at this time. Tusmore in Oxfordshire is almost the only village in that county which seems to have been abandoned after the plague. It paid no tax in 1355 and in 1357 it was said to be 'void of inhabitants since their death in the pestilence'. In Northamptonshire, where more than eighty deserted villages are known, only two, Hale and Elkington, were abandoned because of the Black Death. Certainly many villages were left temporarily devoid of all inhabitants, but within a few years they were repopulated. Cowesfield, in Whiteparish, Wiltshire, was described in 1349 as of no value because the tenants were dead from the plague. But by 1361 'divers tenants' were paying rent and the village still exists, although it is rather small. Similarly, at Combe, near Woodstock in Oxfordshire, the village was abandoned in 1350, probably because of the plague. Yet within fifty years it had been re-established, not on its original site, but on the hilltop above. The new village was apparently planned because it now has a rectangular green and its adjacent church, dated to 1395, also appears to be a new addition. Such evidence of post-plague resettlement accompanied by replanning is not uncommon. At Wawne in north Humberside (Fig. 80), the village in the twelfth and thirteenth centuries consisted of a dozen or so peasants' houses arranged rather haphazardly. In the late fourteenth century this arrangement was abandoned and a new settlement appeared a little way to the south. This consisted of a row of houses laid out on one side of a single street. The rearrangement is unlikely to be anything but a replanning of the village, presumably carried out by the lord of the manor and probably following depopulation as a result of the Black Death. The new village itself lasted only a short while and then it too passed into oblivion.

The most important effect of the Black Death was not that it caused the abandonment of villages but that, combined with climatic deterioration and economic decline, it paved the way for later depopulation in the fifteenth century. Small villages were reduced in size and weakened, large villages became much smaller and people moved from the more marginal villages to those which were better placed with regard to either soils or communications. Thus, by about 1450, when the late-medieval demand for wool for the expanding textile industry began, when the demand for cereals was small because the population of England had not recovered from the Black Death, and when the agricultural labour force was in a position of strength and could demand high wages, it was inevitable that pastoral farming would expand. This took place at the expense of labour-intensive arable and led to the clearance of many of the poorer and smaller villages, such as Easton Neston in Northamptonshire (Fig. 67). In many places villages vanished by the score to be replaced by sheep, although cattle also played their part in some areas. The allegedly rapacious landlords of the late fifteenth century saw that their only means of personal survival was to turn their land over to sheep or cattle and thus where possible they removed or expelled their village tenants. This could only be done in places where the villages were already weakened by plague, climatic deterioration or economic decline. Such villages easily fell prey to enclosing lords or even tenant farmers and the result was that the Midlands and the east of England are today dotted with the sites of villages finally extinguished at this time.

In contrast, those villages which had survived the earlier disasters and changes reasonably well, or had received an influx of new settlers from other declining villages, were difficult or impossible to remove by even the most self-willed lord. At Landbeach, Cambridgeshire, for example, there is evidence that the lords of one of the manors there had for a long time in the late fifteenth and early sixteenth centuries attempted to clear part of the village in order to run sheep. The crisis came in 1549, by which time Richard Kirby, one of the lords, had managed to remove a group of houses in the centre of the village and replace them by grass closes which still exist. Then Kirby came into head-on conflict with the peasantry of the rest of the village as well as the lord of the other manor in Landbeach. Kirby's progress was halted and the village was saved. The fact that Landbeach was a prosperous and well-populated village gave it a distinct advantage over those which were small and weak. This situation was also probably affected by

67 Easton Neston, Northamptonshire *The medieval church in the trees beyond the great late-seventeenth-century house indicates that there was once a village here. Yet it was not destroyed to make room for the house. It was cleared away in the late fifteenth century by Richard Empson who turned the land over to sheep. On the other hand, the village was always very small and Easton Neston House has probably had as many people living in it as there were in the old village. Has the site ever really been deserted or has it merely changed its function?*

the fact that, by the mid sixteenth century, the price of wheat was rising again, the wool market was depressed and the incentive for continued depopulation for sheep was sharply reduced. The pressures and motives that continued to result in changes to and abandonment of villages from now on were to be very different.

Villages also disappeared in medieval times for rather more special reasons. Coastal erosion, especially along the east coast, removed not only inhabitants but the actual sites of villages. A whole group of settlements around the mouth of the Humber disappeared in this way in the fourteenth and fifteenth centuries and others vanished from along the coast of East Anglia at the same period. Milton, in Essex, lay somewhere near the present pier at Southend-on-Sea.

In this long and complex discussion of nucleated villages in the medieval period we have been concerned with those that either still remain as living entities or which can be traced by name or by the existence of upstanding earthworks of former streets, houses and gardens. Almost all these can be shown to have been once surrounded by their medieval fields and located either within one ecclesiastical parish or within a township which was part of a larger parish. That is, these are part of the traditional village – fields – parish pattern of large parts of southern, midland and northern England.

However, recent research has revealed the existence of a hitherto totally unsuspected substratum of medieval settlements which were in some way connected with these villages. These settlements are not apparently the result of colonization of wastes, forests, uplands and marshes, which we will be looking at in the next chapter, though exactly what they do represent is not entirely clear. Their existence has been revealed by the intensive examination of land now under cultivation, which has destroyed all traces of visible remains except for scraps of pottery, bones and other rubbish which can still be found. A good example of the method of discovery and the problems it poses has been provided by work in Haslingfield in Cambridgeshire. The present village is, and always has been. large and prosperous. It shows within it evidence of planning, expansion and contraction. Until 1820 it was surrounded by open fields which occupied the whole area of the parish except along the edges of the River Cam where there was common meadowland divided into small hedged paddocks. Recent field walking along the river has shown that these paddocks were laid out on the site of a small settlement which, to judge from the pottery found, was occupied in the tenth and eleventh centuries. Other than this information, nothing is known of this settlement. It has no recorded name in any document, and no written history. It appears to have come and gone as quickly and as mysteriously as its prehistoric and Roman predecessors, the remains of which have also been found elsewhere in the parish.

Similar un-named and completely unrecorded settlements have been found in many parts of the Midlands, notably in Northamptonshire, and their existence does little except to confuse the accepted view of medieval settlement in this part of England. In southern Northamptonshire, the parish of Furtho has within its boundaries the site of a deserted village, always known as Furtho. Surviving documents tell us exactly what the population was from the eleventh century until the early sixteenth century when it was finally abandoned. This information has been known for many years but recently the ploughed-out site of another small deserted settlement has been found, certainly occupied in the thirteenth and early fourteenth centuries though not later. Again it is unrecorded in documents and seems to have had no name unless it was also called Furtho, a strong possibility. If this was so then all the documents which mention Furtho are in fact referring to two villages. Elsewhere in Northamptonshire, notably in the adjacent parishes of Grendon, Cogenhoe, Earl's Barton, Castle Ashby and Great Doddington, the remains of secondary settlements have been found (Figs. 39, 71). Two were apparently in existence in the eleventh century, three not until the twelfth century and all but one had disappeared by the fifteenth century. Here, at least, four names are known, two were called Cotton and two called Thorpe. But how and why they came into existence, how they related to the main villages in their parishes, and why they vanished is not known.

Work in Bedfordshire has also produced a confusing pattern of medieval settlement in an area traditionally said to be a typical midland county with nucleated villages. The most notable instance is the parish of Carlton cum Chellington, north of

68 Wharram Percy, North Yorkshire *In this well-watered chalk valley the ruined church now stands alone on the site of a once-flourishing village. Yet this village had only a very short life of little more than three hundred years.*

Bedford (Fig. 71). The name suggests that the parish once had two villages, Carlton and Chellington. Carlton still exists and Chellington is a deserted village whose abandoned streets and house sites lie around the now isolated Chellington church. This explanation appeared acceptable until the area was examined more carefully. Then in the eastern, Chellington, part of the parish two other separate deserted villages were found of which there is no record in any documents and which have no known names. Further research showed that the existing village of Carlton was once regarded as two villages. The eastern part, a long north-to-south street, was called Chellington and the western part, an east-to-west street and a separate green settlement, was known as Carlton. The extreme south-west end of Carlton was yet another separate settlement, also perhaps known as Carlton. In addition it was noticed that the parish church of Carlton lay in an isolated position to the west of Carlton village, perhaps indicating an earlier site of Carlton, while further west again a small moated site was proved to be a major manorial settlement of at least thirteenth-century date. This pattern was subsequently found in a number of other adjacent Bedfordshire parishes. The whole landscape there seemed to be dotted with existing and deserted settlements of various sizes and dates in a totally confusing pattern. It is this type of work that indicates how little we know of the complex and constantly changing arrangement of settlement which is obscured by the apparently neat layout of nucleated villages that we can see today.

At the beginning of this chapter it was suggested that, taking the long view from prehistoric times to the present day, nucleated villages with their relatively recent appearance and restricted distribution were perhaps an unusual feature of settlement rather than the norm. This certainly seems to be so, and indeed in many places in England the nucleated village seems to be a transitory feature in the total history of settlement. Nowhere is this to be better seen than at the deserted village of Wharram Percy on the Yorkshire Wolds.

Over thirty years ago Mr J.G.Hurst and Professor M.W.Beresford began excavations there in order to discover when the large nucleated village of Wharram, then judged to be of early Saxon origin, was finally deserted (Fig. 68). Excavations have continued steadily ever since, thus making it arguably the most important archaeological work of any period in this country. While many facts remain to be explained about the history of Wharram Percy, certain features are now clear. Throughout prehistoric and Roman times, perhaps for five thousand years or so, people lived on the land that we now know as the township of Wharram. During those centuries they always lived in dispersed farmsteads and hamlets scattered across the landscape. In Saxon times the picture was no different and by the late eleventh century, when Domesday Book was written, Wharram still consisted of two small separate hamlets. It was not until the twelfth century that the village became nucleated and this seems to have been the result of a conscious piece of planning although the new arrangement was fitted into a pre-existing and perhaps Roman layout of boundaries. Only at this late date did Wharram become a typical English village. Yet by the early sixteenth century, after little more than three hundred years of existence, the village had disappeared and the old pattern of dispersed settlement had reasserted itself. Here, better than anywhere else, the real significance, or rather insignificance, of nucleated villages can be appreciated.

-10-
Hamlets and Farmsteads

Over large parts of England nucleated villages did not appear. Outside the broad north-to-south belt where villages are the normal form of settlement, hamlets and farmsteads predominate, reflecting a pattern of settlement which has been established for millennia. It is not at all clear why this dichotomy between the areas of nucleated and dispersed settlement should have developed. Non-nucleated settlement was certainly a feature of some areas where the population remained generally low and where there was therefore little or no pressure on the land. This is obviously true of large parts of south-west England. But there are many other areas, such as Essex, where there was considerable population growth in the early medieval period and yet where the dispersed pattern of settlement remained. In such areas there is no obvious explanation for what happened, or rather did not happen – there are no apparent physical causes, or obvious racial, political, tenurial or social factors which could explain the continuing existence of dispersed settlement. As so often in the history of rural settlement in England, we have some idea of what happened and when but cannot explain the mechanics involved.

The classic area of dispersed settlement, largely as a result of the work of W.G.Hoskins, is south-west England. There ancient farmsteads and small clusters of houses dot the landscape and such villages that do exist can be proved to be of relatively late date, often resulting from quite recent growth. A splendid example of the settlements typically found here is Zennor, on the coast of Cornwall, where the medieval parish church stands almost alone except for a scattered group of farmsteads (Fig. 69). Perhaps even more typical is Luppitt, in Devon, where winding lanes link isolated farmsteads like beads on a string (Fig. 70).

The history of farmsteads such as these shows that they are part of a dispersed pattern of settlement that has been there since at least late Saxon times. For example, Exbourne to the north of Okehampton in Devon still shows the same pattern of settlement that existed in the late eleventh century (Fig. 71). The name Exbourne refers to a tiny village and also to an area of land or township. Today this township contains ten isolated farmsteads as well as the village and Hoskins has shown that all ten farmsteads were in existence in 1086, occupied by people listed in Domesday Book as villeins. In effect there has been no change in the number of settlements, or in their dispersed arrangement, since that date, though whether all the farmsteads remain on their original sites is a question to which we shall return later.

This dispersed pattern, which is common to large areas of Devon and Cornwall, has often been explained as a cultural phenomenon. It is obvious that the Saxons arrived in south-west England much later than in south-eastern England, perhaps not until the seventh century, and then only in small numbers. There is therefore a case for arguing that such a dispersed pattern of settlement is a remnant of the late prehistoric or Roman one. This is indeed likely, though there is good evidence that not all the

69 Zennor, Cornwall *The parish church does not stand in a village, for there was never a village here, but close to a group of farmsteads. These farmsteads have been here for at least a thousand years, though not perhaps on exactly the same sites. They may have been here for much longer as some of the adjacent fields are prehistoric in origin.*

70 Luppitt, Devon *A typical scene in south-west England where only scattered farmsteads exist amongst the tiny, irregular fields. Most of these farmsteads were certainly in being by the eleventh century but they are probably much older. They perhaps stand on or near sites occupied since at least the Bronze Age, though we cannot tell at the present time.*

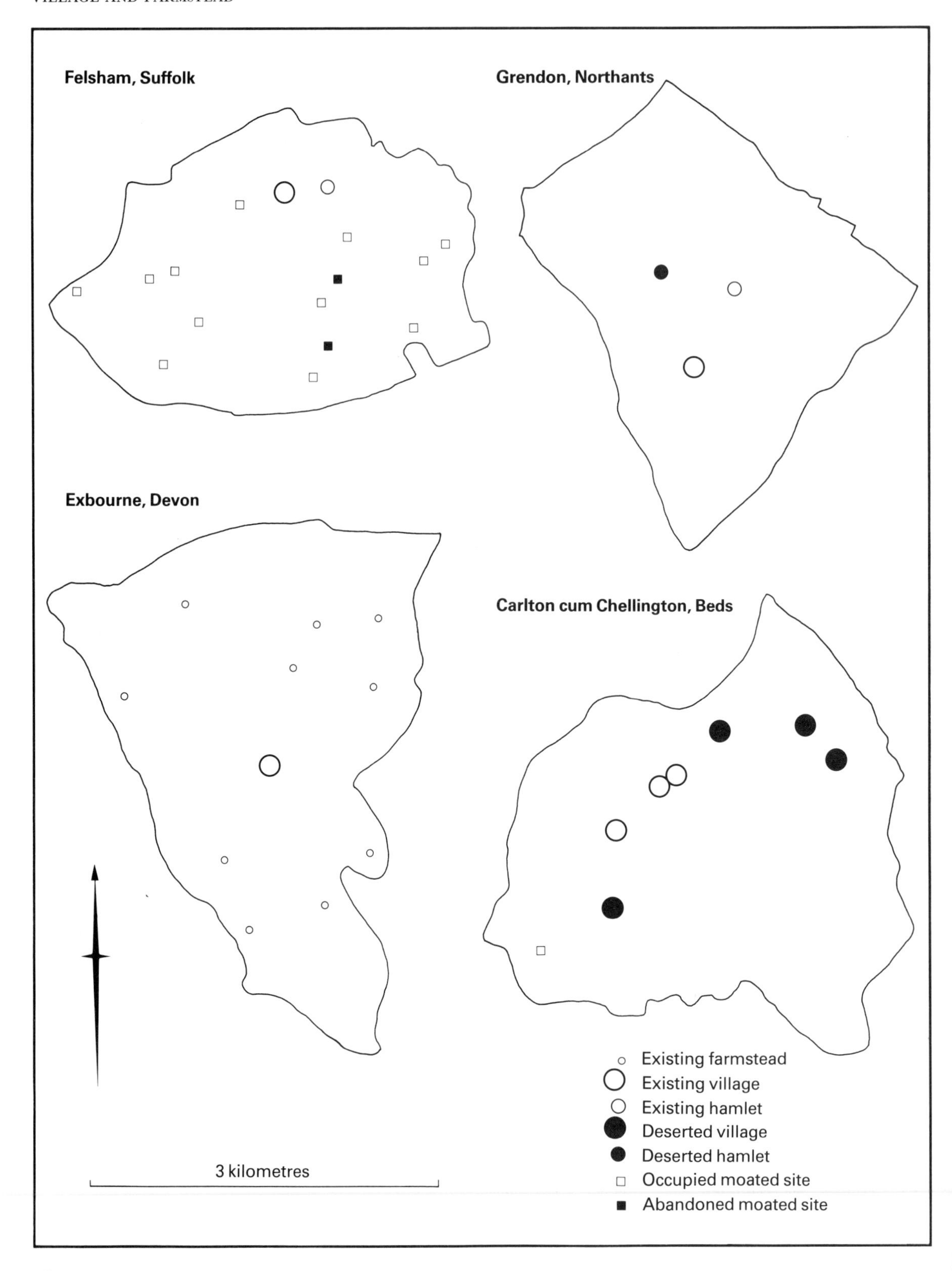
Felsham, Suffolk
Grendon, Northants
Exbourne, Devon
Carlton cum Chellington, Beds
Existing farmstead
Existing village
Existing hamlet
Deserted village
Deserted hamlet
Occupied moated site
Abandoned moated site
3 kilometres

actual sites were necessarily occupied continuously. At least some of the individual farmsteads seem to have changed their positions between Roman and late Saxon times, just as they did in the prehistoric period. There are several ancient farmsteads whose land also contains the site of a late prehistoric or Roman 'round', probably indicating the earlier positions of the present farmsteads.

Nor have these farmsteads necessarily remained in their late Saxon positions. Without massive excavation, it is obviously difficult to prove that farmsteads have indeed moved, but in some cases such movement has been identified. Penhallam, in north-east Cornwall, is a typical Cornish settlement with an isolated parish church and a scatter of farmsteads set in a deep sheltered valley. One of these farmsteads, Berry Court, has a moated and embanked ringwork adjacent to it which has been excavated. Domesday Book suggests that this ringwork was the site of the manor house of Penhallam before the Norman Conquest. Excavations by Mr G. Beresford, however, revealed that the ringwork was probably not constructed until after 1066 and was then occupied until about 1260 when it was abandoned. Though there was some late-Saxon occupation beneath the ringwork, there was nothing earlier. Thus, though the 'site', in its widest sense, may possibly have been occupied for a very long time, the excavation showed that on at least one part of it occupation lasted for only four hundred years at the most. In addition the occupied area had two different functions and layouts during that time and the occupation both before and after lay elsewhere. Thus even in the area of England that is alleged to have the oldest settlement pattern, movement and change are visible and may be proved.

Moving a little further east, in south-east Somerset, too, the predominant pattern of modern settlement is one of hamlets and farmsteads. Work by Mr M. Aston has indicated that this pattern is not only an old one but that it too has been subjected to change and movement. Here the classic example is the parish of Mudford, just north of Yeovil. Today the parish contains Mudford itself, technically a village but one of very recent growth, the four small hamlets of Up Mudford, West Mudford, Mudford Sock and Hinton, together with one old farmstead known as Stone Farm. From medieval documents and fieldwork it has been shown that there were, by the early fourteenth century, eight settlements in the parish, including all the above but in addition the hamlets of Nether Adber and Mudford Terry, both of which have now disappeared. It is also clear that Hinton and West Mudford were then much larger and have subsequently shrunk in size and that Up Mudford too is somewhat smaller than it was once.

Of these eight settlements, Mudford, Stone, Nether Adber and Up Mudford are listed in Domesday Book and thus must have existed at that time, though not necessarily in the form nor indeed on the exact sites that they had later. It is also likely that Hinton is recorded in Domesday Book, though under a different name, and that one other settlement is also listed under Up Mudford, which is recorded twice. This suggests that of the eight settlements in the parish in the fourteenth century at least seven existed in 1086. It is therefore impossible to explain the pattern of settlement in Mudford as the result of later medieval colonization. If it is colonization then it dates from the end of the Saxon period at the latest, but it is more likely to be part of a much older arrangement.

Here then, as in Devon and Cornwall, the evidence indicates an ancient pattern of dispersed settlement, typical of the Celtic west. If, however, we look at some parts of England known to have been settled by the Saxons at an early date, we find much the same pattern. Rivenhall, in Essex, which has been the subject of long-term research by Dr and Mrs W. Rodwell, shows this well. Rivenhall is typical of much of Essex in that there is no old village in the parish and until recent development the church and manor house stood alone. Beyond is a scatter of individual farmsteads, almost all of which are recorded by name in thirteenth-century documents. Excavation has shown that the area round the church has had a long history of almost continuous occupation from an Iron Age farmstead, through a Roman villa, to a succession of Saxon and medieval halls or manor houses, all of which seem to have lain in slightly different positions. These occupation sites all seem to have been the centre of a large estate, probably the present parish. Detailed documentary analyses and fieldwork have shown

71 Medieval Dispersed Settlement Forms *These maps of four widely separated medieval parishes indicate the variety of medieval settlement patterns. At Felsham and Exbourne the pattern was mainly a highly dispersed one, perhaps originating in prehistoric or Roman times. At Grendon and Carlton villages and hamlets predominate. Subsequent desertion, with a resulting simplification of the pattern, is visible in all the parishes except Exbourne.*

that the existing farmsteads were on or adjacent to their present sites by early medieval times, and perhaps since the late Saxon period. On the other hand, they all seem to have had Roman or in some cases even Iron Age predecessors sometimes situated very close by, or at least within their associated fields. Here then, in a truly 'Saxon' area, there is a pattern of dispersed settlement very similar if not identical to that of the 'Celtic' west.

Evidence for the continuation of the old pattern of dispersed settlement can also be found in another area deep in the zone of 'primary Saxon settlement', the Weald of south-east England. It has always been assumed that the first Saxons settled in Kent and Sussex around the edges of the great forested area now called the Weald. They then subsequently pushed into the forest, clearing the woodland and establishing the farmsteads and hamlets that exist there, thus producing a true landscape of secondary or colonizing settlement. Again, place-name evidence supports such a theory for there are numerous names which are indicative of late woodland occupation. Inevitably, however, the true picture is not as simple as it seems at first sight.

The dispersed pattern and the secondary names certainly exist but the traditional interpretation conflicts with the evidence from another source. In a number of places an accident of ancient tenurial history has preserved Saxon land charters which describe the boundaries of large areas in the seventh and eighth centuries. One of these, dated 765, refers to a number of settlements in the deepest recesses of the Weald between Lewes and East Grinstead, in East Sussex. In West Hoathly parish the present farmsteads of Stonelands, Chiddingly and Phillpotts are all recorded, as is Walstead Farm in Lindfield parish. The usual explanation is that these places had been settled by colonizing Saxons by the eighth century. What is rarely questioned is that, if such places were recorded almost by accident in the eighth century, could they really be of such recent origin? Stonelands and Walstead are described in the charter as swine pastures of Stanmer, a place on the South Downs near Brighton, almost 20 kilometres to the south. This implies a complex relationship between settlements which is unlikely to have come into being in the eighth century. In other words, these Wealden settlements must have been at least two hundred or three hundred years old by the time they were recorded in 765, which would mean that they may be of fifth- or sixth-century origin. Such a date puts them less than two hundred years away from similar Roman settlements in the Weald which may also have been the centres of swine pastures for the Roman villages which lay along the South Downs.

It may be that these Wealden farmsteads, far from being the results of Saxon colonization, are merely the successors of a much older pattern of settlement which existed in Roman times and may indeed have originated in the prehistoric period. Work by Mr T. Tatton-Brown on the trackways linking the major settlements of north Kent to the minor swine pasture settlements of the Weald has suggested that these tracks are actually earlier than the system of Roman roads in the same area. Once more the antiquity of the dispersed pattern of settlement over much of England seems apparent.

While it is thus likely that the pattern of dispersed settlement in some parts of the country is very old, it is also possible to identify settlements of this type which are the result of medieval colonization of hitherto unoccupied marginal land i.e. medieval secondary settlement in its usually accepted sense. The most notable areas where this took place were the upland moors of south-west and northern England, the estuarine marshes of south-eastern and eastern England, the relatively recently forested areas of the Midlands and southern England, the Somerset Levels, the eastern fenlands and the open heaths of the south. In addition there was other 'secondary settlement' in all those regions dominated by nucleated villages. Even where such colonization seems obvious, however, the true picture may be more complicated than it appears. An area which shows this well is Shenstone parish, near Lichfield, Staffordshire. The parish lies on the eastern edge of, and extends into, what was in medieval times the Royal Forest of Cannock. In addition to what was, before modern development, the rather straggling and small village of Shenstone, there are the hamlets of Upper and Lower Stonnall, Chesterfield, Hilton, Thornes, Lynn, Little Aston, Footherley, Little Hay and Woodend, as well as a number of isolated farmsteads. The location of the parish, its scattered settlement and the obvious 'secondary' and 'woodland' names of some of the hamlets suggest that it is a classic example of late colonization of the woodlands.

Yet this obvious and superficial interpretation may be challenged. First of all, while there may have been woodland there in the medieval period it is doubtful whether much existed in Roman times or even earlier. Immediately north of the parish is the site of the small Roman town of Letocetum (Wall). Within the parish Roman settlements are known to have existed near Shenstone itself, near Hilton and at Chesterfield. Roman coins have been found at two other places, while at Upper Stonnall further Roman material is known from a small Iron Age fort there. The fort implies at least a centre of Iron Age control in the area at that time. In addition, the discovery of a later Bronze Age hoard of tools, together with a burial, in the south of the parish, may well be evidence of a Bronze Age settlement in that area.

When we turn to the historic period we find that only Shenstone and Hilton are mentioned in Domesday Book: Stonnall is first recorded in 1192, Woodend, Footherley and Little Aston in 1278, Lynn, Thornes and Chesterfield in 1300, while Little Hay does not appear in documents until 1633. This appears to confirm the idea of a slow process of colonization, perhaps from a single ancient centre, Shenstone itself. However, there are indications that there was once a clear division between the eastern part of the parish centred on Shenstone and the western part based on Stonnall. Indeed, during the medieval period special provision was made in Shenstone church for the inhabitants 'across the brook' in Stonnall. Further, though Stonnall is not recorded until 1192 the actual reference makes it clear that Stonnall was in fact a manor described as 'land in Shenstone' granted to the Abbey of Osney, Oxfordshire, in 1129. This would suggest that the single entry in Domesday Book for Shenstone actually includes another place and the relatively high population recorded there also indicates that the inhabitants probably lived in other settlements besides Shenstone itself. It looks very much as if by the late eleventh century at least Shenstone, Upper and Lower Stonnall and Hilton already existed in some form. The other settlements in the parish may well have come into being at a later date. If this is so then they may be regarded as true secondary or colonizing settlements produced as a result of expansion into what was woodland by the twelfth or thirteenth century.

Much medieval secondary colonization is, of course, well documented and well known to most historians. Its salient features have been noted in many academic works as well as in more popular writings. Yet it is usually described in fairly simple terms as the massive growth of farmsteads, hamlets and even new villages which began in the late Saxon period and continued unchecked until the fourteenth century when disease, climatic change and economic decline all combined to halt and indeed reverse the process. However, as with all settlement history, the real story is far more complex, even if basically correct in outline. The process of medieval colonization was not 'one long assart', as it has often been described, but was the result of a complex interplay between economic, social, political and climatic conditions at both local and national levels. The late medieval 'retreat from the wastes' is an equally complicated process and long before it was completed it was overtaken by a new wave of expansion.

Nevertheless, there was clearly large-scale expansion of settlement by colonization in the late Saxon and medieval periods. The best-known example of this was within the great forested areas of England, which themselves were often relatively recent secondary woodland dating from the post-Roman period. In these regions clearance of land and its reduction to cultivation, usually known as assarting, went on apace. Alongside this assarting of land was the establishment of farmsteads, hamlets and even villages. Usually hamlets and farmsteads predominated (Fig. 72), for much of this forest clearance was carried out by individuals and small groups of farmers, though of course subsequent expansion of population could easily turn a single farmstead into a small village within three or four generations. The process was often centred on an existing settlement outside the forest area and took place on land which was associated with that place, its parish or township. The result of this assarting was that the forests were gradually replaced by a mass of irregularly shaped fields, or in some cases by small strip or open-field systems associated with a dispersed pattern of hamlets and farmsteads. This can be seen today in any area which was once forested such as Sherwood in Nottinghamshire, Needwood in Staffordshire and in south-east Cambridgeshire.

The process is particularly well marked and documented in the Vale of Blackmoor, Dorset, the major part of which was a Royal Forest from the twelfth century. Because of its Royal status, the clearance of woodland and the establishment of farmsteads is well recorded, for the Crown treated such activity as a criminal offence for which fines were paid. In fact, the proceedings became a legal fiction, the fines being merely a licence to assart land. From Domesday Book it appears that there were two villages in the parish in 1086, Stalbridge and Stalbridge Weston, though of course whether that was actually so is another matter. The two villages certainly existed by the mid fourteenth century but by then there were at least eight isolated farmsteads scattered across the parish. The names of these farmsteads are recorded for the first time in a variety of thirteenth- and fourteenth-century documents. These are Gummershay Farm (1285), Thornhill (1244), Antioch Farm (1244), Newnham Farm (1244), Frith Farm (1244), Cook's Farm (1327), Bibberns Farm (1327) and Hyde Farm (1327). Around these farms were fields, at least some of which had recently been cut out of the surrounding forest. For example, in 1269 'Richard de Stapelbrigge occupied anew and holds at Nywenham two acres of land . . . and enclosed them'. Here there seems to be ample evidence for massive secondary colonization in the high Middle Ages.

The same process is also visible on the open heathlands of Dorset and Hampshire, on the upland hills of the Pennines and around the edges of the moors of south-west England. Professor Hoskins has used the farmstead of Cholwich in Devon as a model of what seems to have occurred on moorland. The farm lies on the lower slopes of Dartmoor over three kilometres from the village of Cornwood in whose parish it is situated. In the thirteenth century a number of new farmsteads, including Cholwich, were set up on the moorland pastures.

Cholwich itself seems to have originated in a grant by the Lord of Cornwood of 200 acres of land at Cholleswyt to Benedict, son of Edric Siward, a small peasant freeholder. Similar colonization apparently took place on some of the higher downlands of central southern England and within the fenlands of eastern England. In the Cambridgeshire fens, for example, the thirteenth-century records of the estates of Ely Abbey are full of details of reclamation and settlement. In the 1251 survey of the Bishop of Ely's manor of Downham, thirteen new free tenants are listed as holding recently reclaimed land at a place called Apesholte. Though most of these tenants actually lived in Downham some occupied the farmstead of Apesholt which still stands alone on a low gravel ridge out in the fens.

On the estuarine marshes of south Lincolnshire extensive colonization is visible and the relative chronological development is also clear. There successive intakes or 'innings' were made by embanking areas of marsh to protect them from the sea and these were followed first by new villages, then by hamlets and finally by farmsteads as the intakes were extended further out into the marshlands. In parts of south Lincolnshire it is possible to see the results of both fenland and

72 Gore Farm, Margaret Marsh, Dorset *This unprepossessing building, though apparently of eighteenth-century date, is basically sixteenth-century. Yet the farm existed in 1282 and probably originated long before. It may have come into being as the result of forest clearance in the ninth or tenth centuries, but it could be even older.*

estuarine colonization side by side. The parish of Moulton, near Spalding, is a good example. The village of Moulton and its neighbours lie on what, in late Saxon times, was a seashore ridge, behind which lay ill-drained fenland. The actual date of the foundation of the village is not known but we may presume that some occupation existed there by the eleventh century. In the succeeding centuries the estuarine marshes north of the village were slowly reclaimed and soon after 1250 were protected by a massive rampart known as the Sea Bank. Behind this bank a small hamlet, known as Moulton Seas End, had appeared as well as three individual farmsteads. To the south of the village the same reclamation and colonization took place across the fenlands. Again by the mid thirteenth century a whole host of farmsteads, including the moated Snake Hall and even a hamlet, Moulton Chapel, had appeared.

Even in the Midlands, the outer wastes of parishes

were often reclaimed and farmed by individuals living in farmsteads though, as the numerous 'Newton' villages suggest, there were often completely new villages established on the contemporary wastes. Many years ago W.G. Hoskins described an instance of this at Groby, in Leicestershire. Groby is recorded as a sizable place in Domesday Book but more importantly it had a wood 'two miles long and half a mile wide' associated with it. By 1288 large rents were being paid for assarts in Groby and a few years later peasants of Groby were holding assarts at Newton Linford, immediately to the north. Hoskins suggested that these assarts were the same and that Newton Linford was a daughter hamlet of Groby, set up in the old woodland by the early fourteenth century.

In addition to all these new settlements there were also, in certain areas, very special forms of colonization which produced different habitations. It is impossible to describe them all but amongst the most notable were the sheep farms of Cistercian abbeys which were themselves often established in remote places. This is particularly true of northern England though there the picture is often complicated by the fact that the abbeys sometimes cleared existing villages (as was noted in the previous chapter) and replaced them by single farmsteads from which sheep were run on the former arable land. In Derbyshire, over forty outlying farmsteads are known to have been monastic granges. Many still exist as farms but others have long since been abandoned and their sites are now marked only by low earthworks. A splendid instance is Roystone Grange, Ballidon, once the property of the Cistercian Garendon Abbey, in Leicestershire. The remains of its buildings lie neatly equidistant from those of two Roman settlements abandoned centuries before. Other religious orders also founded new farmsteads and these too have sometimes survived as existing farms. Often, however, these farms were abandoned during the reorganization of former monastic estates after the Dissolution. The abandoned moated site at Cottesbrooke, Northamptonshire, is an instance of this (Fig. 73).

Other even more specialized settlements, usually in the form of single dwellings, were associated with upland and heathland rabbit warrens, which acquired warreners' houses, and with the deer parks in the remaining forested areas, which required park keepers' houses within or near them. Out on the Breckland of Norfolk, on Thetford Warren, are the ruins of the medieval warreners' lodge. In such an isolated place the warreners needed protection against marauders so the building is a small tower-like structure with a heavily protected doorway and few windows. From it the warreners managed vast numbers of rabbits, an important source of income at a time when fashion demanded fur-lined and edged cloaks and dresses. The same isolated houses often accommodated the men who ran the deer parks and other woodland activities.

The modern landscape also contains the remains of what may be termed temporary colonization. These consist of herdsmen's and shepherds' huts, used only in the summer when flocks were taken on to higher ground. Many of these sites are known from the Wiltshire and Dorset downlands where the earthwork remains have often been assumed to be of prehistoric or Roman date. Subsequent examination has shown their true origins. On Oakley Down, in the parish of Wimborne St Giles in Dorset, modern ploughing has exposed the remains of a small two-roomed stone hut with a yard, apparently of the thirteenth century. This was undoubtedly a shepherd's hut. In the north of England, especially, there are numerous 'shielings' or summer dwellings where the herdsmen lived during the summer months when the flocks and herds were brought up from the lowlands and grazed on the upland pastures. These shielings usually consist of rectangular huts, often arranged in groups. Not all are of the same date, and many were being built and used well into the seventeenth century. Thereafter many were abandoned though others were turned into permanent farmsteads in the eighteenth century when a more efficient system of pasture management was introduced. The custom of transhumance was, of course, very old and had certainly been practised in the upland hills since Neolithic times. However, it is not until the thirteenth century that documents begin to record the process. Thus Askerton North Moore in Cumbria was returned to the de Melton family by Lanercost Priory in 1256 in exchange for another tract of moorland on which the monks were given the right to build a cowfold, sheepfold and two shielings.

In Cumbria, many former shielings had become farmsteads associated with small areas of arable land even by the eleventh century, and the same change took place later on in the thirteenth century in Northumberland. Many of these farmsteads were later abandoned but their sites, associated enclosures and areas of former ploughed land still survive. Others are still occupied today and only their names, such as Winter Shields Farm, on Askerton North Moor, and Town Shields on Haughton Common in Northumberland, show their origins and distinguish them from their neighbours which were established at a much later date.

The medieval period also saw the development of 'industrial' rural colonization. Certainly by the thirteenth century settlements associated with the mining of minerals, coal and stone had come into being, in the upland areas in particular. On Dartmoor, for example, the development of tin streaming led to the establishment of small communities in the moorland river valleys. Also in south-west England there was a notable appearance of nucleated villages, probably for the first time, as the fishing industry developed. The classic old-world villages of Looe, Mevagissey (Fig. 74) and Gorran Haven all originated as secondary settlements set up as fishing became important. Thus, Gorran Haven, set in a sheltered cove some distance from the original hamlet of Gorran, acquired its own harbour, streets, houses and even a beautiful medieval chapel. At Mevagissey a close examination of the layout of the surviving street pattern reveals a former market place, now built over, of a

73 Kalendar Moat, Cottesbrooke, Northamptonshire *This well-preserved moated site, together with paddocks and a fishpond near the stream, was the site of a grange farm belonging to the Premonstratensian Abbey of Sulby. It was established soon after 1155 and abandoned in the mid sixteenth century.*

74 Mevagissey, Cornwall *A typical Cornish fishing village with a huddle of houses and winding streets set around the ancient harbour. Actually it is a planned village, established quite late in medieval times. A close examination of the centre of the village reveals the existence of a rectangular 'green' or 'square' fronting the harbour, around which the first houses were laid out. Subsequent encroachment has almost totally destroyed it.*

very regular form which suggests that it was indeed constructed on a previously almost empty site. The fact that its name is not recorded until 1410 might suggest that it came into existence at a relatively late date.

The form of the various types of settlement associated with colonization obviously varies. Some of the villages, as in the case of those connected with fishing, have all the characteristics of a planned origin. Others seem as if they grew up around existing road junctions, while many have a straggling appearance which suggests gradual expansion from one or more original farmsteads. The existing hamlets of the colonization phase often support this latter origin, for they usually consist of four or five farmsteads arranged either in an irregular pattern or strung out along a winding road and, incidentally, are generally almost indistinguishable in plan from hamlets of prehistoric, Roman or Saxon date.

A very characteristic form of medieval settlement, often found in the damper areas of colonization, is the moated site. While these settlements vary greatly in detail, there is typically a rectangular area in which the farmhouse and often some farm buildings are situated, surrounded by a wide deep wet ditch or moat. A splendid example is that on the side of the main road to Aylesbury, near Aston Clinton in Buckinghamshire (Fig. 75).

Not all moated sites are the result of colonization. They appear to have been a fashionable way of identifying a reasonably prosperous farmer in the twelfth and thirteenth centuries, the period when most of them were constructed. Consequently moats are found around village manor houses and the dwellings of other successful farmers, where they were principally a status symbol rather than a means of defence. Nevertheless, in many parts of England the numerous isolated moated sites dotted about the landscape (Fig. 71), especially within areas once forested, are usually said to mark the process of colonization of the woodlands and this certainly seems to be the case if we look at their distribution over the country at large or in detail in a

75 Moated Site, Aston Clinton, Buckinghamshire
A typical example of the thousands of moated sites, mainly of twelfth- or thirteenth-century date, that can be found in many parts of England. The original farmhouse stood on the main moated island. The outer enclosure below it in the foreground contains a group of fish ponds and must also have had the barns, stables and outbuildings of the farmstead within it.

particular area. Taking England as a whole moated sites are concentrated mainly in areas of heavy soils. They are very common in the Forest of Arden in Warwickshire, in Essex, Suffolk, and on the claylands of Hereford and Worcester, Bedfordshire and Hertfordshire. They are often associated with place-names that suggest secondary and late occupation and in many cases can be seen to have appeared during periods of forest clearance or assarting. In Hereford and Worcester moated sites with names such as Newlands Farm (at Norton) and Breach Farm (at Hunnington) indicate their establishment on newly-cleared land, while the close correlation of thirteenth-century free tenants with moated sites in the Forest of Arden implies that there was a class of enterprising farmers engaged in removing woodland and establishing new homes there at that time.

Looking at an individual parish in detail the same process can be seen. Thus at Boxworth, in Cambridgeshire, the main village lies in the centre of the parish and was surrounded by its common fields until enclosure in the nineteenth century. However, in an isolated position in the east of the parish, beyond the limits of the former common fields and associated with an area of irregular hedged fields, is a moated site now hidden within a wood called Overhall Grove. The sub-manor of Overhall is first recorded in documents in 1386 and thus the moat may be interpreted as a late secondary settlement established on the waste of the parish towards the end of the medieval period.

The normally accepted period for most of this colonization includes the twelfth, thirteenth and early fourteenth centuries. While some colonization certainly took place at this time the evidence on which the dating of most sites is based is often suspect and few dates can be regarded as absolutely correct. For example, the record of most of the woodland clearances comes from documents of the late twelfth and thirteenth centuries which are often long lists of the names of individuals who were clearing new fields and establishing their homes. Gore Farm at Margaret Marsh in Dorset is apparently a splendid instance of a farmstead established during medieval woodland clearance (Fig. 72). But the basic problem is that the organization which required documents giving such details did not come into being until the mid twelfth century and so it is not surprising that there are few references to forest clearances and new settlements before that time. Yet such clearances and their settlements were probably being produced for hundreds of years before they were recorded.

A study on forest clearance and settlement by the writer, based on the parish of Whiteparish in Wiltshire, fell into this trap. A convincing story was produced, based on the very detailed documentary record, which purported to show that assarting of the woodland began in the twelfth century and was accompanied by a whole series of newly established farmsteads. Yet in fact there was other documentary proof that at least one farmstead existed in the tenth century and in any case the actual documented area of forest cleared was less than 10 per cent of that which was ascertainable on the ground. Even assuming that much woodland was cleared without record, which is unlikely as the area was a Royal Forest, it is obvious that clearance and indeed settlement must have started well before the twelfth century. The story of Whiteparish and the expansion of settlement there may be correct in its relative sequence but the absolute chronology is likely to be quite wrong.

This is probably true not only of all forest clearances but also of colonization of the heaths and uplands. In Dorset, for example, if we take the documents that survive at their face value, we can see a veritable rash of farmsteads being built on the southern heathlands in the thirteenth and fourteenth centuries. This is based on the fact that all the farmsteads are first recorded by name at that time. Yet these farmsteads could have originated much earlier and not been recorded. Occasionally there is proof of this in that one or two places, as a result of accidents of tenure, are recorded much earlier. One such is Hethfelton (Heath Farm), which stands in a most exposed and inhospitable position on the windswept wastes of the parish of East Stoke. It is mentioned by name as a single farm in Domesday Book in 1086 and thus apparently predates the generally accepted main period of expansion.

The same problem can be seen in northern England. In the Lake District there were, until the nineteenth century, no real villages at all. All the present-day villages, such as Coniston and Windermere, are either modern industrial villages based on quarrying or mining, tourist villages or both. Elsewhere only isolated farmsteads or small hamlets

76 Watendlath, Cumbria *This small, remote hamlet at the head of Wastwater is first mentioned in documents in 1209, yet its name indicates that it was occupied by Norsemen in the tenth century. It is probably much older and is perhaps even prehistoric in origin.*

77 Dale Foot Farm, Bishopdale, North Yorkshire *This farmstead is dated 1640 but the existing building is only a replacement for a much older farm whose origins are lost. It was certainly here in medieval times.*

exist. But what date are these? Many are not recorded in documents until late medieval times or even later yet have names which suggest that they were there centuries before. Watendlath, tucked away at the head of Wastwater, is typical of these (Fig. 76). It is first mentioned in 1209 but its name is Old Norse meaning 'end of the lake' which suggests that it was founded in the tenth century. Yet can we be sure of this? There were certainly Saxon people in the area by the eighth century and it is possible that Romano-British or even prehistoric people settled here too. It may well be that man has lived in or around Watendlath for millennia, rather than centuries. Other places, such as Dale Foot Farm in Bishopdale, North Yorkshire (Fig. 77), show in their architecture that they were built in the seventeenth century or sometimes even earlier and documents indicate that the site was occupied before this. But their true origins remain lost to us.

This kind of evidence might suggest that the whole process of medieval colonization began much earlier than has hitherto been supposed. On the other hand it is possible to turn the whole argument on its head and ask if any dispersed settlement should be interpreted as colonization at all. The apparently newly-created farmsteads of the twelfth and thirteenth centuries which dot the former woodland, ancient heaths, estuarine marshes and fen edges may be much older than the documents seem to tell us. Could not such isolated farmsteads be the remnants of a much earlier mid-Saxon dispersed pattern of settlement, as we noted earlier in Devon, Somerset, Essex and Sussex, which had remained reasonably stable, whereas in other areas it was replaced by nucleated villages? In any case the idea of the 'colonization phase' of the twelfth to early fourteenth centuries was originally based on the supposition that it was the result of expansion from villages of much earlier date. But from the evidence discussed earlier it is clear that the establishment of many villages was broadly contemporary with the colonization.

In a very real sense, only archaeology can get to the root of the problem by identifying, with reasonable certainty, the date by which such alleged new settlements came into existence. But archaeology is a slow and expensive method of recovering historical data and it is only relatively recently that its techniques have been applied to the problems of these apparently late settlements. Even so, though few results have been produced as yet, they do show that these so-called secondary and late settlements probably did not originate all at the same time.

Sometimes, of course, archaeology has revealed impeccable evidence of late colonization, as at the site on Fyfield Down in Wiltshire. A small group of abandoned structures there was excavated by Dr P.J. Fowler and proved to be a small farmstead comprising a long rectangular dwelling house with associated barns, all set inside a paddock. It was occupied for no more than a century or so and was dated to around 1200. Because of the remarkable survival of some documents it was also discovered that the place was known as Raddun and was in existence in 1248. It was abandoned in the early fourteenth century. This site, together with its surrounding area of contemporary fields, is a superb example of the traditional idea of the medieval colonization of the chalk downland.

Elsewhere archaeology has merely confused this simple picture. We have already noted the site at Ribblehead on the Yorkshire Pennines which could easily have been interpreted as a medieval farmstead but which was revealed to be a ninth-century building of short duration. On Dartmoor, at Hound Tor, a small hamlet comprising a cluster of eleven stone buildings set within paddocks seems to have been occupied in the eighth century and to have existed until it was abandoned in the early fourteenth century (Fig. 78). Yet only seven kilometres to the south-west at Dinna Clerks, and in a much better position, the farmstead there was not erected until about 1200 and was then abandoned in the late thirteenth or early fourteenth century: a life of perhaps no more than a hundred years.

There have been many excavations of the very common moated sites and this work has proved that

78 Hound Tor, Devon *These foundations are of a medieval peasant's house which was one of a group situated on the lower slopes of Dartmoor. The settlement was established in the eighth century and finally abandoned in the early fourteenth century.*

the moats date mainly from the thirteenth and fourteenth centuries. The great majority of those examined, however, have been associated with villages or hamlets. Far fewer of the completely isolated moated sites, whose origins are usually said to lie in the same period and thus to represent the expansion into the wastes, have been excavated. Of those that have, many were undoubtedly constructed to enclose farmsteads at this period. Archaeological investigation on a site at Newstead in North Yorkshire indicated that the moat was built in the late thirteenth century to surround a flimsy timber building which was later rebuilt and improved on a number of occasions. The same general story has been noted at a number of similar sites and these moats do probably represent a new phase of outlying settlement in the late twelfth to early fourteenth centuries.

On some isolated moated sites there is evidence of occupation before the construction of the moat. Finds from one at Caxton in Cambridgeshire indicated a late tenth- or early eleventh-century origin while at Streatham, near Steyning in East Sussex, excavation has shown that though a moated site was occupied around 1000 the moat itself was not constructed until the thirteenth century. At another moated site near Horley in Surrey archaeological work revealed that the moat was dug in the twelfth or thirteenth centuries on a site which had been first occupied in the late eleventh century.

On the whole the archaeological evidence supports, in general terms, the accepted idea of the medieval explosion of secondary dispersed settlement. Yet archaeology also hints at more complex patterns which may indicate a much longer period of expansion, a more mobile pattern of settlement, or an earlier fossilised pattern of perhaps Saxon settlement, or conceivably all three.

The patterns of settlement in north Essex and east Bedfordshire, which are very similar, illustrate these points and the difficulties involved in unravelling the history of any particular area. In both there is a similar pattern of hamlets and farmsteads, either scattered for up to a kilometre along winding roads or grouped in small clusters around greens, as at Roe Green, Sandon (Fig. 79). Names such as Wood End, Woodleys, Green End, Morley Green and Elmdon Lee suggest that their origins lay in cleared forest. In addition all the settlements lie on relatively heavy clay land where considerable areas of woodland still survive. Nowhere, apparently, could there be better evidence of the late colonization of woodland. Yet detailed archaeological studies have produced very different and conflicting evidence. In north Essex, work by Mr T. Williamson has shown that the dispersed pattern of settlement there developed from an equally dispersed Iron Age and Roman one and that there was no more woodland in the eleventh century than there is today. The names, far from indicating clearance of woodland, appear to mean only that these settlements were in a landscape with more trees than the adjacent areas. Once again the place-name evidence seems to be misleading us.

In Bedfordshire the writer has carried out an examination of two areas of dispersed settlement only four kilometres apart and almost identical in form, both being made up of houses and cottages strung out along a road. The results were extraordinarily confusing. At Scald End in Thurleigh it was clear that the present hamlet evolved from a large number of evenly-spaced farmsteads which had come into existence in the twelfth century (Fig. 80). Most of them seemed to have disappeared by the sixteenth century so producing the present widely-spaced dispersed settlement pattern. But perhaps the most unusual feature was that these farmsteads had not been founded following woodland clearances but had been established on land which was arable. The primeval forest, as so often, disappears from the explanation.

The other hamlet, Bletsoe North End, proved to lie on the long abandoned remains of a small but perfectly laid out village which originally consisted of about a dozen houses on either side of a single straight street. Each house lay in equally-sized crofts, thus indicating that the village was almost certainly a planned settlement. The date that this village began its life is not known, though here again there is no evidence of early woodland in the area. Once more two apparently similar and neighbouring settlements have very different origins and later histories.

This brings us to the problems connected with the end of this period of settlement expansion. For just

79 Roe Green, Sandon, Hertfordshire *This is not the village of Sandon. It is one of four greens that exist in the parish, as well as three other medieval settlements without greens. It is not clear how or why such a pattern evolved. Detailed study of similar sites in Essex has shown that they have Roman or sometimes Iron Age beginnings and were even occupied all through Saxon times as well. The actual greens, however, seem to date from the twelfth or thirteenth centuries.*

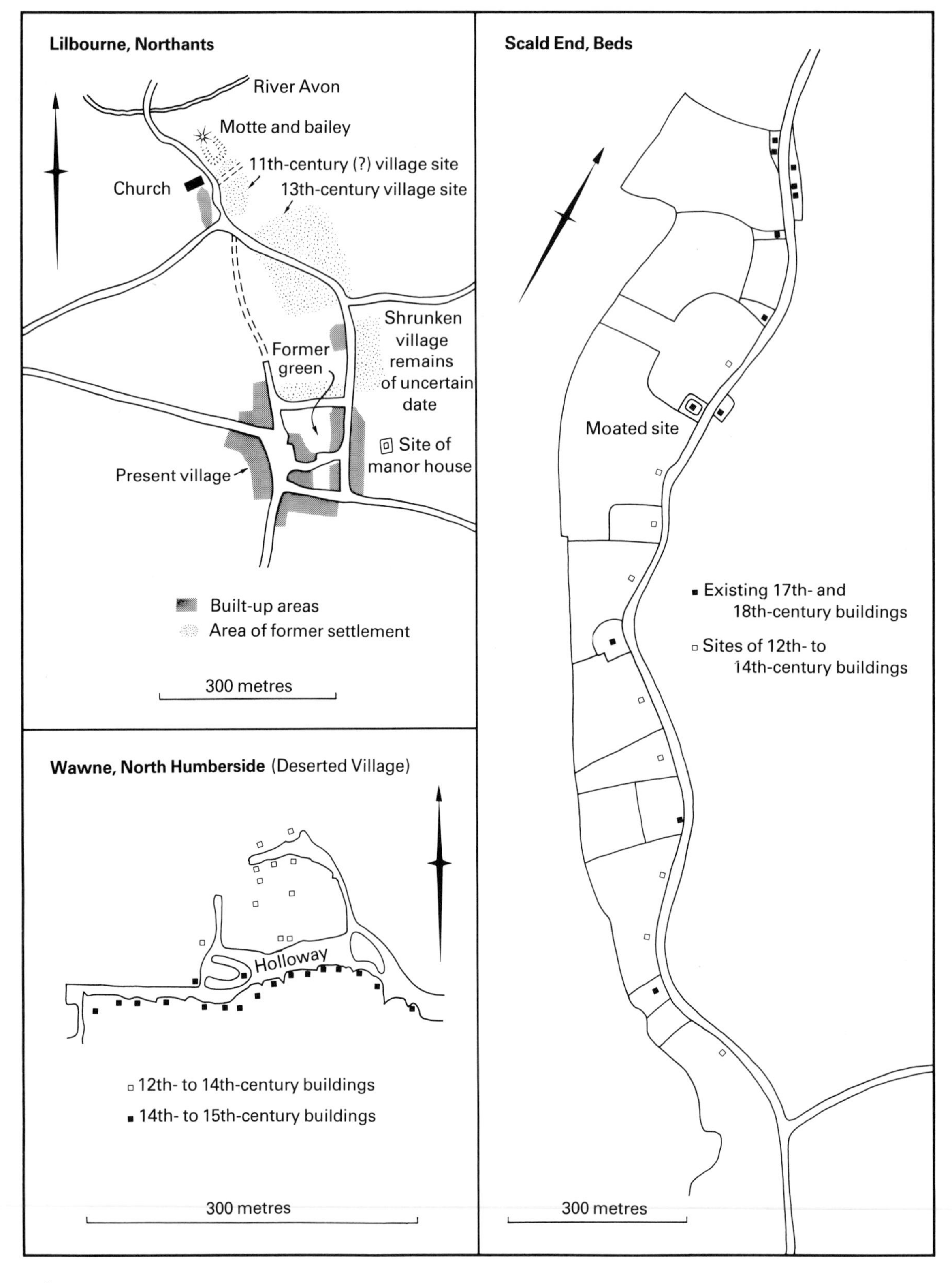
Lilbourne, Northants
River Avon
Motte and bailey
11th-century (?) village site
Church
13th-century village site
Shrunken
village
remains
of uncertain
date
Former
green
Site of
manor house
Present village
Built-up areas
Area of former settlement
300 metres
Scald End, Beds
Moated site
Existing 17th- and
18th-century buildings
Sites of 12th- to
14th-century buildings
300 metres
Wawne, North Humberside (Deserted Village)
Holloway
12th- to 14th-century buildings
14th- to 15th-century buildings
300 metres

as changing climatic conditions, economic decline, disease and changes in land-use played their part in reducing or removing nucleated villages, these factors were also to halt the colonization phase of medieval settlement and to bring about what is usually known as 'the retreat from the margins'.

This contraction of settlement is often said to have taken place on a massive scale in the fourteenth and fifteenth centuries and thus to have produced the thousands of abandoned, isolated moated sites which lie all over the Midlands and East Anglia, as well as the almost countless deserted farmsteads which dot the moorlands and uplands of northern and south-west England. While this is broadly true in outline, archaeological research has once again indicated other complex changes at work as well. As we have seen, at the site of Raddun at Fyfield the farmstead there was certainly abandoned in the early fourteenth century. This was perhaps because it became difficult to grow crops on the high downland at a time of deteriorating climate and economic decline. Equally, small farms on the north Cambridgeshire fens were given up in the fourteenth century, ostensibly, according to contemporary documents, because of constant flooding, but more plausibly assisted by a fall in crop values which made the necessary repairs of dykes and flood-banks uneconomic. Similarly, at Hound Tor on Dartmoor, the poor climate, the marginal situation and vacant tenements in settlements on lower ground may have persuaded the occupants to move down on to more viable land in the early fourteenth century when the site appears to have been abandoned.

Yet not all such places were given up in this period. Excavations have shown that occupation of many now empty moated sites went on far beyond the traditional period of abandonment. At the Newstead moat, noted earlier, occupation did not cease until sometime between the late fifteenth and mid sixteenth centuries. In Bedfordshire, a small moated site on the margins of Milton Ernest parish began life, typically, as a small farm in the twelfth century but was not abandoned until the sixteenth century. In other words, though archaeology can indicate that climatic alterations and economic decline could cause retreat of settlement, we may still be seeing this process in too simplistic terms, and in the end the documentary record, if analyzed correctly, may indicate more complex reasons. For example, on the north side of Dartmoor, near Okehampton, excavation has shown that some isolated moorland farmsteads, set up on the wastes, were abandoned in the early fourteenth century after a relatively short-lived existence. Yet others nearby, in identical situations, were occupied for much longer and indeed some are still inhabited today. The reasons for this apparently curious feature have now been established. The abandoned farmsteads belonged to major landowners who leased them to minor tenants. With the onset of climatic deterioration and economic decline these farmsteads no longer provided a reasonable return on capital for their lordly owners and were thus, in accounting terms, written off, or in actual terms abandoned. The farmsteads which survived were those which were owned by small freeholders. When times became hard these farmers had nowhere to go and had only to produce enough to live on, not to make a profit. They thus remained and their homes have survived as living entities. Again the interplay between man and his environment at a very local level can be seen at work. Such examples make nonsense of the easy generalizations about economic conditions and physical determinants.

Of course, many so-called medieval secondary or colonization settlements were never abandoned at all, even in the remotest areas, and are still occupied today. In deepest Suffolk numerous medieval moats still surround splendid late medieval and later houses. The heathlands of Dorset are still dotted with farms whose names, at least, go back to the thirteenth or fourteenth centuries, and the same is true of the former forested areas and the coastal marshes. These places, at least, seem to show a high-tide mark of medieval colonization from which there was no retreat. Or do they? Can we be sure that all these places occupy exactly the same site now as they did six or seven hundred years ago? Is it possible that settlement 'drift', so common at other periods, also occurred here?

Certainly with many isolated moated sites this is so. For every moated site completely abandoned, or still occupied, there is another which has an existing farmstead just outside it or a little distance away.

80 Change, Movement and Dispersal of Medieval Villages *Lilbourne is an example of a village that has gradually moved and also exhibits a final planned form. Wawne is a deserted village which, when examined by archaeologists, indicated that its form had been entirely altered in the last century of its life. At Scald End the evidence from both existing buildings and the sites of former farmsteads indicates a very regular pattern of occupation, here laid out over former arable land in an area of dispersed settlement.*

The reasons for this undoubted movement or drift may be convincingly explained in individual cases as the result of the rising status of the occupants, shortage of space on the moated island, damp conditions or a desire for an improved standard of living. Yet collectively the evidence points to a general trend that is identical to that which we have noted in all settlements and in all periods. Sometimes the movement must have occurred relatively early, for the farmsteads outside the moats are of fifteenth- or sixteenth-century date. But sometimes the movement occurred much later, as at Maghull Manor, Lancashire, where the moated site was not abandoned until about 1780, when the present house to the south-east of it was built.

Even many of the high moorland farmsteads, though technically deserted, still actually remain in existence on a nearby site. On Dartmoor, the abandoned hamlet at Hutholes has been excavated. It was shown to have consisted of six small buildings set within a group of stone-walled paddocks. The site was abandoned in the fourteenth century and thus could be interpreted as an example of the retreat from marginal land. Yet the adjacent Dockwell Farm is first mentioned in a document of 1545 and thus is almost certainly older than that date. It may well be the direct replacement of the abandoned site and thus the whole arrangement is an instance of settlement drift rather than desertion.

An even more complex example has been noted at Whiteparish in Wiltshire. There, deep within the area once forested, is a small farmstead called Blaxwell Farm. Its name is first recorded in 1242 when its occupants were apparently engaged in removing the surrounding woodland. It is documented that its land increased from 80 acres in 1328 to 108 acres in 1358. Yet the present farmhouse, an eighteenth-century structure, is probably not on the site of the medieval farm. Examination of the adjacent land has shown that occupation in the thirteenth and fourteenth centuries lay some 150 metres to the north and that by the sixteenth century it had moved 200 metres to the south-west. In essence Blaxwell Farm seems to have moved in a circle over the centuries. This type of drift is probably by no means unique, though impeccable evidence from archaeological excavation is still required for absolute proof.

All this evidence shows that, as with earlier periods, the pattern of so-called medieval colonization is far more complicated than has previously been believed.

-11-
The Development of the Modern Countryside

The countryside of England in the sixteenth century is usually seen as reflecting a time of rising population and recovery from the deprivations of climatic deterioration, disease and rapacious landlords. The late Tudor period, in particular, is often regarded as a kind of ideal rural world, full of 'merry England' characters who lived and worked in an unchanging landscape which lasted until the brutal realities of the eighteenth-century Agricultural Revolution brought it to an end. Yet we shall see how far this was from the truth. Perhaps more than any other period of history, except for the last century or so, the late sixteenth and early seventeenth centuries were characterized by a ferment of new ideas and techniques stemming largely from the Renaissance. These changes were reflected in the rural landscape, particularly in the emparking movement. The popular idea of an unchanging rural landscape after about 1550 is a myth and all the processes that we have seen so far continued into this period – villages still disappeared or declined in size, were replanned or expanded, and new farmsteads appeared within recently enclosed fields and on newly cleared or reclaimed areas.

Although there is a wealth of historical material dating from this time, the reasons for desertion are not always known. A study of lost villages in Staffordshire by Mr P. V. Bate and Dr D. M. Palliser has shown that at least a dozen places there disappeared in the seventeenth century, though the reasons for their abandonment are unclear. Only one feature is certain; all the villages concerned were extremely small after centuries of decline and were thus probably very vulnerable to any pressures. A typical example was Godwick in Norfolk (Fig. 81). It was always a tiny place yet it survived the Black Death and by 1508 still had at least ten homesteads. During the sixteenth century these were gradually removed, not by the landlord, but by the tenant farmers who wished to increase their holdings. By 1585 only the two main tenanted farmhouses of the village remained. Then Chief Justice Coke built a new hall and later on his successors laid out a formal garden across the remains of the old village. In the seventeenth century the last two farmhouses vanished and the hall itself survived only for another hundred years before it too was pulled down.

This instance of the creation of a garden brings us to the most notable reason for village abandonment between 1550 and 1700, that of emparking. It may come as a surprise to those who know of the extensive clearances for landscaped parks in the eighteenth and nineteenth centuries to learn that these also occurred in the seventeenth century. Indeed, the earliest known village clearance for emparking, or rather gardening, was in the late sixteenth century, at Holdenby in Northamptonshire.

In medieval times there were two small villages at Holdenby, one at the top of the hill and the other around the parish church some 300 metres away at the bottom of the same hill. In 1579 Sir Christopher Hatton began to build a magnificent new house on a site midway between the two villages. This house was planned to have extensive and elaborate gardens around it which involved the removal of the lower village, except for the church. Flower beds were laid out across its site. The upper village lay just outside the garden area but it too was cleared away. It was however rebuilt on the same site but with a new plan. The old village had an extremely irregular plan but its replacement was given a square green with houses laid neatly around it. This arrangement was part of the garden layout and was an integral part of the latter's rectilinear plan. Indeed there were open decorative arches through the garden walls and across the outer courtyard to give views of the new village green. The whole scheme of house, garden and replanned village was completed in 1587, a remarkable achievement, and perhaps one of the first examples of what was to become very common in later years. It is worth noting that, as with the earlier desertions, even such a clearance as Holdenby was achieved only because the two villages there were already very small and had been reduced in size by earlier events and processes.

The same is true of the seventeenth-century example of clearance for a garden at Kirby, also in Northamptonshire. Here too there was a medieval village, though it was never very large, and it seems to have been in decline for a long period before 1485 when part of its land was enclosed for sheep and a number of houses removed. In 1570 the magnificent Kirby Hall was built on the site of the medieval manor house by Humphrey Stafford. This hall lay to the east of the remaining village which then comprised the medieval church and eleven or twelve houses. The hall was bought by Sir Christopher Hatton in 1585 but in this case the village remained untouched. Then, in 1685–6, Sir Christopher Hatton III laid out the elaborate gardens, which still exist, to the west of the house. To achieve this he had to remove the church and all the houses. Kirby village thus vanished overnight.

Both Holdenby and Kirby are examples of complete village clearances, but there were also many cases of partial removal where gardens or

81 Godwick, Norfolk *This village finally disappeared in the seventeenth century after a long and slow decline. In 1508 it still had at least ten houses. During the sixteenth century all but two were removed. Then, in 1585, a new country house was built and the last two farmsteads disappeared in the early seventeenth century. Now only the church tower remains, together with the marks of former streets and houses. The great house too has gone leaving only its foundations and the traces of its formal garden.*

parks were obstructed by parts of a village. The classic example of this is Wimpole in Cambridgeshire (Fig. 82), not the least because of its subsequent history. The story began in 1638. A map of that date shows the moated manor house and the parish church surrounded by houses. To the north was another group of dwellings while a small hamlet lay a little further east and yet another to the east again. Wimpole appears to have been a polyfocal village of the type discussed earlier. In 1640 Thomas Chicheley acquired the estate and rebuilt the manor house. Sometime in the later seventeenth century this house was surrounded by a highly elaborate formal garden, the construction of which involved the clearance of that part of the village around the new hall and the church but left intact the other three parts of the village beyond the garden boundary. In the mid eighteenth century these

82 Wimpole Hall, Cambridgeshire *This magnificent house, together with the parish church, is all that remains on the site of Wimpole village. The village itself was gradually removed between 1638 and 1840 as the hall and its park were extended.*

gardens were swept away and replaced by a landscaped park which was extended on a number of occasions in the late eighteenth and nineteenth centuries as the hall itself grew in size. The first park extension involved the removal of that part of the village north of the hall and the later extension to the park led to the successive clearance of the two remaining parts. In fact, the final end of medieval Wimpole did not occur until the 1840s. Then, and only then, a replacement village, now called New Wimpole, was built well beyond the nineteenth-century park boundary.

Returning to the seventeenth century, Chippenham, in Cambridgeshire, is another example of park clearance. As Mrs M. Spufford has shown, the village has a remarkable history of decline and shrinkage. In the late thirteenth century Chippenham was large with some 150 households there. By 1377, probably as a result of the Black Death, there were fewer than 70 households and even in 1544 there were still only 60 households and 64 plots empty and 'clere decaed'. Thus the village was probably weak enough to be taken advantage of by a suitably inclined lord. In 1696 Edward Russell, later Lord Orford, bought Chippenham Hall where he said that he desired 'to make a park'. In 1702 he obtained permission to block off the streets in the southern half of the village and then went ahead and cleared the 40 houses there. Orford then rehoused at least some of the displaced villagers in new dwellings built along a separate street. In essence, what had once been a large village with an L-shaped plan, became a short single-street village with a planned extension to one side. Chippenham, as with so many other examples in this book, shows the dangers of reconstructing ancient arrangements from present shapes.

Other partial removals of villages resulting from seventeenth-century emparking include Dingley, probably in 1680, and Rockingham in 1618, both in Northamptonshire. Emparking also changed the shape of villages by processes which did not involve actual destruction, as particularly well seen at Weekley, also in Northamptonshire. By the sixteenth century the village comprised a single street with a small green adjacent to the church at its northern end. In the early seventeenth century the Montagu family, who had acquired most of the land there, began to extend the great park around Boughton House which lay some distance to the north-east of Weekley. In order to obtain the maximum size for this park the main road from Northampton to Stamford, which passed along the village street, was closed and a new one was laid out around the park to the west. This new road not only bypassed Weekley but made the main street a cul-de-sac. The boundary of the new park actually abutted against the northern edge of the village green. As a result, in later years when Weekley grew in size it was unable to expand along the old road north from the green as this no longer existed. It was forced to develop to the south and took on an L-shaped form along a connecting road to the seventeenth-century bypass.

Though these changes to villages as a result of emparking in the seventeenth century are now known to be much more common than hitherto realized, the main alterations to villages at that time were due to other causes. The most important feature of this period was expansion as villages increased in size, often after earlier shrinkage in the fourteenth and fifteenth centuries. This expansion is not obvious from the present plans of most villages but a careful examination of all the remaining buildings and early maps where these exist can indicate the extent to which some villages altered at this time. Gamlingay in Cambridgeshire is a good example. The main part of the medieval village appears to have been arranged around a very large triangular green, giving it a planned aspect. By the late medieval period, while houses still lay around two sides of the green, the third side had been abandoned. In addition, there had also been encroachment on the green as well as expansion to the east and west which had amalgamated the village with two other small and formerly detached hamlets, Green End and Dutter End. Thus, by the late sixteenth century Gamlingay seems to have been both a planned and a polyfocal village and to have suffered shrinkage and movement.

In 1601–2 a splendid map was made of the village which shows its layout at that time in very great detail. If this map is compared with the existing buildings of seventeenth-century date we can see how, during the seventeenth century, a number of plots scattered throughout the village were gradually filled by neat timber-framed farmhouses of a fairly standard type. These empty plots had, of course, been occupied much earlier, were then abandoned and were now being built up again.

A similar picture is visible in another Cambridgeshire village, Toft. There the original village seems to have been laid out on a grid plan, though this was apparently much distorted by later expansion and alteration. The latter must have occurred before the end of the fourteenth century when Toft was small and in a state of decline. There is no indication of any improvement in this situation until the seventeenth century when a series of new houses was erected in various places, mostly on older abandoned crofts.

At the same time as many villages were expanding and despite a population which, in national terms, was certainly increasing, many settlements also declined in size in the seventeenth century and in doing so left abandoned streets, house sites and empty paddocks identical to those of earlier periods of abandonment or shrinkage. The reasons for individual cases of decline vary, though there was a general country-wide factor which must have played a part. As we have seen, in the fifteenth and early sixteenth centuries many villages were finally wiped out or markedly reduced in size as a result of the growth in sheep farming with its associated enclosure of the common or open fields for pasture. By the late sixteenth century, the market for wool had declined and so the rate of enclosure and depopulation slackened. However, almost immediately, as the population of England grew again there was a demand for more meat and cereals and this prompted a new if less extensive process of enclosure. As a result, the old sheep pastures were subdivided and more intensively grazed, ploughed up again for crops or worked on an intensive arable/pastoral rotation. Elsewhere, and especially in places where improving landlords could easily achieve it, existing open fields were enclosed and the land cultivated more efficiently or turned over to cattle ranching. These changes generally involved practices that called for less labour than before so that in areas where such enclosures took place the villages declined in size, though few were actually deserted.

We lack many examples of seventeenth-century shrinkage which can be definitely related to this process but there are a number of places where shrinkage seems to have taken place at this time. At Farnborough, in Warwickshire, a commission of inquiry into depopulation in the early seventeenth century reported that there were thirteen empty houses there that were almost certainly the result of recent enclosure. At Cransley, in Northamptonshire, a map of 1598 shows a long main street with houses on both sides of it. Some of those on the south side of the street were certainly removed in the nineteenth century when the park of Cransley Hall was laid out, but most of those on the north side of the street seem to have disappeared in the seventeenth century. Their sites were later incorporated into the adjacent fields and ploughed over. It may be that the removal of these houses was connected with the enclosure of the open fields of the parish which probably took place soon after 1600.

More positive proof of seventeenth-century shrinkage comes from Strixton, also in Northamptonshire. Again Strixton was a village which had suffered some shrinkage in the later medieval period. Medieval taxation records, the remains of abandoned house sites and a fine map of 1583 all combine to prove this. But, as this map shows, there were still sixteen houses and only six empty plots in the village by the late sixteenth century. By 1720 there were only two houses left and the county historian, writing at that date, noted that before the enclosure of the open fields of the village, which took place in 1619, 'there appear to have been more houses'. Even this was not the end of the story, for a late-eighteenth-century map shows four houses in the village and appears to mark the beginning of an increase in its size. Further cottages were erected in the nineteenth century. Strixton is still very small, but it has managed to survive the many vicissitudes of its history.

Another example of a village which seems to have suffered shrinkage in the seventeenth century, again in Northamptonshire and very close to Strixton, is Easton Maudit. The village today is a very small one with houses aligned on each side of a short single street. Beyond the houses, abandoned house sites extend some distance to the south. Some of these, now ploughed, contain pottery up to the late sixteenth and early seventeenth century in date. Again the county historian reported in 1720 that the population of the village had decreased considerably since the enclosure of the common fields in 1636. Apart from these examples of shrinkage related to enclosure, villages occasionally disappeared or changed their shape as a result of natural events or disasters, as they have done in any period. At Nettleton, in Lincolnshire, a massive landslip overwhelmed some twenty-five houses in the late seventeenth century. The houses were never rebuilt and the landslip is still there.

The existence of abandoned house sites, dated to the seventeenth century, need not always be related to shrinkage. As in earlier periods considerable settlement movement often took place at this time. Usually this seventeenth-century movement or drift was only part of a long, continuing process which had started centuries before and which was to go on sometimes into the nineteenth century. At Harringworth, in Northamptonshire, the slow change already described, whereby the village was slowly turning from a north-to-south linear settlement to an east-to-west one, certainly went on in the seventeenth century and the process was not finally completed until the late eighteenth century. Other examples may be taken from the work carried out in Norfolk by Dr P. Wade-Martins. The village of Weasenham St Peter, like its neighbours, has evidence of a long period of movement and change (Fig. 44). The village was founded in the tenth century around the now isolated parish church but with a subsidiary centre to the east. During the eleventh to fourteenth centuries, settlement expanded further south around the edges of a large area of common land. Additional growth took place both to the north and west of the church and in the small hamlet to the east. In the later Middle Ages, probably in the late fourteenth and fifteenth centuries, the whole of the original village site, its southward extension and the additional settlements on the southern common were abandoned. In the seventeenth century other new hamlets appeared further north and north-east again, and the settlement to the west developed into a true 'green village'. Later in the same century the new hamlets declined to a few scattered houses and gradually all settlement was concentrated around the green to the west. A similar, if less complicated, movement of a village may also be seen at nearby Longham.

Beyond the villages the pattern of settlement also continued to change in the seventeenth century as the enclosures of open or common fields, limited though these were, inevitably led to a new wave of expansion. There was a tendency to build new isolated farmsteads within the recently enclosed fields. In many parishes known to have been enclosed in the seventeenth century, some at least of the existing farmsteads which are scattered over the fields can be shown to date from that time. This is certainly true of Strixton, which we looked at earlier, where at least one farmstead is known to have been established in the mid seventeenth century. Similarly at Wimpole, where enclosure took place between 1638 and 1686, in the part of the parish beyond the great park there are at least three isolated seventeenth-century farmhouses.

In other areas new seventeenth-century farmhouses were more common. This was particularly so in areas of former forest, as despite all the assarting and clearance of medieval times there still remained large stretches of woodland. Some of these forests, especially those still in the hands of the Crown, were 'disafforested' in the early seventeenth century, cleared of trees and divided into new fields. This work was followed by the establishment of farmsteads. For instance at Motcombe, in north Dorset, a very large area of old woodland, the remains of the Royal Forest of Gillingham, was cleared in 1624 and soon afterwards a group of farmsteads appeared on the new agricultural land. The name of one of these, Wolfridge Farm, indicates the former woodland environment. The present building is certainly of seventeenth-century date but is not shown on a map of 1624.

This type of enclosure was not confined to great forests. In any area of former woodland there were small patches of waste or common land, even after the massive medieval clearances. At Hillfield, in Dorset, 180 hectares of such land were enclosed by agreement in 1697–8. At nearby Lydlynch, Haydon Common remained unenclosed until the late sixteenth century when it was divided into fields and a new farmstead laid out. The great heathlands too were slowly reclaimed, sometimes by major landlords, as they strove to improve the value of their land. On the east Dorset heathland, just before 1598, Sir Matthew Arundel of Hampreston enclosed 80 hectares and Mr John Avery of Uddens had broken up 160 hectares of heath. But far more frequent in these areas was the establishment of squatters' cottages along the edges of the heathland by poor labourers who at a time of rising population had nowhere else to live. The Enquiry into the State of Holt Heath, in Dorset, in 1598 which recorded the large enclosures mentioned above also noted that 'there is ... a little plott of grounde conteyning aboute an acre at a place called Croked Wythes inclosed by one Thomas Carter ... uppon which is erected a cottage ... which is verie inconvienient'. Inconvenient or not, the enclosure remained and still exists today, with its cottage, at Crooked Withies on the north-eastern edge of Holt Heath. Gradual encroachment by squatters on to heathland was to increase steadily in the seventeenth, eighteenth and nineteenth centuries as the population continued to rise. Many areas of former and existing heathland in England are characterized by this form of dispersed settlement.

The same feature is also visible on the edges of the upland moors of northern England. Thus at

Northowram, in West Yorkshire, it was reported in 1604 that sixty-two people had made enclosures from the waste and in 1633 the Justices recorded that many new houses had been built on these enclosures. The results of this process are still visible today in many parts of Yorkshire. The upper slopes of the valleys and the moorland edges are characterized by small fields with seventeenth- or eighteenth-century farmsteads scattered amongst them.

The seventeenth-century enclosure movement also led to a concerted attack on the open downlands of southern England. For example, in 1620 three major landowners in the adjacent parishes of Hooke, North Poorton and Toller Porcorum, north-west of Dorchester in Dorset, agreed to divide and enclose most of the downland there in order to run sheep. Many of these downland enclosures resulted in the establishment of new, outlying farmsteads. At Piddletrenthide, also near Dorchester, there are still 180 hectares of downland which are known to have been enclosed in the seventeenth century. In the centre of this land stands Dole's Ash Farm, a seventeenth-century structure. The parish of Whiteparish, in south-east Wiltshire, lies partly on chalk downland and partly on formerly forested clayland and here new farmsteads appeared associated with both woodland clearances and downland enclosures. Broxmore Farm in the old woodland was built soon after 1610 and Ash Hill House, nearby, was erected at the same time. Dry Farm on the downlands was also built in the early seventeenth century, situated in the centre of 60 hectares of new enclosures.

In eastern England the seventeenth century saw a remarkable expansion of dispersed settlement into the fenlands. On the waterlogged peat fens of Cambridgeshire especially no settlement had ever been possible, except on the drier fen edges and on the sandy and clay 'islands'. But the 1630s saw the beginning of a major attack on these watery wastes using improved and newly-developed engineering techniques for cutting channels and lifting water. Despite many difficulties and failures, from the 1650s onwards a rash of isolated farmsteads appeared everywhere but in the very deepest and wettest parts of the fens. The process continued throughout the eighteenth and nineteenth centuries but there are many farmsteads which can be definitely dated to the late seventeenth century. For example, we know that a block of land to the north-west of the Old Bedford River was not drained until 1654. But in 1665, when describing the position of a break in the bank of the Bedford River, the Bedford Level Corporation recorded that it lay 'in Bedford North Bank neere Tubbes his house'. This is exactly where the present Tubb's Farm stands today. A document of 1683 refers to French refugees having recently settled on newly-reclaimed fenland near Thorney. The existing French Farm is almost certainly the site of one of their original farmsteads. The same growth of seventeenth-century farmsteads on reclaimed land is also visible on the estuarine marshes further north in south Lincolnshire and north-west Norfolk.

This phase of seventeenth-century colonization was not one of continuous expansion. Associated with it there was also contraction of settlement though this took place to a lesser extent. Some of the new settlements themselves failed as a result of over-optimistic aims, poor land, bad management or merely farm reorganization. Certainly many of the poor squatters' cottages came and went with monotonous and tragic rapidity. A recent fire on Horton Heath, Dorset, revealed that the ubiquitous gorse and bracken was hiding the banks and collapsed walls of a group of paddocks and buildings which are known to have been established in the mid seventeenth century by squatters but which had certainly disappeared by the mid eighteenth century.

In other areas much older farmsteads suddenly disappeared from the landscape and in many cases it is not clear why. At Harlton, in Cambridgeshire, an isolated moated site north of the village, certainly occupied from the thirteenth century, was abandoned in the seventeenth century judging by the finds discovered on the site but the reason for this desertion is not known. Sometimes there have been rather odd reasons for a site being abandoned. A small moated farmstead apparently established in the thirteenth century on a high clay-covered hillside on the edge of Rockingham Forest at Aldwincle, in Northamptonshire, was swept away in 1597 by Sir Thomas Tresham in order to provide space for an elaborate garden to go with a new house. Tresham's death in 1604 meant that neither house nor garden was ever completed, so the clearance was wasted. The farmstead was never reoccupied and only slight traces of its surrounding moat remain today.

Numerous excavations on moats have indicated similar desertions at this period though, as was noted earlier, many other moated sites were occupied for

another century or more before being abandoned. Others show that settlement drift was still taking place at this time with the desertion of the moated interiors and the establishment of new farmsteads close by.

During the eighteenth and nineteenth centuries, everything that has been described as occurring in the seventeenth century continued, though on a much larger scale. Perhaps the most obvious and certainly the best known feature of settlement change was the removal of villages as a result of emparking. One of the most famous examples is that at Nuneham Courtenay, Oxfordshire, where in 1760 the village was cleared away by the Earl of Harcourt and replaced by the gardens and park of his new house. At the same time a completely new village was laid out just beyond the park to rehouse the displaced inhabitants. Another well known example is Milton Abbas, Dorset (Fig. 83). There, between 1771 and 1790, Joseph Damer swept away what was virtually a small market town to provide space for his new park. The replacement village of neat thatched cottages was erected to the west, well away from the house.

These are only two instances of what was a very common occurrence in England throughout the eighteenth and nineteenth centuries. Every English county has some examples. In Staffordshire the great park at Shugborough was created just after 1737 when Thomas Anson moved the old village to a place which was suitably out of sight of his house. This was not the only move, for in the early nineteenth century Thomas Lord Anson moved the village yet again as the park was enlarged and attached it to the adjacent village of Great Haywood. In Shropshire in 1780 the village of Acton Reynold still consisted of a long main street and two side streets lined by twenty or so houses. By 1810 the old manor house had been enlarged, a park created, all the roads abandoned and the village removed. In West Yorkshire the original village of Harewood was cleared away between 1660 and 1670 when the park around Harewood House was laid out by the First Earl Lascelles. The new village was designed

83 Milton Abbas, Dorset *Perhaps the classic emparking village. The original Milton Abbas stood outside the gates of the great medieval Benedictine Abbey in the valley bottom. The village survived the dissolution but was entirely destroyed between 1771 and 1790 to make way for a landscaped park around the new Milton Abbas House. The displaced inhabitants were rehoused in this neat new village set in a side valley.*

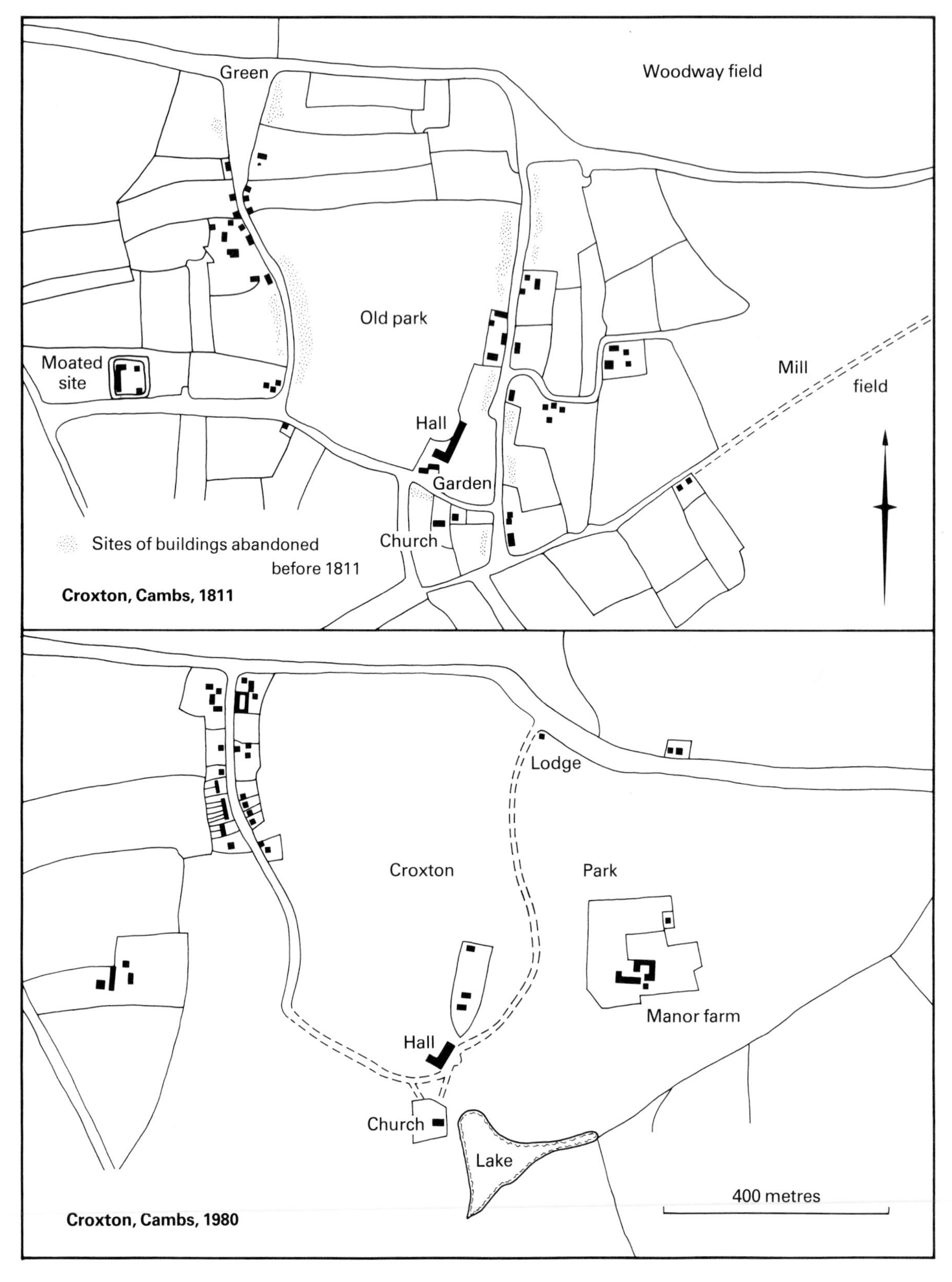
Green
Woodway field
Old park
Moated site
Mill field
Hall
Garden
Church
Sites of buildings abandoned before 1811
Croxton, Cambs, 1811
Lodge
Croxton
Park
Manor farm
Hall
Church
Lake
400 metres
Croxton, Cambs, 1980

by an architect and was laid out with its houses set on either side of a wedge-shaped green just outside the park gates in order to present a vista from those gates.

There are so many examples of either total or partial village clearance as a result of eighteenth- or nineteenth-century emparking that more instances would be superfluous. Certainly far more exist than has been realized. One county, Northamptonshire, has been looked at in some detail and though not perhaps entirely typical, it does show the scale of these clearances. Between 1720 and 1850 eight villages were completely cleared away, only one of which was replaced by a new settlement. The county also contains a much greater number of places which, though not completely removed, were altered to a greater or lesser extent by emparking. No less than twenty-five villages show this. In detail the actual operations vary considerably. At Thorpe Malsor the houses on one side of the main village street were removed in the eighteenth century. At Norton, the eastern part of the village was destroyed and a new estate added to the west just before 1850. This was laid out at a road junction so producing a village green which the village had not possessed before. At Marston Trussell the houses along the street opposite the rebuilt manor house were removed in the 1870s to improve the view. At Newnham, until 1765, the village had a remarkable plan with four separate parts, three with greens, one of which seems to have been a medieval planned addition. Then one whole section, including its green, was removed and replaced by a new manor house and garden.

This partial destruction was probably much more widespread than we imagine. Certainly it has been noticed in many places. At Croxton, in Cambridgeshire, one half of the village was swept away soon after 1811 (Fig. 84). Croxton is a splendid example of a village with a complex history in which emparking was only the final episode. It is clear that, in late medieval times at the latest, the village had two quite distinct parts each arranged along a north-to-south street. The western part had a green at its northern end while the eastern section had the parish church and a much smaller green at its southern end, and perhaps another green to the north. Both parts of the village later shrank in size leaving many abandoned house sites though when and why this took place is not known. Then, in the early nineteenth century the eastern portion, except for the church and hall, was entirely removed for a landscaped park. The western part was subsequently altered and remodelled as an estate village. The village of Madingley, also in Cambridgeshire, shows a variant on this partial removal. There the single long street village had its centre removed in 1743–4 when the park around the adjacent hall was extended and a 'view' created through the village. The result was to produce a polyfocal village of a very curious type. At nearby Conington, yet another variant is visible (Fig. 85). There the medieval village consisted of two quite distinct parts, thus being truly polyfocal. The main centre was arranged around a crossroads with the parish church adjacent. The other part of the village lay 300 metres to the north on either side of the 'High Street'. In the early eighteenth century a modest country house was erected within a small park to the north-west of the village. In 1849 this park was extended to the edge of High Street. All the houses there were demolished leaving only the banks and scarps of their foundations and former gardens in the park on the north side of the street. On the south side a row of four semi-detached cottages of varying designs, but generally Tudoresque in idiom, was erected to replace them. Thus the village retained its overall form but was changed in detail.

84 The Village and Emparking *Here is the result of early nineteenth-century landscaping and emparking on a small village. As can be seen in the upper diagram, Croxton had already passed through a period of major changes before this date.*

Related to this emparking were villages which were either rebuilt to a completely new plan or actually established as new settlements by philanthropic and improving landlords at this time. Again in Northamptonshire the small hamlet of Hulcote was turned into the estate village of Easton Neston House in the 1840s. The irregular green with houses scattered around it was replaced by a triangular one with neat gothic-style cottages on two sides. At Thorpe Achurch, in the same county, the simple single-street village was totally removed in 1830 and estate cottages erected on the old site but only on one side of the street. Here, no great house or park was involved – the changes were the result of agricultural improvement and lordly philanthropy. Other examples of this kind are to be found all over the country but particularly in north-east England where, in addition, there are known to be some completely replanned villages. For instance, Acklington in Northumberland, a typical eleventh- or

twelfth-century planned village, with houses arranged on either side of a broad open green, was completely remodelled by its owner soon after 1800. The green disappeared, all the property boundaries were realigned and new estate cottages erected. Even if villages retained their original form their character could be changed entirely by the work of landowners. At Cardington in Bedfordshire (Fig. 86) many of the houses around the medieval green were rebuilt in the late eighteenth century by John Howard, the philanthropist, who lived there.

It is necessary to exercise some care in the interpretation of the history of villages which appear to have been cleared or altered as a result of emparking at this period as detailed research can sometimes disclose a rather different sequence of events. At Roudham, in Norfolk, the remains of streets, former house sites and paddocks surround the Hall and might easily be suggested as a good example of clearance for emparking. In fact, Roudham, which had survived all the vicissitudes of medieval plagues and economic decline, began to shrink in the late seventeenth century as the lord of the manor reorganized his estate. A long process of

85 Estate Cottages, Conington, Cambridgeshire
These houses were built in 1849 for people removed from an adjacent part of the village destroyed during the enlargement of a park.

buying-up of freeholders took place which was not complete until 1770. By this time most of the village as well as its land was in the lord's hands and the village had contracted to one large farmstead and a handful of cottages. It was only later that part of the former village was landscaped for a park. Thus the shrinkage was the result of agricultural improvement and not emparking as such. The same, possibly misleading picture can be seen at Easton Neston in Northamptonshire (Fig. 67). There church, park, gardens and great house all give the impression of village removal following emparking. Yet the village actually disappeared in the fifteenth century as a result of enclosure for sheep.

Despite the national picture of increasing population, individual villages still shrank during the eighteenth and nineteenth centuries. It is of some interest to note that, although these changes can be closely dated, usually because of surviving maps, the reasons for them are in most cases quite unknown. This is an important point for, if we cannot explain movement and shrinkage in villages at this date, how much more difficult is it to understand the same processes in earlier periods? Two Northamptonshire examples illustrate the variety of this type of change. The village of Rothersthorpe (Fig. 89) now has two roughly parallel east-west streets which converge at their eastern ends. It had this form by 1884 as the first large-scale Ordnance Survey map clearly shows but the 1810 Enclosure Map depicts a third street to the south of and parallel to the more southerly of the two streets. This third street is still lined with some houses though others have already vanished. Within sixty years, for no reason which can be established and without anyone apparently recording it, the southernmost street and all its houses except one farm disappeared, leaving only a rough holloway and the abandoned house sites and garden plots. Green's Norton is somewhat different. An eighteenth-century map shows it as a compact street village with a green at its northern end near the church and with three separate small hamlets to the south, south-east and south-west of it. By the late nineteenth century these hamlets had vanished except for two houses, and the old green had been built over.

At Hanging Houghton, in the same county, an earlier alteration is also a mystery. A map of the mid-seventeenth century shows the village with a basic L-shaped plan with houses on both sides of the two streets. But by the mid-nineteenth century the northern arm, including street, houses and gardens, had disappeared completely. Meanwhile, to the east

86 Cardington, Bedfordshire *Here, in the late eighteenth century, John Howard the philanthropist rebuilt many of the houses around the old village green, with the result that the village entirely changed its character.*

of the surviving street, a triangular green had appeared with houses along two sides.

Similar examples of equally late shrinkage or movement have been noted in many other places. According to a map of 1632, the village of Ogle in Northumberland comprised a very large irregular green with the manor house at its eastern end and houses on its north and south sides. By 1830 all the houses on the north side had disappeared and only a few buildings remained on the south. Later still some of the latter houses went. In recent times new houses have appeared, some on former house sites on the north side of the old green and others, opposite them, on the green itself. The result is that a new 'street' village has developed. Yet the old green and the sites of most of the abandoned houses and their gardens still remain preserved in the surrounding pasture to show the complex recent changes in the village.

The Enclosure Movement of the later eighteenth and nineteenth centuries, though it was largely concerned with the final removal of the medieval open or strip fields over great parts of midland, north-eastern, central and southern England, also had a major effect on settlement. Its most important aspect, that of inaugurating a new phase of secondary settlement, will be dealt with later, but the process also had a considerable and lasting influence on many villages. The formal Acts of Parliament, which gave approval for enclosure, were usually concerned with all the land over which there were common rights. In most parishes this land was a mixture of arable, usually cultivated in strips, open heath, moorland, fen and downland. But in many villages the existing greens were, for various reasons, also regarded as common land and were included in the areas which were to be enclosed. As a result a large number of ancient greens were divided into paddocks and allotted to the owners of adjacent properties, a process that is well illustrated at Cold Kirby in North Yorkshire (Fig. 46). In some cases there was subsequently a further development, for the small paddocks, existing as they did in front of houses in the centre of a village, had little agricultural value. Thus, especially in the nineteenth century when population was expanding, these plots were often sold off for building development.

A classic example of this process can be seen at Great Shelford in Cambridgeshire (Figs. 45, 87). The great green which existed in later medieval times was the result of earlier accretion from two older village centres. By the early nineteenth century this green had houses all around it. In 1834 an Act of Parliament allowed all the open arable land in the parish and the green to be enclosed. Every house on the edge of the green was allotted a long narrow strip of land in front of it and almost immediately new buildings began to appear on these strips. This process of infilling took place over a considerable period as the existing structures show, for they include a mid-nineteenth-century public house, three cottages of the same date, a row of late nineteenth-century terraced houses, some Edwardian gentlemen's residences, a telephone exchange of the 1950s and an ultra-modern bungalow of space-age design. This slow development has changed the layout of the village centre entirely and it is now difficult, though not impossible, to see the outlines of the older green. On the other hand, a new green has appeared with the demolition of one of the Edwardian houses and the transformation of part of its garden into a public open space.

The same process has been noted elsewhere in Cambridgeshire. At Orwell the large rectangular medieval green, almost certainly a planned addition to the original village in response to a market grant, had already been reduced to a small irregular open space by 1680 according to a map of that date. This green survived until 1836 when it was divided into six plots which were allotted to the owners of adjacent houses. In the later nineteenth century new houses were built on some of these plots. At nearby Hardwick, in medieval times, there was also a neat rectangular green at the northern end of the village with houses all around it and with the parish church on its southern side. Again this green was enclosed as part of the general Act of Enclosure for the parish in 1836 and was divided into plots. Four of these remained as paddocks, one had a cottage built on it in the late nineteenth century and another had the new Rectory, a fine red-brick Tudoresque structure, erected on it just before 1850. Comberton had a central green, almost certainly a medieval planned addition, which was finally enclosed in 1839 (Fig. 88). Again the land was allotted to the owners of adjacent houses and long front gardens appeared. However, in a few places earlier encroachment on the green had taken place so that the present garden walls actually show two stages of development.

Perhaps the most remarkable effect of the enclosure of a village green is to be seen at Kingston, again in Cambridgeshire (Fig. 89). The original,

87 Great Shelford, Cambridgeshire *This 'green' occupies part of the great medieval High Green of the village but it is not its direct successor. The medieval green was enclosed in 1834 and houses, including those in the background, gradually spread over it. The present open space was created a few years ago when an Edwardian house was demolished.*

perhaps late Saxon, village consisted of houses set around a small green with the parish church at its north-east end. By the fourteenth century a large rectangular green had been added to the south, perhaps as a result of the market grant of 1306, and this was soon surrounded by houses. By the eighteenth century the original green had been built over and the later one reduced in size by encroachment. In addition there had been large-scale shrinkage elsewhere. In 1815 the green was enclosed and subdivided and in the following hundred years new houses were erected on it and others along the former edges of the green were abandoned. In effect, the village collapsed inwards on to its former green and in doing so completely altered its shape.

The effects of enclosure were not confined to the obliteration of greens. Alterations to road systems also led to changes in the shape of villages. At Spridlington, in Lincolnshire, where four roads met, the abandonment of the old curving medieval road running north out of the village and its replacement by a new straight one led to a re-allotment of the adjacent land which was followed by the establishment of new houses and farmsteads. An older T-shaped village changed to one with an X-shaped plan.

One other form of village alteration, in fact the most common of all, was the result of straightforward expansion. In the late eighteenth and early

88 Village Green, Comberton, Cambridgeshire *The houses in the background stand on the edge of the former green. The garden wall and the gate in the middle distance indicate encroachment on the green of seventeenth- or eighteenth-century date. The wall and the building in the foreground were built after the formal enclosure of the green in 1839.*

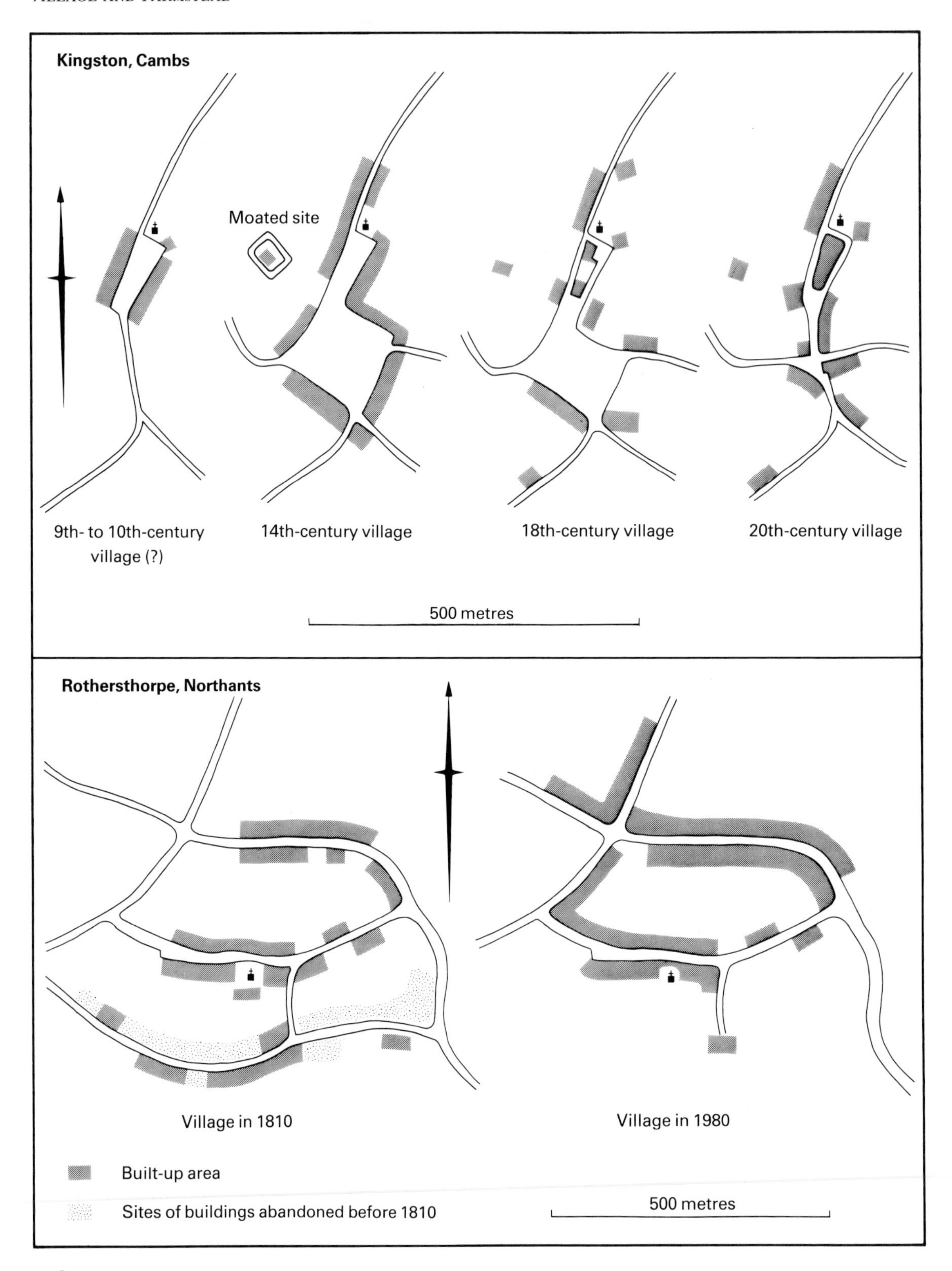
Kingston, Cambs
Moated site
9th- to 10th-century village (?)
14th-century village
18th-century village
20th-century village
500 metres
Rothersthorpe, Northants
Village in 1810
Village in 1980
Built-up area
Sites of buildings abandoned before 1810
500 metres

nineteenth centuries most villages grew in size and, especially between 1800 and 1850, many places doubled their population despite often extensive emigration to the growing industrial towns and to the New World. Part of this new population was housed in existing buildings which were often subdivided into crowded tenements. Elsewhere new cottages were crammed into existing plots in front of or behind houses already there. The writer's own village, Whittlesford in Cambridgeshire, still shows traces of this sort of development in spite of more modern changes. The main village street was lined with individual farmsteads on fairly large plots up to 1800. Then many of these plots had semi-detached cottages built on them and by the end of the nineteenth century the village appeared more strongly nucleated than it ever had been.

In most places, however, expansion usually took the form of steady ribbon development on land often newly enclosed from the former open or strip fields. Again such expansion tended to distort the earlier shapes and give the villages entirely new plans. The village of Meldreth, in Cambridgeshire, is a good example of this. Even before the expansion of the 1950s the village was stretched out along a winding road for a distance of no less than three kilometres in addition to dwellings extending along various side lanes. To attempt to explain the history of Meldreth on the basis of this form would be difficult, if not impossible, but a look at the Enclosure Map of Meldreth showing the village in 1820 displays a very different place. The village was then made up of six quite distinct and separate parts and in fact Meldreth can be seen as a superb example of a polyfocal village.

Developments in communications and transportation systems from the late seventeenth century onwards not only altered existing villages but also produced entirely new settlements in the countryside. In the late seventeenth and eighteenth centuries, turnpike roads often gave rise to new places. At Whiteparish, Wiltshire, a stretch of road was created in 1756 as part of the Salisbury-Romsey Turnpike. The building of a tollgate and tollhouse on it led to the development of a group of cottages which became known as Cowesfield Gate.

Even more common are the small semi-industrial hamlets which appeared in the late eighteenth and early nineteenth centuries along the then new canals. Wharves were often built to serve the needs of adjacent villages and these were followed by the construction of warehouses, cottages and small industrial concerns. Mr T.Rowley has described a number of such places. Amongst the best of his examples is Shardlow in Derbyshire which lies near the point where the Trent and Mersey Canal meets the River Trent. Between 1800 and 1815 an entirely new village appeared quite separate from the old village of Shardlow, lying alongside the canal and around a group of wharves. As well as warehouses, mills and a brewery, rows of neat terraced houses came into existence and in the end the place grew much larger than the original village.

The coming of the railways had an even greater impact, particularly as many rural stations lay well away from the villages they served. If the distance was not great, subsequent ribbon development tended to extend towards these stations, thus altering the shape of the old settlement. In places where the station was quite remote, entirely new settlements grew up, usually with an inn, railway workers' cottages and often a chapel. Such places can be seen all over England but perhaps the most remarkable is the village of Halwill Junction in north Devon. Until the late nineteenth century, apart from a few scattered and ancient farmsteads, there was no settlement in the remote eastern part of Halwill parish. Then, in 1878, the London and South Western Railway began the construction of the line from Okehampton to Holsworthy. In January 1879 both the line and the new Halwill Station were opened and a new settlement came into existence. In 1886 a branch line to Launceston was built and both lines were later extended to Bude and Padstow respectively. The subsequent railway working, whereby regular trains between both these rapidly expanding resorts and London had to be joined and split at Halwill, led to an increase in the size of the new settlement now known as Halwill Junction. In 1925 the Southern Railway built a third line from Halwill to Torrington, later extended to Barnstaple. For a few short years the Atlantic Coast expresses were divided at Halwill. Stopping trains, calling at places such as Egloskerry, Dunsland Cross and Meeth Halt, paused at Halwill, and slow freight trains were assembled there. Its life in

89 Change in Villages *At Kingston the present arrangement of the village bears little resemblance to its original form laid out round a planned green. Today, both this green, and a much larger later one, have almost entirely disappeared. Rothersthorpe shows how a village can change its plan in little more than a century and a half with one of its streets vanishing entirely.*

the early part of this century has been described as 'an oasis of activity' in a slumbering rural world. This lasted until October 1966 when British Railways closed all the lines. Now only the abandoned cuttings, embankments, sidings and buildings remain of the railway, but the settlement of Halwill Junction still survives as the economic and social centre of the area.

There is one other addition to the village landscape that arrived during the eighteenth century. This was the industrial village, particularly linked to the large-scale extractive industries such as coal mining and quarrying. Entirely new settlements grew up, villages in all but the fact that the population did not work on the land. They were often a type of estate village, founded and controlled by an individual or company which owned the industrial site. Some of the best examples are in Northumberland where places such as East Cramlington, Seghill and Sharkhouse are all colliery villages, aesthetically a long way from their rural counterparts but villages nonetheless. All over the Northumberland and Durham coalfield colliery owners constructed new villages. Percy Main on Tyneside was described in 1887 as 'a village of modern growth containing several good streets of artisans' dwellings'. Later development has often obscured the origins and form of these villages. Ashington was a single farm in the mid nineteenth century. In 1880 a new village was laid out with 665 cottages arranged in eleven parallel rows – these still remain in the centre of the modern town.

Another area which shows the same pattern of industrial villages is the former Somerset coalfield around Radstock, and there are many others. For example, in the Lake District, the village of Threlkeld, which lies in the deep valley below the craggy slopes of Blencathra, was a small rural hamlet until the nineteenth century. Then the rapid

90 Styal, Cheshire *A 'model' village, built in the 1780s to house the workers at a new mill. Yet, as this view shows well, its arrangement and appearance were not based on old-established rural villages but foreshadowed the darker side of the industrial urbanization of the next century.*

exploitation of the mineral deposits there, which between 1880 and 1900 produced over 10,000 tons of lead and 13,000 tons of zinc, caused the equally rapid development of the hamlet into a prosperous mining village.

The growth of the textile industry in the late eighteenth century also produced small villages which grew up or were laid out around the new mills that they served. Many of these rapidly expanded into towns but a few still remain much as they were. Some are of particular interest for, as with mining villages, they were often planned by their entrepreneurial owners. Styal, in Cheshire (Fig. 90), laid out in the 1780s next to a new cotton mill, illustrates well not only the 'village' size of these settlements but also their primarily industrial base.

Some industrial villages developed in unexpected places out of much older settlements as a result of the exploitation of a local resource. For example, Stonesfield in Oxfordshire (Fig. 91) suddenly became an industrial village in the seventeenth century after five hundred years of agricultural obscurity. Its inhabitants began to work the stone which lay beneath it and which was widely used for roofing slates. For a little over two hundred years the stone mining and quarrying flourished and produced a village of highly irregular plan as cottages appeared along existing roads and near the quarries. Then the demand for stone slates waned, the industry declined and only the abandoned spoil heaps and the scattered form of the village now remain.

The development of many other extractive industries and their associated settlements was also often followed by sudden and precipitous decline as lodes failed and seams ran out. Desertion of these semi-rural settlements, both planned and unplanned, went on side by side with their establishment and growth. In Shropshire, the important lead deposits there were worked as early as the Roman period but the peak time for their exploitation began in the mid nineteenth century. The main area was around the old village of Shelve, north-west of Church Stretton. The industry was carried out in a piecemeal fashion and the miners erected their own houses on the edges of common land, each of which had a small group of fields to supplement their income. The Earls of Tankerville, lords of the manor in the nineteenth century, actively encouraged such settlement and the result was the appearance of sprawling hamlets covering large areas. Two of these, Pennerley and Perkins Beach, began in the early nineteenth century and by 1847 had some 93 smallholdings between them covering 1000 hectares. Even more houses were built subsequently but by 1902 abandonment had started and this has continued ever since.

In this period, then, the villages of England once more exhibited all the characteristics of change so familiar to earlier centuries. The same is true of the land beyond the villages. For the 'colonization' of land earlier occupied by open fields, heathland, downs or upland moors, which had begun in the seventeenth century, increased dramatically in the eighteenth century when parliamentary Acts of Enclosure came into force and continued well into the nineteenth century. All over the Midlands, southern and north-eastern England tens of thousands of hectares of arable land were enclosed, and in addition even larger areas of heath, moorland, downland, forest and fen were divided into new fields. Within a few years of the new hedged, walled or ditched fields being established farmsteads appeared within them whose owners or tenants were to farm there. The landscape of Leicestershire, with its scatter of red-brick farmsteads, is perhaps the most typical result of this process, but the stone-built moorland farmsteads of North Yorkshire (Fig. 92), the mottled brick and thatched houses of the Hampshire and Dorset heathlands and the soft grey-brick farms of the eastern fenlands are also part of the same development (see title-page illustration). In many places what had been for centuries a relatively empty landscape was suddenly filled with a new pattern of settlement. The following examples are typical of the changes that took place.

In north-east Cambridgeshire, along the fen edge, is the parish of Swaffham Bulbeck. By the late eighteenth century the old village was the only centre of settlement. To the south-east, on rising ground, lay the village's open fields and beyond them its open downland. North-west of the village lay the fenland, part of which had been enclosed and drained in the seventeenth century. The Act for the enclosing of the wastes and commons of the parish was passed in 1800 and within two years all

OVERLEAF **91 Stonesfield, Oxfordshire** *A seventeenth-century and later industrial village whose inhabitants found their livelihood working the stone roofing slate from the adjacent quarries and mines. The result is a village with no clearly defined plan.*

92 Arkengarthdale, North Yorkshire *A typical northern enclosure farmstead of the late eighteenth century, set amidst its contemporary rectangular field system on the high moorland at a height of over 400 metres.*

the open fields, downland and the remaining fenland were divided into neat rectangular fields. On the old downland Four Mile Stable Farm, its name taken from its position on the seventeenth-century Newmarket racecourse, was built soon after 1800. Below it, in the area of the old open fields, Chalk Farm appeared just before 1812, while not far away New England Farm is dated 1833. Nearer the village, but still within the former open-field land, Hill House Farm was built about 1830. Out on the fen, Adventurers' Ground Farm, situated on land enclosed in the 1650s, is dated 1839 and Red Hill Farm is known to have been established about 1840. Further out on the newly-enclosed deep fen, four other farmsteads appeared before 1850.

Throughout medieval and later times a large area in the west of Oxfordshire comprised the Royal Forest of Wychwood. By the early nineteenth century, though the actual woodland had been encroached upon around its edges and there were many clearings, it was, as Arthur Young saw it, a 'fine wild tract of country'. But in 1856 the Parliamentary Act for the disafforestation of Wychwood came into force. The first trees of the 850 hectares of unreclaimed forest were cut in October 1856. Sixteen months later, in January 1858, the first tenants were living in their new farmhouses, seven of which had been built 'on sites judiciously selected'. The same process took place in many of the remaining areas of Royal Forest such as Delamere in Cheshire and Needwood in Staffordshire, and in these cases too a pattern of new farmsteads appeared. In the latter area the tiny hamlet of Newchurch developed around the building erected to serve the spiritual needs of the new community living in scattered farmsteads.

All these settlements were established *de novo* without any older neighbours. In other places new farmsteads were inserted between a much older pattern of dispersed farms. At Sturminster Newton,

in the heart of the medieval Forest of Blackmoor in Dorset, isolated farms had appeared in fields created after woodland clearance by at least the fourteenth century. Perry Farm, in the south of the parish, is one recorded by name in a fourteenth-century document. Encroachment on the forest went on, perhaps almost continuously. There are a number of isolated farmsteads which are not recorded in documents but which, from their suriving architecture, are clearly of considerable age. Lower Bagber Farm has a reset datestone of 1581 and Poplar Farm, though massively rebuilt, contains some sixteenth-century material. Even so, by the early seventeenth century there were still nearly 900 hectares of open common land or woodland in the parish. This, too, was partially enclosed in the seventeenth and eighteenth centuries and a number of farmsteads of this period lie within these later enclosures. The final removal of the wastes, by Acts of 1834 and 1844, produced a rash of late nineteenth-century farmsteads and cottages, dotted about within the new rigidly rectangular field system.

Even where there was no formal enclosure, the establishment of new settlements went on apace. On the estuarine marshes of south Lincolnshire and north-west Norfolk reclamation continued as it probably had done since Roman times. Here, as elsewhere, the very names of the new farmsteads tell us the period of their origin. Balaclava Farm, built in 1855 on Terrington Marsh, Norfolk, is a splendid instance of this phenomenon.

Large parts of the moorlands of England were totally altered in the nineteenth century. One of the best examples, for a number of reasons, is Exmoor. In 1815 a large block of land in the most inaccessible part of the moor was subject to an Act of Enclosure. The land was Crown property, but of little value, so plans were drawn up to enclose it and plant trees on 400 hectares. However, the need for timber did not materialize and in 1818 the Crown decided to sell its allotments by auction. A number of local magnates sent in sealed bids, but to the surprise of all John Knight, a wealthy Worcestershire ironmaster, offered the immense sum of £50,000. Knight thus paid over £12 per hectare for an empty piece of moorland with no mineral resources, roads, hedges, trees or settlement, except for a single farmstead at Simonsbath in the Barle Valley. The latter had been set up in 1654 in an earlier phase of expansion.

For twenty years Knight tried to reclaim the moorland and to work it. To do this he employed many labourers and shepherds who needed accommodation. They lived in cottages at Simonsbath, which thus developed into a hamlet, and in two outlying farmsteads which were built around 1825. The project was financially disastrous and it was not until Knight's son Frederick took over the management of the estate in 1841 that things improved. From 1844 he divided the land into areas of 150 to 300 hectares and leased the new blocks at very low rents. The first new farmstead appeared in 1841, four more in 1844 and others in 1845, 1846 and 1847. Another three were occupied in 1849, a further one in 1852 and two more in 1861. Simonsbath itself acquired a church, a hotel and a post office, as well as new cottages, and by 1871 had a population of 339.

In the end Knight made very little money out of the venture, but perhaps he did not intend to. He had been brought up on Exmoor, being only six when his father acquired the estate. He enjoyed the life of a hunting squire, the battle against nature and the prestige of land ownership. Mere economics did not come into the argument. This story is a timely reminder that the ebb and flow of settlement history is not always related to geographical determinants or economic reality. The 'human factor', often the result of decisions by eccentric, stubborn and illogical people, has an enormous influence.

Alongside this expansion there continued the inevitable contraction and desertion of settlement in some parts of the country. Because this period of history is so well-documented the reasons involved can either be presumed with reasonable certainty or proved without doubt. The growth of agricultural estates and the rationalization of farms as a result of the development of new machinery and techniques played their part, and times of economic depression had a particularly devastating effect in certain areas.

On the fenlands of eastern England the agricultural depressions of the late nineteenth and early twentieth centuries produced a massive reduction in settlement, with the abandonment of many small farmsteads which were often relative newcomers to the landscape. Despite drainage and enclosure these fens remained marginal land and their owners could not always compete with those holding better land elsewhere. On Burwell Fen, in Cambridgeshire, there was no settlement until the 1840s. Then the drainage of the fen was improved by the establishment of a Drainage Commission who, amongst other measures, built a powerful steam engine to draw water from the fen. Almost immediately the poor land, which was used mainly for pasture, became potential arable and with farming entering a prosperous era it was worthwhile to cultivate large areas. By the 1860s no less then eleven new farmsteads had appeared scattered across the fens, as well as three more on the fen edge. But the 1870s saw the onset of a major agricultural depression. It became unprofitable to use the fen as arable land and much of it reverted to summer grazing. By 1903 five of the new farmsteads had been deserted. During the First World War, when agriculture again prospered, two of these deserted farmsteads were reoccupied. Then, in the 1920s and 1930s the agricultural depression returned and by 1940 only one farmstead remained out on the fen which had been largely given up to nature and was classified as derelict land. The single survivor gained new life in 1941 when the local War Agricultural Committee poured in vast sums of money to improve the land and its drainage at a time of national crisis.

In other places farmsteads disappeared to be replaced by new buildings, often on different sites. At Croydon, also in Cambridgeshire, a map of 1797 shows a major farm and four labourer's cottages on land probably enclosed for sheep in the early sixteenth century. By 1900 only one cottage remained though the land which had been worked from the earlier farm was now run from two separate farmsteads, one 250 metres to the south-west, the other 600 metres to the south-east. Both of these are mid-nineteenth-century structures. In this case these changes probably resulted from a combination of farm reorganization and a desire to establish new farmsteads with better access to a changed communication pattern. Both the new farmsteads lie on a road which, until the nineteenth century, was a minor trackway but which, in 1826, was turnpiked and made the main route from Cambridge to Biggleswade.

Elsewhere in England farmsteads of a much older origin were abandoned in the eighteenth and nineteenth centuries. Work in west Somerset has shown that a number of isolated farmsteads, documented as being in existence in the thirteenth and fourteenth centuries, and thus probably much older, disappeared between 1750 and 1850, mainly as the result of farm amalgamation and estate consolidation. Even hamlets vanished at this period. At Spargrove, near Bruton, there were six houses and a medieval moated manor house in 1791, but now only the Victorian replacement of the manor house remains.

The same abandonment of settlement is also visible in areas such as north Hertfordshire where, especially in the late nineteenth century, there was a major contraction of settlement. Here there was, and still is, a dispersed pattern of isolated farmsteads and small groups of houses and cottages, often set around tiny greens. Archaeological and documentary work has shown that many of these were in existence in late Saxon or early medieval times and some may go back to the late Roman period. Yet between 1850 and 1900 many of the farmsteads disappeared and the hamlets shrank in size or even vanished. For example, in the parish of Anstey in north-east Hertfordshire, though the main village actually grew in size after 1850, the surrounding hamlets of Puddocks Green End, Puddocks, North End and Snow End all lost a large proportion of their dwellings. But the reasons for this abandonment, even at such a late date, are not clearly understood.

-12-
The Modern Landscape

No one can doubt that rural settlement in England has changed in the last eighty years and that we now live in an environment which is subject to constant and increasingly rapid alteration. Because of this we tend to look back at the past and to regard it as stable, and therefore comforting, in contrast with our own unstable and mobile world. But all we have today is the latest phase of change, more violent perhaps than before, certainly faster than that in previous centuries, but a direct descendant of it and merely part of the same ebb and flow of the tide of human occupation.

In the last half century people have been driven from their homes to produce military training areas and airfields at times of national crisis. The village of Imber, in Wiltshire, suffered in this way as did Tyneham, in Dorset (Fig. 93), together with a host of farmsteads. At Stanford in Norfolk three villages and a large number of farms were cleared of their inhabitants in 1940. At all these places the rapacious landlord, in this case the Ministry of Defence, still maintains its grasp on the land for its own purposes, despite the cries of the dispossessed and the political promises of a democratic government. In Bedfordshire the airfield at Thurleigh lies across the site of the hamlet of Whitwick Green, while during the construction of Little Staughton airfield half the village of Little Staughton was obliterated.

Similarly, the demands of the great urban areas for ever-increasing supplies of water have not only resulted in the flooding of large tracts of high-quality agricultural land, as well as some of the most beautiful valleys in the country, but they have also led to depopulation. This process began in the late nineteenth century and still continues. In general, it is farmsteads that are literally swallowed up by these man-made lakes but villages and hamlets have also been lost. In 1940 the hamlet of Mardale Green, in the Lake District, vanished beneath Haweswater. Here again powerful lords, in this case Manchester Corporation Water Works, were the villains. Although these changes are particularly dramatic, there have been examples of landlords acting in the same manner, for various motives, throughout history, and with the same inevitable results.

Yet at the same time the State, acting in its capacity as an authoritarian landlord, can and has created new settlements, as did medieval lords. In northern England, for example, new hamlets and even small villages have appeared within or close to areas afforested on a vast scale by the Forestry Commission. The new woodland and the new settlements have provided much needed work and homes in these remote regions. Some new settlements have been created by commercial concerns. In Bedfordshire, the village of Stewartby (Fig. 94) was built in 1927 to provide homes for brickyard workers, while Shortstown was created even earlier, in 1917, by Short Brothers for the families of men engaged in aircraft construction. In essence these new settlements are not very different from eleventh-century planned villages – only the centuries separate them.

Modern planners, with their concern for compact

rural housing estates and the better use of land, have held back ribbon development but they have still changed the shape and appearance of villages. There must be few villages in England that have not at least a small line of council houses or a modern estate of private dwellings, while many have had considerable blocks of new houses grafted on to them. Sometimes these modern houses have been inserted into the gaps left by medieval or later shrinkage, or have filled in empty spaces which have separated foci dating from late Saxon times. In other places whole new estates have been laid out around the edges of old villages, in the same way as medieval lords added planned extensions to their villages and with much the same visual effect.

In some places authority at a much more local level has played an important role. Whittlesford, in Cambridgeshire, lost its village green by encroachment, probably in the thirteenth century (Fig. 95). Yet in the 1950s the parish council took the opportunity of acquiring for recreational purposes the abandoned garden of an eighteenth-century

ABOVE LEFT **93 Tyneham House, Dorset** *This magnificent building, mainly of sixteenth-century date but including part of a fourteenth-century hall, is now, together with the rest of the village of Tyneham, derelict and abandoned. Tyneham survived until 1940 when it was taken over by the army for a military training area. It remains in the possession of the Ministry of Defence.*

ABOVE **94 Stewartby, Bedfordshire** *Despite the 'obvious' Danish name, this village was founded in 1927 by the firm of B. J. Forder and named after the company chairman, H. Stewart. It was built to provide homes for the workers in the adjacent brickyards.*

BELOW LEFT **95 Whittlesford, Cambridgeshire** *This 'green' has an appearance and a function very similar to those of other village greens centuries old. It was, however, created in 1958 out of a long-abandoned eighteenth-century garden. Only the council houses which edge it show its modern origins.*

country house, long since demolished. Subsequently the planning authorities decided to build council houses around its boundaries and it now has the same appearance and function as other village greens which are centuries old.

In Northamptonshire a very different effect was achieved as a result of a local authority decision. The village of Faxton (Fig. 43), which was probably a post eleventh-century foundation and which subsequently had two major planned additions to it, followed by a period of considerable shrinkage, just managed to survive until the 1950s. Then, because the County Council found it uneconomic to make up the roads leading to the village, it finally died. If it had survived for another ten years then almost certainly it would have expanded as a commuter village.

Local authorities can sometimes have an even greater effect on the landscape. A recent example is the deliberate policy of clearance and desertion which was implemented in County Durham. The infamous scheme by which the so-called 'Category D' industrial villages were bulldozed away and their inhabitants rehoused in new towns has been a major source of contention in the declining parts of the coalfield there. East Howe, near Sedgefield, and Burnhope, near Lanchester (Fig. 96), are only two of many examples of villages swept away by an authority which arbitrarily decided that they had no future. Other villages have been changed by individual owners in recent years exactly as in the remote past. Until 1900 the village of Ashton in Northamptonshire consisted of a single short street with small triangular greens at each end where incoming roads met. Then the Rothschild family, who owned Ashton, cleared the whole village. They rebuilt it on the same site but they gave it a broad rectangular central green edged by neat thatched and stone-built cottages as well as a traditional public house.

In contrast to these changes, which can be seen as the continuation of processes that have been acting over centuries, some aspects of change in villages are new and directly related to the conditions and demands of twentieth-century life.

96 Burnhope, Co Durham *The isolated church, surrounded by traces of former houses and streets, produces the appearance of a deserted medieval village. In fact, Burnhope was a nineteenth-century mining village, ruthlessly destroyed in the 1950s when its life was alleged to be over.*

97 Barton Park, Great Barton, Suffolk *Suburbia in a rural setting. Here middle-class needs and hopes have been achieved by a pseudo-village, complete with a green, established in the parkland of a demolished country house.*

They have not occurred before, or at least not on the scale that they do now. One important modern phenomenon is the rise of the commuter village. Such villages have indeed existed since medieval times when people living in places close to towns walked there on a daily basis for work. Later, the coming of the railways produced a massive growth of commuter villages, though many were soon swamped by large-scale urban expansion and became merely suburbs. But the arrival of the motor car, coupled with planning restrictions and the concept of the 'Green Belt', has led to the expansion of villages on a scale never seen before. Around most large towns villages have been enlarged, often to the extent that the original small settlement has been completely overwhelmed. Most of the best and the worst of surburban architecture and attitudes has been forced ruthlessly on these rural communities (Figs. 97, 98). Few of their inhabitants now have any connection with the land – these villages are merely places in which to live in surroundings that are cleaner, safer and more pleasant than the adjacent towns. Yet the needs of people who are still psychologically urban dwellers produce neat suburban estates, schools, playing fields, supermarkets and other services. In essence these commuter villages have become little more than detached suburbs. On the other hand, in some cases the arrival of the commuter has revitalized many dying villages and saved them from the otherwise inevitable slow decay.

The same is true of what may be called tourist and weekend villages, though these have been less successful. The weekend villages, particularly common in parts of Norfolk, are a major social problem. Older inhabitants have been driven out, not by rapacious lords or even by bureaucratic authorities, but by the market forces created by middle-class demands for a 'cottage in the country'. In many of these villages the greater part of the population lives there only at weekends in the summer. The rest of the time these settlements remain almost dead and, lacking the necessary services for the few remaining permanent inhabitants, continue to decline as real villages.

In the 'tourist villages' the problem is not too few people but too many. For half the year they are swamped by visitors who bring profit to a small proportion of the population but also make life unbearable for the majority. Indeed, at times visitors threaten to destroy, by sheer numbers, the beauty they come to see. Castle Combe in Wiltshire, Finchingfield in Essex and Looe in Cornwall are examples of places where the lifestyle of the inhabitants is continuously under threat and whose form and appearance is being gradually changed as a result of the pressures of tourism.

Elsewhere in England shrinkage, desertion and movement of villages have taken place over the last century and yet all memory of the events has been forgotten. In Northamptonshire, as late as the 1840s, the village of Luddington (Fig. 99) lay in the

bottom of the valley of the Alconbury Brook. During the next hundred years the village virtually disappeared, leaving only two cottages, one farm and the church. The last house was not abandoned until the 1950s. But no one seems to have realized that the village was shrinking and to this day it is not known why it happened. In Wiltshire the land around the village of Snap was acquired in the early years of this century by a family of Ramsbury butchers who turned it into a sheep farm. Deprived

98 Great Shelford, Cambridgeshire *Part of a 1.5-kilometre-long extension which developed in the 1920s and 1930s when the village changed from a rural settlement to a commuting suburb.*

99 Luddington in the Brook, Northamptonshire
The isolated church, Church Farm and the handful of modern cottages seem to indicate a classic example of a deserted medieval village. In fact the village was still here in 1840 and has disappeared only in the last hundred years or so; no one knows why.

of employment the villagers were forced to leave and by 1914 Snap had been abandoned (Fig. 100). Despite a violent outcry which involved the local MP, memories soon faded. By 1950, when M.W.Smith wrote the history of Snap, the local tradition was that the village had been deserted because its water supply had failed.

How much more difficult is it then to explain the desertion, movement or shrinkage of settlements in the medieval period, let alone in Roman or prehistoric times? It is easy to resort to broad generalizations based on evidence of widespread social changes, economic development or climatic alteration. Yet the decisions of individuals or groups of people can have and probably did have a much greater effect, if we did but know what they were. Thus we puzzle over the existence in one area of a dense pattern of prehistoric settlement and a total lack of it a short distance away. We wonder why there are a large number of medieval moated sites in one parish and none in the next. Such situations are common and we cannot explain them either in terms of neat geographical determinism or even with reference to the broad themes of this book. The answers will probably never be known but they almost certainly relate to purely local decisions and events which overrode general trends.

The importance of local factors in influencing events can be seen in the present landscape. In south Cambridgeshire there are two adjacent parishes with almost identical physical backgrounds and with very similar histories until the end of the eighteenth century. In both the medieval fields were enclosed in the early nineteenth century and a scatter of farmsteads appeared in the new fields. The land of one parish came into the hands of two farmers in the 1920s and in the last thirty years reorganization and more effective methods of agriculture have meant that almost all the nineteenth-century farmsteads now stand ruinous. In the other parish a decision made by the County Council, also in the 1920s, to buy up land and to create a number of tenanted smallholdings produced many new dispersed farmsteads. It has

100 Snap, Wiltshire *Another apparently perfect example of a deserted medieval village, Snap was actually removed in the early part of this century by a butcher who wanted to run stock on the land. By 1950 all memory of this event had been lost and only detailed historical research was able to unravel the story.*

recently been suggested that the County Council sell off their land to the sitting tenants. If this comes about the inevitable result, at least in the long term, will almost certainly be the amalgamation of the smallholdings to produce large farming units and, presumably, the abandonment of some of the more isolated farmsteads.

Elsewhere the complex interplay between broad economic events, technological advances and social changes has led to the abandonment of farmsteads, especially in the Pennines (Fig. 101). Hill-farming subsidies have tended to encourage the amalgamation of holdings and modern agricultural techniques do not require the labour force needed half a century ago. At the same time, people are less willing to live in isolated positions. The northern hills are now dotted with derelict farm buildings, many of which are only a century or so old. Without our detailed knowledge of recent events it would be difficult to explain the reasons behind this desertion in a satisfactory manner.

Our ancestors must have been well aware of changes taking place in the landscape. Being as irrational and as apprehensive of change as we are, they probably deplored the destruction of forests in Neolithic times, sneered at the grandiose new villas of the third century AD and stood appalled at the new villages of the eleventh century. Yet inexorably change continued.

As this book has attempted to show, the evidence of these changes is all around us if we care to look for it. In the writer's own village, Whittlesford in Cambridgeshire, where he has lived for over fifteen years, a long and complex story has been unravelled by detailed and assiduous research both in archives and on the ground. Even now not all is clearly understood and there are still large gaps. But one thing is absolutely clear: the village we see now is the result of considerable and perhaps even continuous change over at least 2500 years.

The story appears to begin in the Iron Age for two settlements of that date have been discovered. One of these was soon abandoned, but the other continued into the Roman period and eventually developed into a richly appointed villa. This was perhaps the centre of the estate which later became the parish. Two other small farmsteads grew up elsewhere and across the area which was later to be occupied by the medieval village a very large Roman settlement developed. As yet nothing is known of the Saxon period but by the eleventh century the present village seems to have been in existence, though it then consisted only of a few houses arranged along a street leading to a river crossing.

Between then and 1250 the village grew rapidly in size, its population increasing from around 150 to perhaps over 500. A new planned extension was added to one end of the village with houses set around an L-shaped green. Other dwellings grew up, more haphazardly, along an old road leading north from the village and eventually converged with houses which had been recently established on badly drained meadowland around a small triangular green. Some of this latter expansion seems to have been carried out by enterprising tenant farmers, at least two of whom surrounded their new houses with moats. Even this physical expansion could not contain the growing population and by the end of the thirteenth century the new planned green in the main village had been partially covered by dwellings. As a result, in 1306, when the lord of the manor obtained a grant for a weekly market, he had to lay out a new market place, or green, at the far end of the village. Even so houses grew up around the new market place and indeed extended beyond it.

Then disaster struck. Perhaps as a result of plague, economic decline, or both, the population of the village fell dramatically, perhaps to about 200 by the late fourteenth century, and of course physically it shrank. The original eleventh-century village area was completely abandoned, leaving the church and the manor house quite isolated. In addition, a large gap opened up between the main part of the village and the secondary extension around the triangular green, which itself was reduced to a handful of houses. From then until the seventeenth century the population of the village remained stable and even by the early eighteenth century there were only about 270 people there. Thus, morphologically the village remained static during this period.

By 1801, however, the population had jumped to 416 and by the end of the nineteenth century to almost 900. This increased population was housed in a number of ways. Many dwellings were

101 Coverdale, North Yorkshire *This farmstead, built to house the herdsmen working on the improved enclosed pastures of the moors, is now abandoned and derelict after a life of less than two hundred years. Agricultural technology, and more importantly modern social developments, have made it unnecessary and unwanted.*

subdivided to take three or more families and new cottages were built behind existing houses or on empty plots in the main village. The latter process particularly increased the nucleated appearance of the settlement. In addition, houses began to spread back along the road to the north, reoccupying the area abandoned in the fourteenth century. At the same time houses also appeared along the road to the south so that gradually a T-shaped plan evolved. After enclosure in 1817 the inevitable scatter of farmsteads appeared in the new fields producing a dispersed pattern of settlement.

The arrival of the railway in 1847 led to the construction of a station. This was not situated near the village but in the furthest corner of the parish in order to be equidistant from five adjacent villages. The building of the station was immediately followed by the arrival of a public house, railwaymen's cottages and later some elegant Edwardian villas. In effect a new secondary hamlet appeared, this time actually lying across the parish boundary.

In this century uncontrolled ribbon development continued to the south of the village on the higher dry land, unlike the medieval expansion which had been confined to wet and boggy land. The railway hamlet also expanded towards the village and the two had almost met when post-Second World War planning controls stopped the process. Since then there has been a policy of re-nucleation, with the result that small neat estates of council houses, neo-Georgian private dwellings, and modern-style closes have been set within the old village. Even the secondary medieval hamlet to the north has expanded again with the appearance of both council houses and private dwellings. As we have already seen, the village acquired a new green, made from the grounds of the eighteenth-century manor house (Fig. 95). At the time of writing the possible expansion of Stanstead Airport, only a short drive along the M11, threatens to produce a new growth in population and thus another alteration to the shape of the village.

The word 'palimpsest' has often been used to describe the English landscape, implying that it is the result of the superimposition of one set of features on another throughout time; but the reality is somewhat different. The history of settlement in England is not just the story of man's adaptation to dull geographical determinants, grinding social pressures, inevitable economic change or anything else that geographers, historians and archaeologists tell us. It is all these but it is much more. Most of all it is a wonderful, richly coloured, whirling kaleidoscope of movement and change. If we appreciate this then we may understand our past, present and perhaps even our future that much better.

Bibliography

This bibliography is not intended to be comprehensive. It is merely a selection to indicate the range of evidence for, the modern techniques applied to, and the scholarly interpretation of, the great variety of rural settlements in England.

Many of the works sited under specific period headings also include material relevant to other chapters. For example, Limbrey, S. and Evans, J.G., *The Effect of Man on the Landscape: The Lowland Zone* is listed in the Mesolithic section as it contains three papers of great relevance to that period. However, it also includes articles on the Neolithic, Iron Age, Roman and medieval periods, all of which are important in the context of this book. Similarly, the Royal Commission volumes on *Northamptonshire*, *Dorset* and *Cambridgeshire* contain a very large amount of important material of all dates, and almost all the examples quoted in the text from these counties are taken from the Commission's work.

PART I PREHISTORIC AND ROMAN SETTLEMENT

General Works of Reference

BRADLEY, R., *The Prehistoric Settlement of Britain* (London, 1978).

CLARKE, D.L., *Analytical Archaeology* (London, 1968).

CLARKE, D.L. (ed), *Models in Archaeology* (London, 1972).

DAVIDSON, D. (ed) and SHACKLEY, M. (eds), *Geoarchaeology* (London, 1978).

EVANS, J.G., *Land Snails in Archaeology* (London, 1972).

EVANS, J.G., *The Environment of Early Man in the British Isles* (London, 1975).

FOX, C., *The Personality of Britain* (Cardiff, 1932).

FRERE, S.S., *Britannia* (London, 1967).

FOWLER, P. J. (ed), *Recent Work in Rural Archaeology* (Bradford-on-Avon, 1975).

LIMBREY, S., *Soil Science and Archaeology* (London, 1975).

MEGAW, J.V.S. and SIMPSON, D.D.A., *Introduction to British Prehistory* (Leicester, 1979).

RENFREW, C. (ed), *British Prehistory: A New Outline* (London, 1974).

SALWAY, P., *Roman Britain* (Oxford, 1981).

SIEVKING, G., LONGWORTH, I. and WILSON, K. (eds), *Problems in Economic and Social Archaeology* (London, 1976).

1 The Beginning of Settlement

CHURCHILL, D.M. and WYMER, J.J., 'The Kitchen Midden Site at Westward Ho!, Devon', *Proceedings of the Prehistoric Society* 31 (1965), 74–84.

CLARK, J.G.D., *Excavations at Star Carr* (Cambridge, 1954).

EVANS, J.G., LIMBREY, S. and CLEERE, H. (eds), *The Effect of Man on the Landscape: The Highland Zone*, Council for British Archaeology Research Report 11 (1975).

GRIEG, A. and RANKINE, W.F., 'A Stone Age Settlement System at East Week, Dartmoor', *Proceedings of the Devon Archaeological Society* 5 (1972), 8–26.

HIGGS, E.S., 'The Excavation of a Late Mesolithic Site at Downton, Wilts', *Proceedings of the Prehistoric Society* 25 (1959), 209–32.

KEEF, P.A.M. et al, 'A Mesolithic Site at Iping Common, Sussex', *Proceedings of the Prehistoric Society* 31 (1965), 85–92.

LIMBREY, S. and EVANS, J.G. (eds), *The Effect of Man on the Landscape: The Lowland Zone*, Council for British Archaeology Research Report 21 (1978).

RADLEY, J., 'The Mesolithic Period in North East Yorkshire', *Yorkshire Archaeological Journal* 42 (1969), 314–27.

RADLEY, J. and MELLARS, P., 'A Mesolithic Structure at Deepcar, Yorks', *Proceedings of the Prehistoric Society* 30 (1964), 1–24.

RADLEY, J., TALLIS, J.H. and SWITSUR, V.R., 'Excavations at Three Mesolithic Sites in the Southern Pennines', *Proceedings of the Prehistoric Society* 40 (1974), 1–19.

RANKINE, W.F., 'A Mesolithic Site at Farnham', *Surrey Archaeological Collections* 44 (1936), 25–46.

SELKIRK, A., 'Hampstead Heath', *Current Archaeology* 60 (1978), 24–6.

SELKIRK, A., 'Broom Hill, Braishfield', *Current Archaeology* 63 (1978), 117–20.

WYMER, J.J., 'Excavations at the Maglemosian Site at Thatcham, Berks', *Proceedings of the Prehistoric Society* 28 (1962), 329–61.

2 The First Villages and Farmsteads

BRADLEY, R., 'Prehistorians and Pastoralists in Neolithic and Bronze Age England', *World Archaeology* 4 (1972), 192–204.

BURGESS, C. and MIKET, R. (eds), *Settlement and Economy in the Third and Second Millennia BC*, British Archaeological Reports 33 (1976).

CASE, H., 'The Neolithic Causewayed Camp at Abington, Berks', *Antiquaries Journal* 36 (1956), 11–30.

CHERRY, J., 'Eskmeals Sand-dunes Occupation Sites', *Transactions of the Cumberland and Westmorland Archaeological Society* 63 (1963), 31–52.

CLARK, J.G.D., 'A Neolithic House at Haldon, Devon', *Proceedings of the Prehistoric Society* 4 (1938), 222–3.

CLARK, J.G.D. et al, 'Excavations at the Neolithic Site at Great Hurst Fen, Mildenhall, Suffolk', *Proceedings of the Prehistoric Society* 26 (1960), 202–45.

DREWITT, P.L., 'The Excavations of an Oval Burial Mound at Alfriston, Sussex', *Proceedings of the Prehistoric Society* 41 (1975), 119–52.

DREWITT, P.L., 'The Excavation of a Neolithic Enclosure on Offham Hill, Sussex', *Proceedings of the Prehistoric Society* 43 (1977), 201–42.

FIELD, N.H. et al, 'New Neolithic Sites in Dorset', *Proceedings of the Prehistoric Society* 30 (1964), 352–81.

JACKSON, D., 'The Excavation of a Neolithic and Bronze Age Site at Aldwincle', *Northamptonshire Archaeology* 11 (1976), 12–70.

MANBY, T.G., 'Neolithic Occupation Sites in the Yorkshire Wolds', *Yorkshire Archaeological Journal* 47 (1975), 23–60.

MERCER, R.M., 'Carn Brea', *Current Archaeology* 5 (1975), 16–18.

PRYOR, F., *Excavations at Fengate, Peterborough I*, Royal Ontario Museum Monograph 3 (1974).

PRYOR, F., *Excavations at Fengate, Peterborough II*, Royal Ontario Museum Monograph 5 (1978).

PRYOR, F., *Excavations at Fengate, Peterborough III*, Northamptonshire Archaeological Society Monograph 1 (1980).

SMITH, I.F., *Windmill Hill and Avebury* (Oxford, 1965).

SIMPSON, D.D.A. (ed), *Economy and Settlement in Neolithic and Early Bronze Age Britain and Europe* (Leicester, 1971).

WAINWRIGHT, G.J., 'The Excavations of a Neolithic Settlement on Broome Heath, Norfolk', *Proceedings of the Prehistoric Society* 38 (1972), 1–97.

WAINWRIGHT, G.J., 'The Excavations of Prehistoric and Romano-British Settlements on Eaton Heath, Norwich', *Archaeological Journal* 130 (1973), 1–43.

WAINWRIGHT, G.J. and LONGWORTH, I.H., *Durrington Walls Excavations*, Society of Antiquaries Research Report 27 (1971).

WILLOCK, E.H., 'A Neolithic Site at Haldon', *Proceedings of the Devon Archaeological Society* 2 (1936), 244–63.

3 The Outlines Established

BRADLEY, R., 'Excavations of a Beaker Settlement at Belle Tout, East Sussex', *Proceedings of the Prehistoric Society* 36 (1970), 312–79.

FLEMING, A., 'Bronze Age Agriculture in the Marginal Lands of North East Yorkshire', *Agricultural History Review* 19 (1971), 1–24.

FLEMING, A., 'Territorial Patterns in Bronze Age Wessex', *Proceedings of the Prehistoric Society* 37 (1971), 138–66.

GREEN, H.S., 'Early Bronze Age Burials, Territories and Population in Milton Keynes', *Archaeological Journal* 131 (1974), 58–139.

GREENFIELD, E., 'The Excavation of Barrow 4 at Swarkstone', *Derbyshire Archaeological Journal* 80 (1960), 1–48.

HIGGS, E. (ed), *Papers in Economic Prehistory* (London, 1972).

MEGAW, J.V.S. et al, 'The Bronze Age Settlement Gwithian', *Proceedings of the West Cornwall Field Club* 2 (1961), 200–15.

POSNANSKY, M., 'The Bronze Age Barrow at Swarkstone', *Derbyshire Archaeological Journal* 75 (1955), 123–39; 76 (1956), 10–26.

RHATZ, P., 'A Neolithic and Beaker Site at Downton', *Wiltshire Archaeological Magazine* 58 (1962), 116–42.

RILEY, D.N., 'Risby Warren', *Lincolnshire History and Archaeology* 13 (1978), 5–15.

4 The Countryside Fills Up

ATHERDEN, M.A., 'The Impact of Late Prehistoric Settlements on the Vegetation of the North York Moors', *Transactions of the Institute of British Geographers* 1 (1976), 284–300.

BARRETT, J. et al, 'South Lodge Camp and Down Farm', *Current Archaeology* 67 (1979), 242–6.

BURSTOW, G.P. and HOLLEYMAN, G.A., 'Late Bronze Age Settlement on Itford Hill, Sussex', *Proceedings of the Prehistoric Society* 23 (1957), 167–212.

BRADLEY, R. et al, 'Two Late Bronze Age Settlements on the Kennett Gravels', *Proceedings of the Prehistoric Society* 46 (1980), 217–96.

BRADLEY, R. and ELLISON, A., *Rams Hill – A Bronze Age Defended Enclosure*, British Archaeological Reports 19 (1975).
CHOWNE, P., 'Billingborough', *Current Archaeology* 67 (1979), 246–8.
COOMBS, P., 'Bronze Age Weapon Hoards in Britain', *Archaeologia Atlantica* 1 (1975), 49–81.
COOMBS, P. and THOMPSON, F.H., 'Excavations at Mam Tor', *Derbyshire Archaeological Journal* 99 (1979), 7–51.
CUNLIFFE, B., 'A Bronze Age Settlement at Chalton, Hants', *Antiquaries Journal* 50 (1970), 1–13.
DAVEY, P., 'The Distribution of Later Bronze Age Metalwork in Lincs', *Proceedings of the Prehistoric Society* 37 (1971), 96–111.
HOGG, A., 'Dodding and Haughton Moors', *Archaeologia Aeliana* 34 (1956), 142–9.
LONGLEY, D., 'Excavations at Runnymede Bridge', *London Archaeologist* 3 (1976), 10–17.
MANBY, T., 'Thwing', *Current Archaeology* 67 (1979), 240–1.
RHATZ, P. and APSIMON, A., 'Excavations at Shearplace Hill, Sydling St Nicholas, Dorset', *Proceedings of the Prehistoric Society* 28 (1962), 289–328.
SELKIRK, A., 'Norton Fitzwarren', *Current Archaeology* 28 (1971), 116–20.
SELKIRK, A., 'The Later Bronze Age', *Current Archaeology* 67 (1979), 229–39.
SELKIRK, A., 'Black Patch', *Current Archaeology* 67 (1979), 249–50.
SIMMONDS, I., 'Environment and Early Man on Dartmoor', *Proceedings of the Prehistoric Society* 35 (1969), 203–19.
WAINWRIGHT, G.J. and SMITH, K., 'The Shaugh Moor Project: The Enclosure', *Proceedings of the Prehistoric Society* 46 (1980), 65–122.

5 A Crowded Country

APSIMON, A. and GREENFIELD, E., 'Excavations at the Bronze Age and the Iron Age Settlement at Trevisker Round, Cornwall', *Proceedings of the Prehistoric Society* 38 (1972), 302–81.
BERSU, G., 'Excavations at Little Woodbury, Wilts', *Proceedings of the Prehistoric Society* 6 (1940), 30–111.
CHRISTIE, P.M.L., 'The Settlement at Carn Euny, Cornwall', *Proceedings of the Prehistoric Society* 44 (1978), 309–434.
COLLIS, J., 'Excavations at Owslebury, Hants', *Antiquaries Journal* 48 (1968), 18–31; 50 (1970), 246–61.
CUNLIFFE, B., *Iron Age Communities in Britain* (London, 1978).
CUNLIFFE, B. and ROWLEY, T. (eds), *Lowland Iron Age Communities in Europe*, British Archaeological Reports, Supplementary Series 48 (1978).
DIX, B., 'Excavations at Odell', *Bedfordshire Archaeological Journal* 14 (1980), 15–18.
DRURY, P.J., *Excavations at Little Waltham*, Council for British Archaeology Research Report 32 (1979).
FRERE, S.S. (ed), *Problems of the Iron Age in Southern Britain* (London, 1961).
FORDE-JOHNSTON, J., *Hill Forts of the Iron Age in England* (Liverpool, 1976).
HALL, D. and HUTCHINS, J., 'Distribution of Archaeological Sites between the Nene and Ouse Valleys', *Bedfordshire Archaeological Journal* 7 (1972), 1–16.
HARDING, D.N., *The Iron Age in Lowland Britain* (London, 1974).
HARDING, D.N. (ed), *Hill Forts* (London, 1976).
JACKSON, D., 'An Iron Age Settlement at Twywell', *Northamptonshire Archaeology* 10 (1975), 31–93.
JOBEY, G., 'Hill Forts and Settlements in Northumberland', *Archaeologia Aeliana* 43 (1965), 21–64.
JOBEY, G., 'An Iron Age Settlement and Homestead at Burradon, Northumberland', *Archaeologia Aeliana* 48 (1970), 51–96.
LAMBRICK, G. and ROBINSON, M., *Iron Age and Roman Settlements at Farmoor, Oxon*, Council for British Archaeology Research Report 32, (1979).
MAY, J., 'Excavations at Dragonby, Lincs', *Antiquaries Journal* 50 (1970), 222–45.
ORDNANCE SURVEY, *Map of Southern Britain in the Iron Age* (Chessington, 1976).
PARRINGTON, M., *Excavations at Ashville, Abingdon, Oxon*, Council for British Archaeology Research Report 28, (1978).
PERRY, B., 'Iron Age Enclosures and Settlements on the Hampshire Chalklands', *Archaeological Journal* 126 (1969), 29–43.
RICHARDSON, K.M., 'The Excavation of an Iron Age Village on Boscombe Down West', *Wiltshire Archaeological Magazine* 54 (1951), 123–68.
SELKIRK, A., 'Village and Farm in Iron Age Oxfordshire', *Current Archaeology* 63 (1978), 106–13.
SMITH, K., 'Excavations at Winklebury, Hants', *Proceedings of the Prehistoric Society* 43 (1977), 131–54.
STEAD, I., 'An Iron Age Hillfort at Grimthorpe, Yorks', *Proceedings of the Prehistoric Society* 34 (1968), 148–90.
WAINWRIGHT, G.J., 'The Excavation of a Durotrigian Farmstead, near Tollard Royal', *Proceedings of the Prehistoric Society* 34 (1968), 102–47.
WAINWRIGHT, G.J., *Gussage All Saints: An Iron Age Settlement in Dorset* (London, 1979).

6 The Impact of Rome

BONNEY, D.J., 'Iron Age and Romano-British Settlement Sites', *Wiltshire Archaeological Magazine* 63 (1968), 27–38.
BRANIGAN, K., 'The Latimer Roman Villa', *Current Archaelogy* 20 (1970), 241–4.
DIX, B., 'The Romano-British Farmstead at Odell', *Landscape History* 3 (1981), 17–26.
FIELD, N.H., 'The Romano-British Settlement at Studland', *Proceedings of the Dorset Natural History and Archaeological Society* 87 (1965), 142–207.

HIGHAM, N.J. and JONES, G.D.B., 'Frontier Forts and Farmers', *Archaeological Journal* 132 (1975), 16–53.

HUNTER, R. and MYNARD, D., 'Excavations at Thorpelands', *Northamptonshire Archaeology* 12 (1977), 97–154.

JONES, R.F.J., 'The Romano-British Farmstead at Lynch Farm', *Northamptonshire Archaeology* 10 (1975), 94–137.

PHILIPS, C.W. (ed), *The Fenland in Roman Times* (London, 1970).

POTTER, T.W., 'The Roman Occupation of the Central Fenland', *Britannia* 12 (1981), 79–134.

RIVET, A.L.F., *Town and Country in Roman Britain* (London, 1958).

RIVET, A.L.F. (ed), *The Roman Villa in Britain* (London, 1969).

ROYAL COMMISSION ON HISTORICAL MONUMENTS (ENGLAND), *Iron Age and Romano-British Monuments in the Gloucestershire Cotswolds* (London, 1976).

SELKIRK, A., 'Gadebridge Park Roman Villa', *Current Archaeology* 18 (1970), 198–203.

TAYLOR, C.C., *Dorset* (London, 1970).

TAYLOR, C.C., 'The Origin of Lichfield', *Transactions of the South Staffordshire Archaeological and Historical Society* 10 (1969), 43–52.

THOMAS, A.C. (ed), *Rural Settlement in Roman Britain* (London, 1966).

WEBSTER, G. and HOBLEY, B., 'Aerial Reconnaissance over the Warwickshire Avon', *Archaeological Journal* 121 (1964), 1–22.

WEBSTER, R.A., 'A Morphological Study of Romano-British Settlements in Westmorland', *Transactions of the Cumberland and Westmorland Archaeological Society* 71 (1971), 64–74.

PART II MEDIEVAL AND LATER SETTLEMENT

General Works of Reference

ASTON, M. and ROWLEY, T., *Landscape Archaeology* (London, 1974).

BERESFORD, M.W., *The Lost Villages of England* (London, 1954).

BERESFORD, M.W., *History on the Ground* (London, 1957).

BERESFORD, M.W. and HURST, J.G., *Deserted Medieval Villages* (London, 1971).

BERESFORD, M.W. and ST JOSEPH, J.K.S., *Medieval England: An Aerial Survey* (Cambridge, 1957 and 1979).

HOSKINS, W.G., *The Making of the English Landscape* (London, 1955).

ROBERTS, B.K., *Rural Settlement in Britain* (Folkstone, 1977).

ROWLEY, T., *Villages in the Landscape* (London, 1978).

SAWYER, P.H., *Medieval Settlement* (London, 1976).

TAYLOR, C.C., *Fieldwork in Medieval Archaeology* (London, 1974).

WILSON, D.M. (ed), *The Archaeology of Anglo-Saxon England* (London, 1976).

7 The Coming of the Saxons

ADDYMAN, P.V., 'A Dark-Age Settlement at Maxey, Northants', *Medieval Archaeology* 8 (1964), 20–73.

ADDYMAN, P.V., 'The Anglo-Saxon House', *Anglo-Saxon England* 1 (1972), 273–307.

ADDYMAN, P.V. and LEIGH, D., 'The Anglo-Saxon Village at Chalton, Hants', *Medieval Archaeology* 17 (1973), 1–25.

ARNOLD, C.J, and WARDLE, P., 'Early Medieval Settlement in England', *Medieval Archaeology* 25 (1981), 145–9.

BELL, M., *Excavations at Bishopstone*, Sussex Archaeological Collections 115 (1977), 1–299.

BONNEY, D.J., 'Pagan Saxon Boundaries in Wilts', *Wiltshire Archaeological Magazine* 61 (1960), 25–30,

CHAMPION, T., 'Chalton', *Current Archaeology* 59 (1977), 364–9.

CUNLIFFE, B.W., 'Saxon and Medieval Settlement Patterns in the Regions of Chalton, Hants', *Medieval Archaeology* 26 (1972), 1–12.

FINBERG, H.P.R., *Roman and Saxon Withington*, Leicester University Department of English Local History Occasional Paper 8, 1957.

HALL, D. and MARTIN, P., 'Fieldwork Survey of the Soke of Peterborough', *Durobrivae* 8 (1980), 13–14.

LOSCO-BRADLEY, S., 'Catholme', *Current Archaeology* 59 (1977), 358–64.

MACKRETH, D., 'Orton Hall Farm – The Saxon Connection', *Durobrivae* 5 (1977), 20–1.

RODWELL, W., 'Rivenhall', *Current Archaeology* 30 (1972), 184–5.

ROWLEY, T. (ed), *Anglo-Saxon Settlement and Landscape* (Oxford, 1974).

SELKIRK, A., 'Bishops Waltham', *Current Archaeology* 10 (1968), 274–6.

SELKIRK, A., 'West Stow', *Current Archaeology* 40 (1973), 151–6.

SELKIRK, A., 'Ribblehead', *Current Archaeology* 61 (1978), 38–41.

THOMAS, C., *Christianity in Roman Britain to 500 AD* (London, 1981).

WEST, S., 'The Anglo-Saxon Village at West Stow', *Medieval Archaeology* 13 (1969), 1–20.

8 The Making of Villages

ALLERSTON, P., 'English Village Development', *Transactions of the Institute of British Geographers* 51 (1970), 95–109.

BERESFORD, G., *The Medieval Clay-land Village*, Society for Medieval Archaeology Monograph 6, 1975.

BROWN, A.E. et al, 'Some Anglo-Saxon Estates and their Boundaries', *Northamptonshire Archaeology* 12 (1977), 155–67.

ELLISON, A., *Village Surveys*, Committee for Rescue Archaeology in Avon, Gloucestershire and Somerset Occasional Paper 1, 1976.

HILTON, R.H. and RHATZ, P.A., 'Excavations at Upton', *Transactions of the Bristol and Gloucestershire Archaeological Society* 185 (1966), 70–146.

HOSKINS, W.G., *Provincial England* (London, 1975).

MUMBY, L.M. (ed), *East Anglian Studies* (Cambridge, 1968).

PEACOCK, D., 'Fladbury', *Current Archaeology* 5 (1967), 123–4.

RHATZ, P.A., 'Holworth', *Proceedings of the Dorset Natural History and Archaeological Society* 81 (1959), 127–47.

ROBERTS, B.K., 'Village Plans in County Durham', *Medieval Archaeology* 16 (1973), 33–56.

ROBERTS, B.K., *The Green Villages of County Durham*, Durham County Library Local History Publication 12, 1977.

ROBERTS, B.K. and AUSTIN, D., *Rural Clusters in County Durham*, Durham County Library, 1975.

ROYAL COMMISSION ON HISTORICAL MONUMENTS (ENGLAND), *Northamptonshire* vols I–IV (London, 1975–1982).

SHEPPARD, J.A., 'Metrological Analysis of Regular Village Plans in Yorks', *Agricultural History Review* 22 (1974), 118–35.

SHEPPARD, J.A., 'Medieval Village Planning in Northern England, *Journal of Historical Geography* 2 (1976), 3–20.

STEANE, J.A., 'Excavations at Lyveden', *Journal of the Northampton Museums and Art Galleries* 2 (1967), 1–37.

TAYLOR, C.C. (ed), *Domesday to Dormitory – The History of Great Shelford*, Cambridge Workers' Educational Association, 1971.

TAYLOR, C.C., 'Polyfocal Settlement and the English Village', *Medieval Archaeology* 21 (1977), 189–93.

TAYLOR, C.C., 'Cambridgeshire Earthwork Surveys', *Proceedings of the Cambridgeshire Antiquarian Society* 64 (1973), 38–43.

WADE-MARTINS, P., 'Village Sites in Launditch Hundred', *East Anglian Archaeology* 10 (1980).

9 The Changing Village

ALLISON, K.J., 'The Lost Villages of Norfolk', *Norfolk Archaeology* 31 (1955), 116–62.

ALLISON, K.J. et al, *The Deserted Villages of Oxfordshire*, University of Leicester Department of English Local History Occasional Paper 17, 1965.

BARING, F., 'The Making of the New Forest', *English Historical Review* 16 (1901), 427–38.

DONKIN, R.A., 'Settlement and Depopulation on Cistercian Estates in the Twelfth and Thirteenth Centuries', *Bulletin of the Institute of Historical Research* 33 (1960), 141–65.

BEAN, J.M.W., 'Plague, Population and Economic Decline', *Economic Historical Review* 15 (1963), 49–106.

PARRY, M.L., *Climatic Change, Agriculture and Settlement* (Folkstone, 1978).

PLATT, C., *The Monastic Grange in Medieval England* (London, 1969).

RAVENSDALE, J.R., *Liable to Floods* (Cambridge, 1974).

ROYAL COMMISSION ON HISTORICAL MONUMENTS (ENGLAND), *West Cambridgeshire* (London, 1968).

ROYAL COMMISSION ON HISTORICAL MONUMENTS (ENGLAND), *North East Cambridgeshire* (London, 1972).

10 Hamlets and Farmsteads

ABERG, F.A. (ed), *Medieval Moated Sites*, Council for British Archaeology Research Report 17 (1978).

ASTON, M.A., 'Deserted Settlements in Mudford Parish, Yeovil', *Proceedings of the Somerset Archaeological and Natural History Society* 121 (1977), 41–53,

AUSTIN, D. et al, 'Farms and Fields in Okehampton Park, Devon', *Landscape History* 2 (1980), 39–57.

BERESFORD, G., 'The Medieval Manor of Penhallam, Jacobstow, Cornwall', *Medieval Archaeology* 18 (1974), 90–145.

BERESFORD, G., 'Three Deserted Medieval Settlements on Dartmoor', *Medieval Archaeology* 23 (1979), 98–158.

BOWEN, H.C. and FOWLER, P.J., 'The Archaeology of Fyfield and Overton Downs', *Wiltshire Archaeological Magazine* 58 (1963), 98–115.

BRANDON, P., *The Sussex Landscape* (London, 1974).

HEBDEN, R.E., 'The Development of the Settlement Pattern and Farming in the Shenstone Area', *Transactions of the South Staffordshire Archaeological and Historical Society* 3 (1962), 27–39.

HURST, D.G., 'Milton Ernest, Beds', *Medieval Archaeology* 8 (1964), 270.

HURST, D.G., 'Horley, Surrey', *Medieval Archaeology* 12 (1968), 193.

LE PATOUREL, J., *The Moated Sites of Yorkshire*, Society for Medieval Archaeology Monograph 5, 1973.

MOORHOUSE, S., 'Stretham, Sussex', *Medieval Archaeology* 15 (1978), 166–8.

ROBERTS, B.K., 'Medieval Colonization in the Forest of Arden, Warks', *Agricultural History Review* 16 (1968), 101–13.

ROYAL COMMISSION ON HISTORICAL MONUMENTS (ENGLAND), *Shielings and Bastles* (London, 1970).

TAYLOR, C.C., 'The Pattern of Settlement in the Vale of Blackmoor', *Proceedings of the Dorset Natural History and Archaeological Society* 87 (1966), 251–4.

TAYLOR, C.C., 'Whiteparish', *Wiltshire Archaeological Magazine* 62 (1967), 79–102.

11 The Development of the Modern Countryside

BATE, P.V. and PALLISER, D.M., 'Suspected Lost Villages in Staffs', *Transactions of the South Staffordshire Archaeological and Historical Society* 12 (1971), 31–6.

BATEY, M., 'Nuneham Courtney', *Oxoniensia* 38 (1968), 108–24.

BROWN, A.E. and TAYLOR, C.C., 'The Gardens at Lyveden, Northants', *Archaeological Journal* 129 (1973), 154–60.

EMERY, F., *The Oxfordshire Landscape* (London, 1974).

GLEAVE, M.B., 'Dispersed and Nucleated Settlement in the Yorkshire Wolds, 1770–1850', *Transactions of the Institute of British Geographers* 30 (1962), 105–18.

HALL, D.N. and NICKERSON, N., 'The Earthworks at Strixton', *Journal of the Northampton Museum and Art Gallery* 6 (1969), 22–34.

HAVINDEN, M., *The Somerset Landscape* (London, 1981).

NEWTON, R., *The Northumberland Landscape* (London, 1972).

NICHOLLS, P.H., 'The Evolution of a Forest Landscape', *Transactions of the Institute of British Geographers* 56 (1972), 57–76.

ROWLEY, T. (ed), *The Evolution of Marshland Landscapes* (Oxford University Department for External Studies, 1981).

SPUFFORD, M., *A Cambridgeshire Community*, Leicester University Department of English Local History Occasional Paper 20, 1965.

TAYLOR, C.C., *The Cambridgeshire Landscape* (London, 1973).

TAYLOR, C.C., *Roads and Tracks in Britain* (London, 1979).

WILLIAMS, M., 'The Enclosure and Reclamation of the Mendip Hills 1770–1870', *Agricultural History Review* 19 (1971), 65–81.

12 The Modern Landscape

BIGMORE, P., *The Bedfordshire and Huntingdonshire Landscape* (London, 1979).

MUIR, R., *The English Village* (London, 1980).

SMITH, M.W., 'Snap, A Modern Example of Depopulation', *Wiltshire Archaeological Magazine* 57 (1960), 386–90.

TAYLOR, C.C., 'The Making of the English Landscape – 25 Years On', *The Local Historian* 14 (1980), 195–201.

Index

References to illustrations are given in italics